Business Leader Reviews

Johnson clearly outlines the opportunity business leaders have to learn from sports. Given sports very public journey through media coverage, they provide many relevant case studies that can be applied across broader business settings. The coverage of exiting the pandemic for example provides many such learnings – capital management, financial strength, the need for agility and flexibility for a variety of risks and opportunities that have to be balanced and managed.

> Tim Ford Managing Director and Chief Executive Officer, Treasury Wine Estates

The reason you hear business leaders use sporting metaphors is because they work. But Johnson goes further by looking at which sports, sporting leagues and businesses have best navigated the trying circumstances of the pandemic to provide new insights and new anecdotes for every leader to use.

> Robert Hillard Consulting Leader, Deloitte Asia Pacific

One of my go-to sporting analogies is "where is the puck going?" which is used in ice hockey to encourage players to move to where the puck is going to be rather than descend on where the puck currently can be seen. It is the same in the tech sector. Look for where the gaps in the market will be in five years time, don't try to build for today, you will never catch up. There are many strong sporting anecdotes in this book that can be applied in the broader business setting.

> Peter James Chair and Non-Executive Director, multiple listed companies.

Running a business and also now a football club, sporting analogies are close to my heart and something I think about every day. It is riveting to reflect on the successes of some leagues using profits to fund future growth while in a position of power. The AFL has done this very well historically to create its national competition. Rugby League now investing in taking the game to the US. The differing approaches of all sporting leagues to their grassroots development provides fascinating business lessons.

> Adam Driussi Co-Founder and CEO Quantium, and Chairman Canterbury-Bankstown Bulldogs

Johnson masterfully intertwines the realms of sports and business, drawing powerful parallels between the two worlds. Through compelling anecdotes and data-driven insights, he highlights essential lessons in grit, accountability, and the transformative impact of incremental improvements. This book is a must-read for anyone seeking to unlock the winning mindset shared by top athletes, sporting organisations and leading a successful business.

> Trudy MacDonald Founder & Managing Director, TalentCode HR

The intersection of sports, business and technology represents the bleeding edge of customer experience. Digital innovation, finding new ways to create value, and finding new ways to create customer connections is a critical ingredient of the pro sports playbook. There are strong lessons there that can be applied in any number of other business settings.

> Clive Dickens Vice President, Television, Content and Product Development, Optus

This book helped me enhance my perspective on business and sport. It is clearly well researched and shows how much business can learn from sport and vice versa.

> Ajay Bhatia Chief Executive Officer mobile.de, and head of Adevinta's global mobility portfolio

Where you have elite competition, financial expectations and performance demands follow. You are no longer restricted by geographical boundaries as technology enables consumer consumption globally. Sports administrators are now challenged with great expectations and a newfound transparency and scrutiny. From capital management to supporting and enabling grass roots development. Johnson demonstrates that the playbook for any business is always underpinned by fundamentals. First principles which are then fueled by creating momentum. When momentum is lost, the road back is challenging.

> Phillip Muhlbauer Principal, Global Investors

I was aware of the history of Australians playing in the NBA. The section on transferrable skills however was a real eyeopener highlighting the number of Australians that have demonstrated skills mobility using their kicking skills developed through AFL pathways, and successfully making the transition into the NFL, excelling as punters. The ties between the US and Australia continue to go from strength to strength.

> Andrew Tulloch General Manager Victoria, American Chamber of Commerce in Australia

This book is dedicated to my wife Kelly and children Keira and Nicola.

Thank you for your support and encouragement.

And for your smiles every time I watched a sporting contest and called it research.

Acknowledgements

In today's world, data is everywhere. No primary research was necessary for this book. Media interviews posted to YouTube or corporate websites, coupled with an expansive array of podcasts, provide direct access to leaders across sport and business. Yes, there is an imperative to ensure that comments are not taken out of context, and yes it does rely on taking comments on face-value. Nonetheless, commentary direct from leaders has never been more accessible.

It should be noted that the author is based on the east coast of Australia. Podcasts contained in this book's references are documented from the lens of that time zone.

I wish to acknowledge the treasure trove of sports data that is available across NFL.com, ESPN, Pro Football Network, Spotrac, Sports Reference and Wisden.

I would like to thank Yohan Ramasundara, Roy Butcher, Daniel Reihana, Stephen Buckman, Jim Whiteside, Jeff Brown, Michael McNamara and Keira Johnson for their reviews and insights over various drafts. Also, a humbling vote of thanks to those business leaders for their reviews and comments.

IRON SHARPENS IRON

HOW BORROWING FROM THE PRO SPORTS PLAYBOOK CAN GIVE BUSINESSES THE WINNING EDGE

Andrew Johnson

First published 2024 by Andrew Johnson

Produced by Independent Ink
independentink.com.au

Copyright © Andrew Johnson 2024

The moral right of the author to be identified as the author of this work has been asserted.

All rights reserved. Except as permitted under the *Australian Copyright Act 1968*, no part of this publication may be reproduced, stored in a retrieval system, or transmitted in any form or by any means, electronic, mechanical, photocopying, recording or otherwise, without prior written permission from the publisher. All enquiries should be made to the author.

Cover design by Catucci Design
Edited by Samantha Sainsbury
Internal design by Independent Ink
Typeset in 12/16 pt Sabon LT Pro by Post Pre-press Group, Brisbane
Cover image: Stadium iStock-1255148856.jpg

ISBN 978-0-9756530-0-5 (paperback)
ISBN 978-0-9756530-2-9 (hardback)
ISBN 978-0-9756530-1-2 (epub)

Disclaimer:
Any information in the book is purely the opinion of the author based on personal experience and should not be taken as business or legal advice. All material is provided for educational purposes only. We recommend to always seek the advice of a qualified professional before making any decision regarding personal and business needs.

Contents

1. Introduction	1
2. Why the NFL is the perfect metaphor for the free-market economy	10
3. The unexpected time out: What happens to sport when a once-in-a-lifetime pandemic hits?	18
3.1 The Australian public policy response to the onset of a health and economic crisis	20
3.2 Australian sports in trouble	23
3.3 US sports pivot	52
3.4 Australian case study: macroeconomic factors that influence public policy decision-making	65
4. Talent identification and acquisition: building a championship winning roster	75
4.1 Assigning value: not all positions are created equal	80
4.2 Evaluating potential	94
4.3 Chip on your shoulder	105
4.4 Transferrable skills	117
5. Talent development	136
5.1 The insights of teammates matter: you cannot fool the players	143
6. The secret sauce of success: grit	149
7. Roster management: where fluidity and proactivity are business enablers	173
8. Scheme and philosophy (aka your north star)	188

9. All in: culture and legacy	205
10. Coaching mindset	
10.1 Iron sharpens iron	237
10.2 Becoming elite and the Tiger Woods model	243
10.3 Team first and the locker room	260
11. Customer experience, go-to-market and your distribution platform	279
12. Politics and sport: there is no escaping the macroeconomic environment	307
13. Exiting the pandemic: How different sports fared	324
14. Conclusion	333
Endnotes	349

1. Introduction

I HAVE A REMARKABLY SIMPLE thesis in writing this book – a firm belief that competition is good, ultimately driving the attainment of excellence. Now instinctively for some, that may come across as old thinking. Peter Thiel in his seminal book *Zero to One* certainly argues the opposite. In the context of startups and building the future, Thiel posits that competition is an ideological construct – in the real-world competition means no differentiation, no profits for the market combatants and a struggle to survive. He argues that the mindset of an entrepreneur should be to look to create a monopoly by initially tackling a small market that you can dominate, and then grow through the characteristics of proprietary technology, network effects, economies of scale and branding.

My own view is that these two positions are not diametrically opposed, and I am confident that I will be able to demonstrate this using anecdotes from the world of professional sport.

My motivation for writing this book has been the observation that many businesses – across the full spectrum of small, medium and large enterprises – have yet to fully bounce back since the onset of the COVID-19 pandemic. There is a sense that many are treading water, trying to manage uncertainty by continuing to batten down the hatches.

Such an approach is not sustainable. It continues to drain resources, while market share shrinks. We have witnessed many businesses die a slow and painful death since the pandemic.

COVID-19 was not a black swan event in the technical meaning of the phrase. It was not an outlier. There have been pandemics before, and there will be pandemics again. But a once-in-a-generation pandemic is pretty darn close to a black swan event. It was near impossible for a business owner, company board directors, CEOs or executives, to accurately predict how government and health bureaucracies would respond to a growing health crisis – not just across countries but within them, given federated levels of government. And then how those government policy levers would impact upon trade given the western world's reliance on global supply chains.

For this reason, in prosecuting the thesis of this book, I have taken a contrarian view to many sports fans who adopt the mantra that sport and politics do not mix. When it comes to the economy, everything is connected. Just like in a salary cap sports league, what goes to Peter cannot go to paying Paul. Changes to government policy at any time will have an impact somewhere else in the economy, taking time to find a new equilibrium.

Some sporting leagues were able to withstand the onset of COVID-19 limiting a declining revenue base to just one financial year, while other sporting leagues have been unable to bounce back at all.

In chapter three, I contrast how sporting leagues from the United States (National Basketball League and National Football League) and Australia (National Rugby League, Australian Football League, Australian Cricket and Australian Rugby Union) responded to the different health levers adopted by federated levels of governments at the onset of COVID-19.

It is unlikely that a global pandemic existed in many risk registers. I assume only for the largest of global businesses. Even then, the risk mitigation strategies would not have been war gamed too deeply.

Chapter three also analyzes the financial performance of these sporting leagues both prior to and after the onset of the pandemic, offering insights as to why some did well, while others did not. The economy and politics were key factors that needed to be navigated. Those with the growth mindset succeed, while others tread water and remain slowly drowning.

I will use the Australian economy as a case study, highlighting the multitude of factors that inform government decision-making, most of which cannot be influenced by an individual business. This will serve as a reminder that variables beyond your control do at times present themselves. How you have insulated the business will go a long way towards both survival and being best positioned to rebound strongly when those variables subside – recognizing in such instances those variables only subside at a time that is not of your choosing.

Thus, I wanted to write a book that would encourage readers to put the recent past to bed, to appreciate that their battle-scars have forged new levels of resilience, to embrace the new normal, to put in place risk mitigation strategies that protect from any future left-field variables, and to focus on realizing their own potential and that of their business.

I could think of no better metaphor for business than the cauldron that is professional sport. Sporting anecdotes are intended as a means for reigniting passion, taking a helicopter view of business in a parallel area of interest – allowing for reflection time and not complicating matters by confronting the issues of the day in your own business.

At a grass-roots level, participation in sports binds local communities, builds tribe mentalities, and creates identities. Sport brings out the best and worst of both competitors and fans. As competitors the best is reflected in the pursuit of excellence, striving to win, and leaving your best out on the field irrespective of the end result. As fans, the best provides a common interest from which a strong connection can be developed and from which tribes are built.

Sometimes the emotional connection is so strong, behavior on the field by players and off the field from fans, extends past what is acceptable.

Memorable moments are not just tied to winning outcomes. Heartbreak is par for the course for any sporting passion and tribe. The highs and lows of being a part of a sporting team's faithful is ... character building ... particularly the lows.

"The Richmond Faithful gather on a crucial night. Win and they stay up. Lose and they go down. They come here full of hope, but as they know all too well, it's the hope that kills you."

– *Ted Lasso Series 1 episode 10*

As countries responded to the threat of COVID-19, professional sport was a unifying activity across communities. In an environment where lockdowns were applied in an on-off manner, broadcast professional sport was a form of reliable entertainment and a reminder of normalcy in a difficult time.

This is not intended to be a book about sports. It is intended to be a book about business strategy using sporting stories to consider and confront business fundamentals. Just like a football fantasy league, I am looking to put you the reader into the seat of a general manager recruiting your roster, into the seat of a coach in squeezing the best out of your playing roster, and perhaps more uniquely, into the seat of a sporting-league commissioner or CEO and strategizing how best to grow the impact and reach of your game.

Professional sport can be a ruthless business - a constant journey to improve playing lists, extracting maximum value from salary caps, letting players go, building a brand, finding and growing sources of revenue, developing young talent, and ultimately playing the game in a way that secures finals participation, culminating in the winning of a championship.

Professional sport is the ultimate meritocracy. In many leagues, player payments are constrained by a salary cap. The best players on the team, playing the most important positions, attract the higher salaries. From there, it is a sliding scale throughout the remainder of the roster.

The objective in professional sport is pure and simple – win. Win individual games, optimize the health and performance of the playing list, make the finals, and be the last team standing holding the championship trophy. It is the ultimate accountable business model.

Coaches and players cannot let emotions get too high or too low, week in week out, and cannot get too ahead of themselves when planning for success. It does not matter how an individual player feels during the week, the measure of success will only be what you put on tape that weekend. You might plan for the big end of season games, but if you lose focus on the here and now, and do not deliver the next weekend, the end of season can quickly become a pipe dream.

You may have a great brand, sell lots of merchandise, generate lots of revenue, but ultimately if you are not winning, the front office is under pressure, and so too the playing group. Fans have limited patience, and are quick to call for coaches, players, CEOs, and boards to be moved on.

And herein lies the paradox of a fan. What fans may expect to be the business approach of their favorite sporting franchise, is rarely an approach that they would support or find acceptable in their own workplaces. Professional sports as a business takes "fail fast" to an entirely different level. There would be few businesses that could match the ruthlessness of professional sport with which players, coaches, CEOs are moved on and boards overthrown, the small amount of time given for teams to reinvent themselves and become competitive before the end of year review results in inevitable casualties, blowing up things, resetting and starting again.

It is here where professional sport becomes a metaphor for a competitive free market economy. Sport cannot exist without competition, and it cannot be fun and appreciated by sports fans unless that level of competition is sufficiently close that it drives standards higher.

Sure, some teams will enjoy longer periods of success than others. It cannot work however if there is simply one team dominant by a significant margin over everyone else. It only works if your competition is strong – if your team can compete, or see others competing, so that you too aspire to greener days and brighter futures. No one has ever praised a strong monopoly. Many may aspire to become a monopoly, but no-one has ever been inspired by one.

The origins of the word compete and competition in the English language stem from the Latin verb "competere" where the prefix "com" holds the meaning of "together" or "with" and "petere" having the meaning "to seek" or "to strive" – in combination holding the meaning to strive together. It is simply about realizing full potential.

That is where the title *Iron Sharpens Iron* comes from. It is a phrase that has become part of the indoctrination process across sports, particularly in the National Football League where you will note coaches and players use the phrase in many a press conference. Titles may be won on championship game day, but titles are most certainly lost well before.

Iron sharpens irons means there is a process to be followed to take the jump from poor to average, average to good, good to great, great to elite. There is no hiding from the daily grind. In fact, hard work does not guarantee success; it just gets you to the starting line enabling you to compete. The grind occurs in the gym pre-season, finetuning the body, working on addressing weaknesses and improving strengths. It occurs during pre-season training during drills with team-mates all designed to make individual players and units stronger.

It continues to occur during the season, where close games and losses provide great insights into where rosters need to improve to continue to gain strides. It is about facing adversity and finding ways to improve.

This is the reason I do not see the thesis of this book being diametrically opposed to Thiel's position. Competition in the sporting sense is much broader than in a market sense, where businesses may compete for the same market with the same product. Competition in sport is really about competing with yourself, fine-tuning and honing your craft to become the best that you can be. This mentality plays out across the roster. The more team members gain strides, the higher the overall standard. The higher the standard, the higher the potential impact on game day. Not necessarily on a specific game day. There are highs and lows to be experienced. Rather, a higher bar and greater consistency that optimizes the chances for achieving desired results.

The same approach is espoused in Thiel's work. Pick your

niche. Build and fine-tune, pursuing excellence until you are best in class. That is, compete with yourself to get better. Then look to scale – your moat will be created through proprietary technology, network effects, economies of scale and branding.

Envisioning success in business can be complex. The ultimate objective of any individual business is often not as clear as what winning looks like in professional sport. That is why businesses spend so much effort crafting and defining what envisioned success looks like, corralling the team behind a common purpose, and regularly reviewing so this evolves over time.

For public companies, there is the driver of doing what is in the shareholders best interest. For privately owned business, it is not always about scaling, growing and capturing the dominant market share. In the absence of a business aggressively pursuing growth and realizing its full potential, Silicon Valley has coined the term "lifestyle" business – intended to reflect instances where drivers for the business owner are not necessarily prioritized according to maximizing profits, but rather the business complements as opposed to impacts the business owner's other lifestyle objectives.

Nonetheless, first principles of business are universal. Why do you exist, what is it that you do, and why do you do what you do? What is your vision, your purpose, your target market, your ideal customer profile, your go-to-market strategy? How will you attract and retain talent? What is the culture you need to be successful?

This book is not a deep dive into theoretical frameworks on strategy, but rather the approach is to share interesting stories and anecdotes from professional sport that offer parallels to any business setting. Crafting a vision, determine a scheme and philosophy to get you there, building a culture and identity to execute on that scheme and philosophy. Finding the right talent and developing that talent. Being clear on your intended market, and then finding the best way to access and satisfy that market.

It is hoped that these parallels enable you to reflect on your own current business and assist in identifying those decisions that need to be prioritized in order to keep your business heading in the right direction.

As a general heads-up, what follows includes a lot of data. The genuine sports fan enthusiastically embraces data – using it for justification of their views on the trials and tribulations of their favorite franchise. Business leaders need to be data-driven too.

2. Why the NFL is the perfect metaphor for the free-market economy

In 2020, Athletic Panda Sports[1] produced a list of the top eleven highest grossing sports leagues in the world. Intuitively, it would not be unexpected that a number of these sporting leagues are based in the USA. The US is after all the world's largest economy and by a significant margin.

Highest grossing sports leagues:
1. National Football League (NFL) – $13 Billion
2. Major League Baseball (MLB) – $10 Billion
3. National Basketball Association (NBA) – $7.4 Billion
4. Indian Premier League (Cricket) – $6.3 Billion
5. English Premier League – $5.3 Billion
6. National Hockey League (NHL) – $4.43 Billion
7. Australian Rules Football – $2.5 Billion
8. La Liga (Spanish Football League) – $2.2 Billion
9. Serie A (Italian Football League) – $1.9 Billion
10. Ligue 1 (France/Monaco Football League) – $1.5 Billion
11. Nippon Professional Baseball (Japanese Baseball league) – $1.1 Billion

Only two leagues are based in countries outside the largest ten economies, being Australian Rules Football and the Spanish Football League. Four of the top six are based in the US. Perhaps somewhat counterintuitively, the US league with the most franchises based outside of the country, is the National Hockey League with seven teams based in Canada. Yet despite the broader direct access markets, it is the smallest grossing of the four US-based leagues.

While this list of highest grossing leagues has continued to evolve since 2020, what has not changed is the clear domination of the NFL in holding the top spot. Let's take a quick helicopter view of the NFL, before landing on some governance structures that have enabled it's continued success.

In terms of the structure of league delivery, the NFL is split into two equal conferences of sixteen franchises, the American Football Conference (AFC) and the National Football Conference (NFC). Each conference is further divided into four divisions of four. Previously, there was an annual season of 16 games which had been the way for the 43 years. The 2021/22 season saw the competition expanded by one game to 17 through the CBA negotiations and at the expense of reducing the number of pre-season games from four to three.

Franchises play each team in their division twice every season. As there are far fewer games than franchises, the NFL uses a rotation system to make sure each team plays all other teams outside their division at least once every four years.

A total of 14 teams competes in the playoffs, being seven from each conference. The franchise with the best record in each conference has a bye in the first round of the playoffs (named the wild-card round). The wild-card round is sudden death and is scheduled as seeds 2 v 7, seeds 3 v 6, and seeds 4 v 5 playing in sudden death.

With four teams now remaining in each conference, the next playoff round is called the divisional round with the number one seed who had the bye playing the lowest remaining seed, and the two remaining teams meeting.

The following week is then the championship game in both the AFC and NFC conference. The winners of both conferences then meet in the Superbowl.

American Football Conference (AFC)		National Football Conference (NFC)	
AFC East	**AFC West**	**NFC East**	**NFC West**
Buffalo Bills	Denver Broncos	Dallas Cowboys	Arizona Cardinals
Miami Dolphins	Kansas City Chiefs	New York Giants	Los Angeles Rams
New England Patriots	Las Vegas Raiders	Philadelphia Eagles	San Francisco 49ers
New York Jets	Los Angeles Charger	Washington	Seattle Seahawks
AFC North	**AFC South**	**NFC North**	**NFC South**
Baltimore Ravens	Houston Texans	Chicago Bears	Atlanta Falcons
Cincinnati Bengals	Indiana Colts	Detroit Lions	Carolina Panthers
Cleveland Browns	Jacksonville Jaguars	Green Bay Packers	New Orleans Saints
Pittsburgh Steelers	Tennessee Titans	Minnesota Vikings	Tampa Bay Buccaneers

Forbes produces an annual list of the World's 50 Most Valuable Sports Teams. For the 2023 year[2], the list comprised of thirty franchises from the NFL, seven from soccer across four separate leagues, six from the NBA, five from the MLB, and two from Formula One. The Dallas Cowboys are the biggest brand globally of sporting teams valued at $8b having held the top spot since 2016.

National Football League (NFL)
#1 Dallas Cowboys ($9b), = #3 New England Patriots ($7b), #5 Los Angeles Rams ($6.9b), #6 New York Giants ($.86b), #7 Chicago Bears ($6.3b), #8 Las Vegas Raiders ($6.2b), = #9 New York Jets ($6.1b), #12 Washington Commanders ($6.05b), = #13 San Francisco 49ers ($6b) #16 Philadelphia Eagles ($5.8b), #17 Miami Dolphins ($5.7b), #19 Houston Texans ($5.5b), #21 Denver Broncos ($5.1b), #22 Seattle Seahawks ($5b), #26 Atlanta Falcons ($4.7b), #27 Minnesota Vikings ($4.65b), #28 Baltimore Ravens ($4.63b), #29 Pittsburgh Steelers ($4.625b), #30 Cleveland Browns ($4.62b), #31 Green Bay Packers ($4.6b), #33 Tennessee Titans ($4.4b), #34 Indianapolis Colts ($4.35b), #35 Kansas City Chiefs ($4.3b), #37 Tampa Bay Buccaneers ($4.2b), #38 Los Angeles Chargers ($4.15b), = #39 Carolina Panthers ($4.1b), #42 New Orleans Saints ($4.075b), = #43 Jacksonville Jaguars ($4b), = #47 Arizona Cardinals ($3.8b), #49 Buffalo Bills ($3.7b).
Soccer (English Premier League, French Ligue 1, German Bundesliga, Spanish La Liga)
#11 Real Madrid ($6.07b), = #13 Manchester United ($6b), #18 Barcelona ($5.508b), #20 Liverpool ($5.288b), #23 Manchester City ($4.99b), #24 Bayern Munich ($4.86b), #36 Paris Saint-Germain ($4.21b).
National Basketball Association (NBA)
= #3 Golden State Warriors ($7b), = #9 New York Knicks ($6.1b), #15 Los Angeles Lakers ($5.9b), = #39 Chicago Bulls ($4.1b), = #43 Boston Celtics ($4b), = #45 Los Angeles Clippers ($3.9b).
Major League Baseball (MLB)
#2 New York Yankees ($7.1b), #25 Los Angeles Dodgers ($4.8b), #32 Boston Red Sox ($4.5b), = #39 Chicago Cubs ($4.1b), = #49 San Francisco Giants ($3.7b).
Formula One
= #45 Ferrari ($3.9b), = #47 Mercedes ($3.8b).

Despite the highest revenues of all US sporting leagues, the NFL has the smallest core product – only 17 games per franchise in the normal season (excluding playoffs). Yet these franchises represent 30 of the top 50 most valuable sporting brands.

A standard season in the Major League Baseball (MLB) consists of 162 games per team. The National Basketball Association (NBA) normally hosts 82 games per team (the 2020–21 NBA season was 72 games for each team due to COVID-19). The National Hockey League also hosts 82 games per team.

Even if you wanted to use aggregate regular season games as the baseline, in the NFL there are 17 games for each of the 32 franchises (divided by two teams in each game) for a regular season total of 272 games. There are 82 games for each of the 32 teams in the NHL for a regular season total of 1,312; 82 games for 30 franchises in the NBA for a regular season total of 1,230; and 162 games for each of the 30 franchises in MLB for a regular season total of 2,430.

Given the small number of games relative to other sports, one of the great attractions of the NFL is that every game matters. At the division level, one team must qualify for the playoffs each year. That is one in every four teams in each division makes it into the post season. On top of that, the next three teams with the best record in each conference also qualify for the playoffs. In the 2020-21 season, Washington had a 7-9 win-loss record in the NFC East Division with a winning percentage of .438. Despite this losing record, it was the best record in the NFC East and thus saw Washington qualify for the playoffs. In the main, a 10-6 winning record has been sufficient to qualify for the post season. A new normal will be set over coming years with the extension to a 17-game season.

While the NBA is full of world class athletes, the reality is that once players reach 28 years and older, they are rarely available for the full number of games in a season. There are injuries that need to be managed, and for the best of the best players particularly in their thirties, maintenance breaks used to get players refreshed prior to the playoff run. A frustration for fans is that there are too many games where the best players are not available and makes for a noticeably clear difference in quality between play in the regular season and that being witnessed in the playoffs.

For the team that comes last of the 32 NFL teams in any given season, the consolation prize (and it is a very significant consolation prize) is the opportunity to pick first in the next

NFL draft. That franchise gets to take their pick from often 400 plus college players nominating for the draft each year.

There is no minor league in the NFL such as there is in baseball, or the G League represents for the NBA, or the English Football League Championship performs for the promotion/relegation system in the English Premier League (EPL). There are two leagues playing in the NFL offseason being the USFL and XFL however neither is formally attached to the NFL (NB. The USFL and XFL will merge in 2024). Similarly, given the global nature of sport, athletes often can play in their sports equivalent league overseas. This does not happen in the NFL (sorry Canada!). College football is the pathway and equivalent of a minor league for the NFL.

The college football system in the US is the epitome of a tribe culture. Your alma mater is often part of the essence of who you are and supporting your former college both in heart and in action creates tribes. The Alabama Crimson Tide, the Georgia Bulldogs, the Ohio State Buckeyes, the Michigan Wolverines, and the Clemson Tigers are household brands in the US. The average attendance at college football games is over 40,000. Then at Christmas, there is a feast of college football which is a staple of American culture. The Bowl Championship Series determines the nation's best college football team.

To be eligible to nominate for the NFL draft, players must have been out of high school for at least three years and are only draft-eligible in the year after the end of their college eligibility. The NFL draft has seven rounds, with each team having one selection per round. There are several additional selections as NFL compensatory picks available as part of the NFL's collective bargaining agreement. This includes losing players during free agency with the intention of the draft filling that void, or compensation for losing minority coaches and executives to competitors in recognition of the development invested by the team losing those personnel.

In the NFL, contracted players can be traded between teams after the completion of the current season in March, and through to the end of week 8 of the regular season. After week 8, there can be no trades again until the completion of the season.

In the first round of the NFL draft, the franchise finishing last the previous season selects first, the franchise finishing second last goes next, and so on through 32 selections (unless there have been trades prior that involved those draft picks). The draft coupled with the salary cap, are mechanisms to ensure talent is more equitably available over time. Then it is over to franchises to identify talent, better develop talent than their competitors, and acquire talent from other franchises through free agency and trades that best position the team for future success.

So why is the NFL at the peak of highest grossing sporting leagues in the US, when it has the smallest core product?

There is a dedicated chapter on customer experience, go-to-market strategy, and distribution channel later in this book. For now, this chapter is focused on governance.

The NFL consists of 32 franchises. Only the Green Bay Packers are publicly owned having been established as a non-profit corporation on August 18, 1923. There are approximately 361,300 people (representing approximately 5,009,400 shares) who are owners of the Green Bay Packer franchise. The remaining 31 franchises are privately owned though holding companies with a clear line of sight to a majority owner.

The NFL itself is not owned by a single entity. The league and NFL brand are managed and governed by an Executive Committee[3] comprising of one representative from each franchise.

Imagine if you were a startup, and you were experiencing some good growth, and now you were at a stage where your early investors were starting to make some noise about formally establishing a skills-based board. If I said you needed a board of 32, you would quite rightly be aghast.

For the NFL, such a governance model works really well in the context of growing revenues. The NFL has a very tight mission: "*We are all stewards of football. We unite people and inspire communities in the joy of the game by delivering the world's most exciting sports and entertainment experience.*"

This mission is the triage funnel for prioritizing and making decisions. Any proposed changes to the league require a three-quarter majority of the Executive Committee to pass. Within this context, it is a pure market with very little intervention or any market distortion by external factors. Each franchise owner operates under the same rules to attract and retain talent under a salary cap framework. Each franchise is empowered to earn revenue from its target demographic.

Players have no seat at the Executive Committee table. Underpinning terms of employment including the setting of a salary cap occurs in negotiation between the Executive Committee and the NFL Players Association (NFLPA). The agreed framework is then set out in the Collective Bargaining Agreement.

While the salary cap creates equity and a level-playing field for competition, it also caps the cost base meaning all stakeholders are aligned to delivering the mission of '... *delivering the world's most exciting sports and entertainment experience*'. The laws of supply and demand play out without external influence. The NFL is the perfect metaphor for a free-market economy.

3. The unexpected time out: What happens to sport when a once-in-a-lifetime pandemic hits?

IT WAS DURING DECEMBER 2019 that word started filtering through into Australia that a highly contagious virus had been discovered transmitting in China, and that it may have global implications.

During January 2020, it became clear that both the federal and state governments of Australia were doing their research, undertaking scenario planning, and developing risk mitigation strategies. The World Health Organization declared the novel coronavirus outbreak a public health emergency on January 30, 2020. But as Australia is on the other side of the world, panic did not set in. There was some comfort in being an isolated island on the other side of the world. Yes, shipping, and international passenger arrivals could be a risk – but it was a watching brief at this stage.

On February 11, the virus was named severe acute respiratory syndrome coronavirus 2 (SARS-CoV-2) by the International Committee on Taxonomy of Viruses. On the same day, the World Health Organization correspondingly named the disease caused by SARS-CoV-2 the coronavirus disease (COVID-19).

By March 3, 2020, Australia had confirmed 38 cases of COVID-19 with one death, while across the world there had been 90,846 confirmed cases of COVID-19 with 3,115 reported deaths[4].

The Melbourne Cricket Ground hosted the Women's T20 World Cup cricket final on March 8 with 86,174 fans watching on as Australia beat India by 85 runs. This was just shy of the world-record attendance at any women's sporting event (held by the 1999 FIFA Women's World Cup final held at the Rose Bowl in the USA with 90,185 fans).

Cruise ships were the first seeder of a COVID-19 super-spreader event in Australia. The Ruby Princess cruise ship docked in Sydney Harbour on March 8 having arrived from New Zealand with 158 sick passengers on board, 13 of whom were registering high temperatures. Only nine of those passengers were tested for COVID-19 upon arrival, and all passengers were allowed to disembark. Later that day, 2,700 passengers boarded for another return trip to New Zealand.

The World Health Organization declared the SARS-CoV-2 virus a global pandemic on March 11, 2020.

The National Rugby League season commenced on March 12, with the Parramatta Eels beating the Canterbury Bulldogs 8–2 at Bank West Stadium in Parramatta, New South Wales. There was a crowd of 21,363 in attendance. Over 100,000 attended the eight opening round games of Rugby League that weekend, which would turn out to be the last of crowds for a while.

3.1 The Australian public policy response to the onset of a health and economic crisis

On March 12, 2020, the Australian Federal Government announced the first of its economic measures with a $17.6 billion stimulus package targeted towards keeping Australians in jobs and helping small and medium sized businesses to stay in business.

One day later and in response to the evolving COVID-19 threat, the Australian Government announced a ban on public gatherings of more than 500 was to come into effect from March 16. All major sporting codes continued with their leagues despite the announcement. The second round of the National Rugby League proceeded behind closed doors. The first rounds of the Australian Football League (AFL) and A-League (Football/Soccer) went ahead as scheduled although without crowds. The National Basketball League was midway through a grand-final series with fans unable to attend the remaining games. The Australian cricket team were hosting New Zealand in a three match one-day series that started on March 13. This too proceeded behind closed doors with no spectators.

On March 19, the Ruby Princess cruise ship returned to Sydney Harbour and all 2,700 passengers were allowed to disembark[5]. A number headed to the airport for intrastate travel home. A public inquiry later linked more than 900 COVID-cases and 28 deaths to the cruise ship.

Co-incidentally, that very same day, the prime minister of Australia announced that Australia was closing its borders to all non-citizens and non-residents, with the entry ban taking effect just 24 hours later from 9pm Australian Eastern Daylight Time March 20, 2020. It became clear at this stage, that Australia was responding to the threat of COVID-19 through the lens of a crisis requiring an emergency response. While the general population may have not yet realized it, COVID-19 cases were no longer isolated, and Australia's first COVID-19 wave was gaining momentum.

On March 22, the prime minister announced a further $66.1 billion of economic support, along with $105 billion to deliver easier access to finance. These additional measures injected a total $189 billion economic stimulus into the Australian economy by all arms of government to keep Australians in work and businesses in business.

Just eight days later, the Australian prime minister announced a further economic support package of $130 billion[6] taking total support announced during March to $320 billion and representing 16.4 percent of Gross Domestic Product (GDP). The additional support was predominately two programs: JobKeeper and JobSeeker. JobKeeper allocated funding for a wage subsidy of $1,500 per fortnight for six million workers to encourage employers who were experiencing revenue declines to resist downsizing in the face of uncertain economic conditions, and thus ensuring the economy did not lose capability and infrastructure during the initial wave of COVID-19. JobSeeker provided an additional supplement for those in receipt of government support and looking for work.

By April 12, Australia's first wave had been flattened and COVID-19 was looking manageable particularly when comparing Australia's infection rates to those being experienced internationally. At this stage, there had been 6,313 cases of COVID-19 infection, of which 3,338 had recovered, and 59 deaths[7].

DAILY NUMBER OF REPORTED CASES

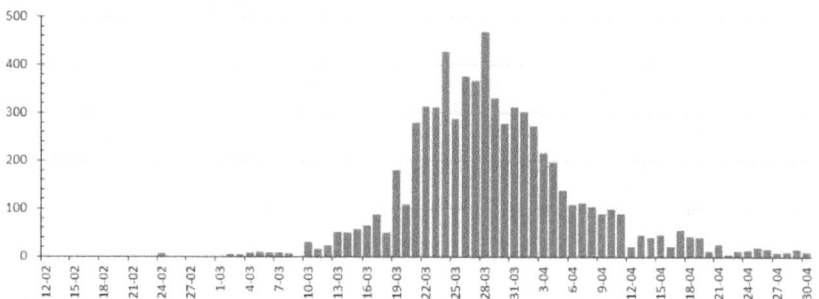

It is customary in Australia for the Federal Government to produce a budget in May of each calendar year. With COVID-19 providing community health and economic uncertainty, there was a need to better understand the economic trends and costs, hence the government pushed back the budget date until October.

Australia's second wave of COVID-19 arrived mid-winter in June 2020 and lasted through to the end of September. Most troubling, and despite every effort to prioritize citizens who were the most vulnerable, residential aged-care facilities in the state of Victoria provided super-seeding events. This was underpinned by poor infection controls, delays in contract tracing, longer sample throughput times from pathology testing to track down infections, depleted staffing levels due to increasing demand across the sector and staff being required to isolate having been deemed a close contact of an infection case. In total, there were 1,962 cases of COVID-19 among aged-care residents in Victoria and 648 deaths[8].

On August 19, 2020, the Australian prime minister announced an agreement with UK-based drug company Astra Zeneca[9]. The University of Oxford COVID-19 vaccine was in stage three clinical trials at the time, and Astra Zeneca had signed a development and worldwide manufacturing and distribution deal for the vaccine with Oxford[10]. This was a strong sign of leadership by the Australian government at the time. You back a mate who has a proven track record. Committing early assured early access to vaccines as part of managing the health pandemic. Supply was secured for all Australians as was the ability to manufacture onshore, assuring future supply and removing any risks of global supply chains failing. There would later be much criticism around execution and poor public messaging causing vaccine hesitancy and inhibiting uptake. Nonetheless, during August 2020 this agreement was an important milestone for the citizens of Australia.

By the end of September, Australia had experienced 27,078 COVID-19 infections of which 24,614 cases had recovered. Total deaths stood at 886.

DAILY NUMBER OF REPORTED CASES

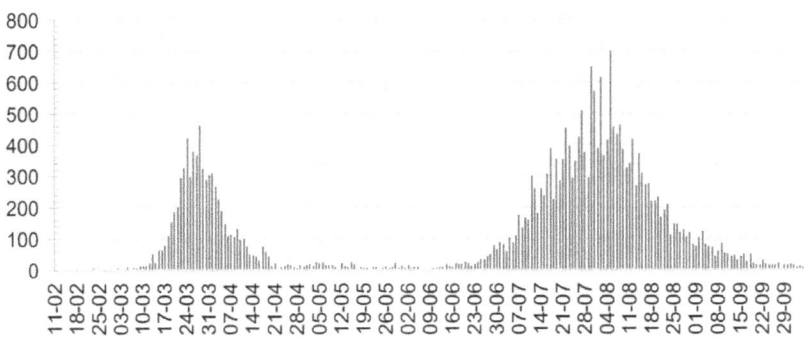

3.2 Australian sports in trouble

The Australian Constitution allocates responsibility for Defence (that is, the national borders), immigration and emigration, and quarantine to the Federal Government. Outside of the constitution, public health is governed and administered at a state and territory level. This means there can be differences in how public health is managed across the country. There are eight states and territories in Australia: New South Wales, Victoria, Queensland, Western Australia, Tasmania, South Australia, the Australian Capital Territory and the Northern Territory. Each of these states and territories addressed the COVID-19 crisis in a slightly different way impacting the sporting codes. The codes in turn responded to the crisis in various ways to differing levels of success.

National Rugby League (NRL)

Rugby League is one of the premier professional sports in Australia, most popular in New South Wales and Queensland. Rugby League was birthed in 1895 when clubs in the north of England broke away from the Rugby Football Union. The same thing happened in Australia in 1907[11] driven by a desire to professionalize sharing in spoils and addressing costs being borne by players such as insurance and injury treatment[12].

Today, the National Rugby League comprises 17 teams, four of which are located in the state of Queensland (the Brisbane Broncos, the Gold Coast Titans, the North Queensland Cowboys and the Dolphins). There is one team, the Melbourne Storm, based in the state of Victoria. There is also one international franchise: the New Zealand Warriors. The remaining 11 teams are based in New South Wales.

The 2020 season of the National Rugby League commenced on March 12. The competition was partly through its second round when on March 19, New Zealand Prime Minister Jacinda Ardern announced that New Zealand's international borders to non-residents would be closed from 11.59pm that very day. Then on March 23, the Queensland State Government announced that any non-resident travelling to Queensland would be required to quarantine for 14 days. The

National Rugby League competition and its weekly playing schedule were thrown into disarray.

The saying "never let a good crisis go to waste" is often attributed to Sir Winston Churchill to reflect the coming together of an unlikely alliance with Franklin Roosevelt and Joseph Stalin – an alliance that would lead to the end of the Second World War.

The saying has been adopted as a mantra in the business world – used as a rallying cry to respond to emergencies by challenging the status quo, looking for new ways of doing things, acting with a sense of urgency, and creating opportunities to respond successfully to an evolving new normal. During a crisis in particular, leaders are the early movers.

The new chairman of the National Rugby League Peter V'landys, who had been in the post less than six months, was determined to see the competition back up and running as soon as possible.

This involved taking advice from biosecurity and infectious disease experts and forming a dedicated working committee tasked with devising a plan on how to establish a bubble environment. The theory being that a bubble would minimize risks of COVID-19 contagion and thereby ensure the safety of players and the community when the competition was restarted. Those plans developed by the dedicated committee then required tabling and seeking approval from the departments of health in each of the states of Queensland, New South Wales and Victoria.

With approval not yet secured from these departments of health, the National Rugby League announced on April 14 that the competition would be restarted May 28, 2020. This early signaling of intent showed leadership: by being first to market, and then providing the call to action for all stakeholders including health officials, teams, and fans. It showed leadership by demonstrating that due diligence had been undertaken, and then by publicly asking the question and placing the onus back onto public-service bureaucrats, that given these risk-mitigation strategies – why not restart the competition? The advance notice of six weeks was designed to provide sufficient lead time for players to acclimate and ensure appropriate physical conditioning that minimized the potential for injury upon recommencement of the competition.

As recommencement plans matured and were rolled out, it was indicated that the first two rounds of the season would remain counted as part of a shortened competition, as would the competition ladder as it stood after the first two rounds. The competition restarting on May 28, however, would be reduced from the normal 25 rounds to 20 rounds, with the grand final played late October as opposed to the historical early October.

The bubble plan involved six venues: three in New South Wales (Bankwest Stadium, Campbelltown Stadium, Central Coast Stadium), two in Queensland (Suncorp Stadium and QCB Stadium), and one in Victoria (AAMI Park). Risks in travelling across interstate borders would be minimized by establishing accommodation bubbles and restricting movement to inside the bubble only, while inhibiting access to the outside world. For as long as the border restrictions required, the New Zealand Warriors would be based in the regional center of Tamworth in New South Wales. Crowds would not be permitted to attend games.

Now at this stage, once approval was granted by the various departments of health, it would be easy to think all the heavy lifting had been done, and game on. In professional sports, however, the tricker bit with a shortened season is an immediate inability to meet all commitments contained in commercial contracts due to fewer games. Based on the number of games in specific geographies, there are existing contracts with broadcasters, contracts with stadia, contracts with hospitality and caterers, contracts with sponsors, etc. Pricing and business models go out the window with no fans at games. And then there was the impact these financial variables might mean on player contracts. Lots of uncertainty, and lots of stakeholder expectations needed to be managed.

In an environment where emergency public health orders change the regulatory landscape without notice, force de majeure and act of God provisions in contract law can assist in navigating the inability to meet contracted commitments. That said, those contract clauses do not mean your current business partners are going to sign up to a new normal, particularly in an environment where there is economic upheaval. History shows that when these decisions were being navigated Australia's GDP experienced a drop of -7 percent and a drop of -7.6 percent in real net national disposable income for the quarter ending June 2020[13].

Broadcast rights for the NRL are shared between Channel Nine on free to air (the Nine Entertainment Company) and Foxtel on cable for television, with Telstra (a telecommunications company) holding some streaming rights via a deal with Foxtel. On March 30, 2020, Nine Entertainment Company issued a statement to the Australian Stock Exchange which outlined operational initiatives in response to the economic downturn due to COVID-19[14]. Listed in the statement was advice that $130m could be saved by Nine Entertainment over two years should the NRL 2020 season be cancelled. Hence the pressure was on, and the financial lines in the sand drawn for any renegotiations for a shorted National Rugby League season.

On May 28, 2020, coinciding with the restart of the competition, the National Rugby League announced reworked television deals with both Nine and Foxtel[15]. It was reported the reworked deal saved Nine on average $27.5 million per year for the 2021 and 2022 financial years[16]. A reduced revenue base naturally has flow-on effects.

With the first COVID-19 wave in Australia flattened, the NSW Government announced on June 14, 2020[17] that up to 10,000 fans would be allowed to return to each NRL game from July 1 in NSW provided it amounted to 25 percent or less of a venue's capacity. By the end of the season, 37,303 fans attended the Grand Final held in Sydney, NSW at Stadium Australia watching the Melbourne Storm defeat the Penrith Panthers 26–20.

The financial year in Australia ends June 30 each year, meaning the impacts of COVID-19 were only felt in the final quarter of the financial year ending June 30, 2020. Nonetheless, the impacts on Rugby League were keenly felt with revenue dropping $135.7m on the previous year, and net assets declining by 20.5 percent ($122.8m down to $97.6m).

As part of ensuring ongoing sustainability and cutting the cloth to suit the reduced revenue base, the National Rugby League undertook six months of negotiations with the Rugby League Players Association reaching an agreement to reduce the salary cap by six percent in each of the next two years. This meant the 2020 salary cap was reduced from $9.6m contained in the original agreement, down to $9.02m in 2021, and a reduction from the originally intended $9.7m in 2022 down to $9.11m[18].

Table 1. National Rugby League Financial Position 2012–2020 (Year Ending June 30)

Profit & Loss ($'000)			Balance Sheet ($'000)			
Year	Total Revenue	Surplus/ (Deficit)	Year	Total Assets	Total Liabilities	NET ASSETS
2012	181,600	(9,400)	2012	110,740	91,390	19,350
2013	320,612	45,341	2013	188,074	123,383	64,691
2014	344,878	21,842	2014	194,816	108,282	86,534
2015	354,261	(12,466)	2015	192,892	118,824	74,068
2016	366,165	(10,164)	2016	249,304	185,400	63,904
2017	377,320	(7,482)	2017	226,956	170,534	56,421
2018	520,465	47,122	2018	248,431	154,537	93,894
2019	552,941	28,876	2019	267,335	144,564	122,771
2020	417,273	(25,181)	2020	238,553	140,963	97,590

2020 Timeline

March 12	Commencement of National Rugby League season.
March 19	New Zealand's international borders to non-residents closed.
March 23	Queensland State Government introduces 14-day quarantine arrangements for any non-resident travelling to Queensland.
April 14	National Rugby League announces on April 14 that the competition would be restarted.
April 20	National Rugby League CEO resigns with immediate effect.
May 28	National Rugby League recommences.
June 14	NSW Government announcement that fans would be permitted to return at 25 percent of stadium capacity.
July 1	Crowds return in NSW at 25 percent of stadium capacity.
October 25	Grand final held with 37,303 fans in attendance.

Australian Football League (AFL)

The Australian Football League is the most valuable professional sporting league in Australia and ranks seventh as the most profitable sports league globally behind the National Football League (NFL), Major League Baseball (MLB), National Basketball League (NBA), Indian Premier League (cricket), English Premier League (EPL), and the National Hockey League (NHL).

The sport of Australian Rules was founded in 1859[19]. Today, there are 18 teams competing in the Australian Football League, ten of which are located in the state of Victoria (Melbourne Demons, North Melbourne Kangaroos, Collingwood Magpies, Hawthorn Hawks, Carlton Blues, Richmond Tigers, St Kilda Football Club, Essendon Bombers, Western Bulldogs and the Geelong Cats), two in the state of New South Wales (Sydney Swans and Greater Western Sydney), two in the state of South Australia (Adelaide Crows and Port Adelaide), two in the state of Western Australia (West Coast Eagles and the Freemantle Dockers), and two in the state of Queensland (Brisbane Lions and the Gold Coast Suns).

The 2020 AFL season commenced in crowd-less stadiums on March 19 with defending premiers Richmond defeating Carlton 105–81. The decision to proceed with the scheduled opening fixture had only been ratified 24 hours earlier. Before the end of the first round, the season was formally postponed[20] along with advice that a recommencement would not occur before June. The announcement also included the cancellation of the remainder of the women's league which had already completed its regular season and was heading into a semi-final's series.

On May 14, 2020, the Australian Football League announced that clubs would return to training on May 18, and that the premiership season would resume on June 11. Having been unable to convince the state health departments in Western Australia and South Australia of their risk-management plans to recommence the competition, a bubble was established with approval from the Queensland health department which resulted in the four teams from Western Australia and South Australia relocating to the Gold Coast in Queensland. Games were scheduled to be played in Victoria, New South Wales, and Queensland.

COVID-19 protocols included bi-weekly testing of all players at least 24 hours prior to contact sessions. To remain flexible and agile in the evolving environment, the remaining games of the season were to be released in blocks of four to six weeks.

The state of Victoria was the birthplace of the Australian Football League and remains the heartland of the game as demonstrated by the ten clubs domiciled there. Victoria began to experience its second COVID-19 wave at the end of June 2020.

COVID-19 CASES IN VICTORIA[21]

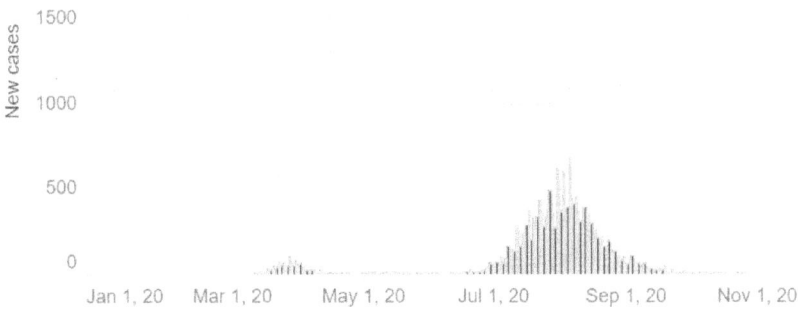

Halfway through the fifth round, on July 3, 2020, the Australian Football League announced the relocation of all ten Victorian clubs for the next two rounds with six clubs moving into Queensland and four into New South Wales[22]. This decision was just in advance of the Queensland Government announcing on July 9 that visitors from Victoria would no longer be able to enter and quarantine in Queensland from noon July 10, 2020[23].

Round 8 of the Australian Football League season was completed on July 27, 2020, at the conclusion of which all six clubs in New South Wales (including the four that had earlier relocated from Victoria) were moved into Queensland. This again, was just in advance of the Queensland Government declaring its borders closed to NSW residents on August 8[24]. The relocations of all clubs into Queensland remained in place through to the end of the season. By this time, the competition had been reduced to 17 games per club (down from the regular 22) and the grand final was played outside of Melbourne for the first time. Richmond beat Geelong 81–50 in the premiership decider, which was held at the Gabba in Brisbane on 24 October 2020. The Gabba's standard crowd capacity is 38,000, however, was limited to a maximum of 30,000 as the safe number determined by the Queensland Government in response to the COVID-19 pandemic. The official crowd number attending the grand final was 29,707.

For the financial year ending June 30, 2020, the Australian Football League experienced a 15 percent drop in revenue ($119m) compared to the previous financial year, with the income and expenditure statement showing an $8.4m loss for the financial year down from a $27.9m profit the year before. The net asset base declined by only 3.5 percent which was easily the best result of the four Australian sports discussed in this chapter.

Key contributors to this financial result were the securing of over half a billion dollars of credit from two major banks in order to navigate revenue losses due to the postponement of the commencement of the season, revenue losses from having no crowds when the competition did return, and the shortened season.

Cost cutting was significant and across the board. Examples of cutting the cloth to fit the suit included an agreement between the Australian Football League and the AFL Players Association for players to take 50 percent pay cuts for April and May, while the central administration of the league stood down 80 percent of its national workforce over this same period, with all remaining roles on reduced hours of three or four days a week[25].

The AFL was able to achieve this line of credit with two major banks because of the asset of Marvel Stadium which the Australian Football League purchased for $200m in 2016 and was reported to be worth more than one billion dollars in 2020[26].

Table 2. Australian Football League Financial Position 2012–2020 (Year Ending June 30)

Profit & Loss ($'000)			Balance Sheet ($'000)			
Year	Total Revenue	Surplus/ (Deficit)	Year	Total Assets	Total Liabilities	NET ASSETS
2012	471,177	8,052	2012	151,726	46,717	105,009
2013	502,699	18,229	2013	174,648	51,410	123,238
2014	528,230	13,320	2014	186,191	49,633	136,558
2015	558,674	3,648	2015	206,260	66,054	140,206
2016	569,856	(15,455)	2016	203,678	78,927	124,751
2017	752,622	60,344	2017	476,649	291,554	185,095
2018	778,596	25,714	2018	536,090	325,121	210,969
2019	793,939	27,858	2019	487,487	248,660	238,827
2020	674,816	(8,378)	2020	628,097	397,648	230,449

2020 Timeline

March 18	Decision ratified to proceed with AFL season commencement.
March 19	AFL season commences in crowd-less stadiums.
March 22	CEO Gillon McLachlan announces the postponement of the 2020 AFL season and the cancellation of the AFLW season.
May 14	Announcement by the AFL that clubs would return to training May 18 and the competition would recommence June 11.
July 3	AFL announces all ten Victoria clubs would relocate interstate for the next two rounds.
July 9	Queensland government announces that visitors from Victoria would no longer be able to enter and quarantine in Queensland from July 10.
July 27	Round eight is completed at the conclusion of which all six clubs in NSW (including the four relocated earlier from Victoria) are moved into Queensland. All clubs in Queensland remains in place through to the end of the season. Competition is reduced to 17 games per club, down from the regular 22 games per club.
October 24	Grand final played for the first time outside of Melbourne with 29,707 fans in attendance.

Cricket Australia

Cricket Australia is a standalone legal entity, incorporated as an Australian Public Company, limited by guarantee. That said, in a similar way where the NFL is structured with franchise owners, Cricket Australia is made up of six member associations: Cricket New South Wales, Queensland Cricket, South Australian Cricket Association, Cricket Tasmania,

Cricket Victoria, and Western Australian Cricket Association. These represent the six states of Australia. The two territories of Australia are non-member associations: Cricket Australian Capital Territory and Northern Territory Cricket.

Previously Cricket Australia was governed by a state-based board of 14 directors. In August 2012, State Associations voted to replace this model with a new, nine-person board with three independent directors and one each appointed by the six State Associations. Any director can be removed if voted down by a two-thirds majority, which means State Associations retain influence over future directions and governance.

Unlike the National Rugby League and the Australian Football League, the driver of revenue for cricket in Australia is not a domestic competition, but rather international match series and competitions, which all fall under the administration of Cricket Australia.

There are several domestic competitions owned and conducted by Cricket Australia including the four-day, first-class competition for men involving the six states (neither of the two Australian territories), 50-over competitions for men and women, and the 20-over T20 competitions for both men and women.

The T20 competition for men was established in 2005 and at that time comprised the same state-based teams as in the four-day competition. In 2011, however, the competition was changed into a franchise competition. While privatization of franchises was considered by Cricket Australia at the time, ultimately the T20 competitions were established with franchises owned and operated by state cricket boards rather than private interests.

These franchise-based competitions were extended by two more teams, with the larger markets of New South Wales and Victoria each having two franchisees being the Sydney Sixers and Sydney Thunder owned by the New South Wales Cricket Association, and the Melbourne Stars and Melbourne Renegades owned by the Victoria Cricket Association. The remaining franchises are the Perth Scorchers (owned by the Western Australian Cricket Association), Brisbane Heat (owned by the Queensland Cricket Association), Adelaide Strikers (owned by the South Australian Cricket Association), and the Hobart Hurricanes (owned by the Tasmanian Cricket Association). Franchises mirror each other in the men's and women's T20 competitions.

While State Associations are autonomous and separate legal entities, a key source of revenue is member distribution from Cricket Australia. For the financial year prior to COVID-19 ending June 30, 2019, this equated to $127.5m and 26.2 percent of Cricket Australia's total revenue of $485.9m which was distributed to the member cricket associations. State and territory cricket associations conduct their own geographically based grassroot competitions.

The first signs of cricket in Australia being under financial pressure due to COVID-19 became apparent when Cricket Australia announced on March 30, 2020, that the annual contract rankings for the national teams would be held off until April 30 to better work through potential scenarios for the upcoming season.

The South Australian Cricket Association had already reduced headcount during this same month of March. It is a smaller association, however, with a unique risk. It co-manages the premier stadium, Adelaide Oval, in that state along with the South Australian National Football League. With AFL matches being relocated to hubs in other states, budgeted revenue expectations from the Adelaide Oval were not being realized. Hence the headcount reduction by the

South Australian Cricket Association was not really foreshadowing the magnitude of what was about to come.

The domino effect impacting cricket started overseas. The Indian Prime Minister Narendra Modi enacted a national lockdown in India for 21 days commencing March 25, 2020. The lucrative Indian Premier League (IPL) had been scheduled to commence on March 29. The IPL has historically been conducted in the April–May window each year, in what is an otherwise cramped international cricket calendar. Due to the national lockdown in India, the IPL was initially suspended until April 15, and then suspended again until May 3. The national Indian team was scheduled to visit Australia for a summer test series in December. With Australia's international borders closed and national lockdowns in India, there was uncertainty whether the tour would proceed.

There is a standard playbook businesses deploy in the face of unexpected financial challenges. This includes stopping any work being undertaken by independent contractors (a separate discussion and business model issue if you are using contractors for the continuance of essential operations and business as usual activities), delaying the entering of any new contracts/liabilities (even if budgeted), running down of inventories, delaying maintenance, and putting a hold on any new hiring decisions. Indeed, this playbook is pretty common in the final quarter of any financial year where a business may be behind on revenue forecasts, and thereby use cost-reduction exercises to bring the bottom-line financial position into somewhere near budgeted expectations.

When financial shocks are looking bigger and likely to last longer, the playbook includes not replacing any staff who leave, mandating shutdown periods to reduce leave liabilities on balance sheets, selling off assets, strengthening the balance sheet by updating independent valuations on assets such as property where there is clear upside, or headcount reductions via redundancies.

To achieve the desired material difference, again the playbook is to go hard and go early, being mindful of not losing critical organizational capacity and capability, so that you can rebound strongly when the financial position is where it needs to be.

Cricket Australia was following the playbook by focusing on the areas within their immediate control. On April 16, 2020, Cricket Australia announced that it would operate on skeletal staff with much of its staff to be stood down from April 27 through to the end of financial year June 30, 2020[27].

At a press conference held April 21, 2020[28], Cricket Australia CEO Kevin Roberts was asked why so many staff were stood down and additional cost cutting measures when the sport did not have significant numbers of matches scheduled in the immediate future, so there could not be much impact on current cash flows.

Roberts response was:

"So on one level cricket is fortunate in terms of the time of year when the coronavirus situation hit, on another level cricket's unfortunate in that it's hit us at the lowest point of our four year cash cycle, so in a pre-coronavirus world we were already projecting that our cash and the investments would reduce to about $40 million at the start of September this year, and that they would bounce back very quickly by the start of the Indian test series, to about $100 million, which is approximately the level of cash and investments that we had in the end of March just gone. So the unfortunate reality of that is that we're anticipating that or we're estimating that we've taken a $20 million impact thus far and we have to anticipate given the unknown nature and fast-moving nature of this situation that they'll be more risks than that $20 million, so $20 million would take us from a low point of $40 million in cash and investments and any further shocks would take us far lower than that, and then if you contemplate the prospect of the international season in particular being affected, we have an issue of hundreds of millions of dollars on our hands, so it's very important that we plan proactively to that, that we do everything possible to stage the season and to navigate our way through this as we go. We certainly hope the situation doesn't go that deep and will be doing everything we can to prevent it, but if it goes there and we haven't taken preemptive action beforehand, we have nothing to fight it with."

Unlike other professional sports leagues which have a domestic focus, cricket at the highest level is a summer sport and an international competition requiring scheduling years in advance of matches that builds in accompanying travel logistics. Cricket is not a sport where you play all other competitors over a 12-month period.

For Australia, the test-cricket series that draw the biggest crowds and broadcast ratings are those against England and India. Australia plays both England and India in a test series every two years on a home and away basis, which means it is a four-year cycle when those teams visit Australia to play test matches.

As a general rule of thumb, visiting national teams from larger markets will play 4–5 test matches, whereas test series against national teams from smaller markets will generally be played over 2–3 test matches, allowing Cricket Australia to schedule two smaller market nations to visit over a summer. Test-match series are accompanied by separate series in the 50-over and 20-over formats.

Due to large expat and migrant communities in Australia, test-match series against England and India are highly popular. Doubly so through tourism, with citizens from both England and India visiting Australia's shores to experience the contests firsthand. These series maximize the bank and investment deposits for Cricket Australia to such an extent that they in turn subsidize the hosting of other nations in future series who do not draw the same size crowds or broadcast audiences.

You really are only able to play at the margins if trying to lower the cost base when opposing national teams who generate less revenue visit. Infrastructure cannot be turned on and off like a tap. Travel and accommodation costs do not change. Wages for players, officials and staff naturally cannot be lowered for periods during revenue troughs – their performance and expertise is required for the same duration, at the same level and output for revenue peaks when England or India visit.

COVID-19 striking Australian at the beginning of 2020 coincided at a time when India was due to visit for the Australian summer of 2020 (December – January). Co-incidentally, England was scheduled to visit Australia in the very next summer of 2021. This is what Kevin Roberts CEO of Cricket Australia alluded to when stating that COVID-19 had hit at the lowest point of Cricket Australia's four-year cash cycle. Should COVID-19 impact crowds or broadcast revenue going forward during what would be expected revenue high points, financial risks would be amplified over the coming four years.

This was the decision-making lens. During April 2020, there was no guarantee the summer series against India would go ahead, and even if it did, there was a low likelihood that crowds would be able to attend.

By the end of May, job losses in Australian cricket across

Cricket Australia and all state and territory associations had reached approximately 200, with Cricket Australia announcing a permanent reduction of 14 percent of its workforce and a reduction of $40m from its annual budget[29].

The central administrative cricket body had focused on the immediate areas it could control. Player wages were much more complicated, as they were part of a revenue-share model that was updated and re-signed in 2017, effective for a five-year period. Under the arrangement, there was a player payments pool of $459m assuming Australian Cricket revenue of $1.67bn (the equivalent of 27.5 percent). If Australian Cricket revenue exceeded $1.67bn, players were to receive 19 percent of the upside to $1.96 billion and grassroots cricket were to receive 8.5 percent. Above $1.96 billion, male, and female players receive 27.5 percent[30].

While negotiations create inevitable tension, eventually it is a win-win, and everyone is happy with a revenue-sharing model while revenue increases.

The difficulty becomes apparent when you come face to face with a financial cliff. The $1.67b milestone was reached after year four of the agreement (June 30, 2021), meaning players were entitled to a greater percentage on the upside with one year remaining, yet the administration was experiencing a balance sheet being reduced by over 40 percent.

By mid-June, Cricket Australia had announced the visit by the touring Indian team would go ahead, even though it was not clear at that stage whether crowds would be able to attend[31]. The IPL eventually commenced on September 19 and concluded on November 10 with a final that saw the Mumbai Indians defeat the Delhi Capitals by five wickets[32]. This timeframe enabled the Indian cricket team to be in Australia, meet quarantine requirements, and participate in a 50-over series starting November 27.

A bubble was created initially with a three-game 50-over series, and a three-game 20-over series played across New South Wales and the Australian Capital Territory only. This plan was to manage movements and mitigate risks of further COVID-19 lockdowns across states and territories. The four match test series of five-day games were scheduled December 17–21 in South Australia, December 26–30 in Victoria, January 7–11 in New South Wales, and January 15–19 in Queensland[33].

History shows that Cricket Australia experienced a 19.7 percent drop in revenue for the year ending June 30, 2020, representing a decline of $95.8m on the previous year. The impact on the bottom line was a $43.2m loss that reduced the asset base by 44.2 percent.

Despite the significant reduction in revenues, the member distribution from Cricket Australia to State Associations increased to $130.5m and represented 33.5 percent of Cricket Australia's total revenue ($390.1m) – up from the $127.5m and 26.2 percent of total revenue the year before.

Financial performance for the financial year ending June 30, 2021 would reflect receipts from a test series with India, while the following financial year ending June 30, 2022 would include a completed summer tour from England. At this point, revenue will have peaked for the next four-year cycle.

There remain storm clouds building on the horizon for Cricket Australia, further complicated by the need to renegotiate the player revenue share model in 2022.

Table 3. Cricket Australia Financial Position 2016–2020 (Year Ending June 30)

Profit & Loss ($'000)					
Year	2016	2017	2018	2019	2020
Total Revenue	339,787	303,490	399,265	485,901	390,098
Total income/(loss) for the year	35,727	(51,295)	(10,759)	9,902	(43,155)

Balance Sheet ($'000)					
Year	2016	2017	2018	2019	2020
Total Assets	371,412	317,717	276,128	240,785	195,178
Total Liabilities	221,517	219,117	188,287	143,042	140,590
NET ASSETS	149,895	98,600	87,841	97,743	54,588

2020 Timeline

March 3	Australia had confirmed 38 cases of COVID-19 in aggregate with one death.
March 8	Melbourne Cricket Ground hosts Women's T20 World Cup cricket final attended by 86,174 fans witnessing Australia defeat India by 85 runs.
March 13	Australian cricket team plays New Zealand in the first of a three match one-day series that went behind closed doors with no spectators.
March 20	Australia closes international borders to all non-citizens and non-residents.
March 23	Queensland State Government introduces 14-day quarantine arrangements for any non-resident travelling to Queensland.
March 25	India enters into 21-day nationwide lockdown.
March 29	Scheduled commencement of Indian Premier League postponed firstly until April 15, and then suspended again until May 3.
March 30	Cricket Australia delays national team annual contract rankings until April 30.

2020 Timeline

April 16	Cricket Australia announces it will operate on skeletal staff with the majority to be stood down from 27 April through to the end of financial year being June 30, 2020.
June 16	Cricket Australia CEO resigns.
September 19	Indian Premier League eventually commences.
November 10	Final of the Indian Premier League held with the Mumbai Indians defeating Delhi Capitals by five wickets.
November 27	Indian cricket team tour to Australia commences with a 50-over match in Sydney.

Rugby Australia

Rugby Union in Australia is a little different to the other three sports discussed. The Australian Football League is solely a domestic competition. Rugby League does have international competitions; however, it is the domestic league that is the driver and enabler of revenue generation. While there is a growing domestic 20-over franchise competition in cricket that has added more value to broadcast deals and attracted new audiences, international series remain the driver of revenue for Cricket Australia.

Drivers of revenue for Rugby Australia has greater similarities with cricket than Rugby League or the Australian Football League. The Australian Rugby Union team, monikered as the Wallabies, visits and hosts other international nations such as England, Ireland, Wales, Scotland, Argentina, Fiji, Japan, Italy, France, Samoa, Tonga, New Zealand, and South Africa.

These match series are drivers of broadcast revenue and crowds. Annually, however, the bigger drawcard in aggregate is an alliance Rugby Australia entered into with South African Rugby and New Zealand Rugby (SANZAAR) for an expanded domestic competition known as Super Rugby. Super Rugby comprised five teams in three geographical national divisions that essentially enable the identification of a winner within each nation, but a broader audience base by having those national divisions also competing with each other.

In 2020, the five franchises in the Australian division were the Brumbies, Rebels, Queensland Reds, NSW Waratahs, and the Sunwolves. The five franchises in the South African division were the Sharks, Stormers, Jaguars, Bulls, and Lions. The five franchises in the New Zealand division were the Crusaders, Blues, Chiefs, Hurricanes, and Highlanders. With the exception of the Sunwolves, all franchises are based in the countries of their division. The Sunwolves were based in Japan.

In Australia, there are additionally state-based competitions in New South Wales, Queensland, Victoria, Western Australia, South Australia, and the Australian Capital Territory. There is also a national women's competition (Super W), a universities competition, and Australia competes internationally in both men and women's seven-a-side Rugby Union competitions.

The major competition, however, is Super Rugby which commenced its season on January 31, 2020, and which was brought to a halt with one game left to be completed in round seven on March 15, 2020. Two days later it was announced that the semi-finals for the Super W (women's competition) that were scheduled for Saturday 21 March, would be postponed until the weekend of May 23–24[34].

Unlike the three other major sporting codes in Australia, Rugby Union was already experiencing a clear downward trend with revenue dropping from $150m in 2017, to $120m in 2018, to $112m in 2019. The total bottom-line performance was on a similar downward trajectory having made of a profit of $17.6m in 2017, returning a profit of $5.2m in 2018, and a $9.5m loss in 2019, which was before COVID-19 hit in Australia at the beginning of 2020.

There is no better indication of how delicate the financial state is of an organization than timelines around decision-making and implementation that are a clear pivot from current direction.

On March 31, Rugby Australia announced[35] that 75 percent of its workforce would be stood down the very next day (1 April) for three months through to the end of financial year June 30, 2020. All board directors had agreed to defer their directors' fees, while the chief executive officer would take a 50 percent salary reduction and the remaining executive staff across the game would receive at least a 30 percent reduction in salary over this same period.

The announcement came with a worst-case scenario projection of a loss of up to $120m should the Super-Rugby season and the entire test calendar for the Wallabies domestic season be cancelled in their entirety.

On April 21, the Rugby Australia board advised it had received a letter signed by eleven former Wallabies expressing their concerns over how the game had been administered in recent years[36]. By April 23, the CEO of Rugby Australia had resigned[37].

To protect capacity and capability in the game, the global governing body World Rugby established an emergency relief fund of approximately $160m available to national unions on an application and evaluation basis. Rugby Australia received $14.2m to assist on May 15, 2020[38]. World Rugby also advised on this date that Wallaby test matches scheduled for

July against Ireland and Fiji would need to be postponed[39]. Eventually these matches failed to find new homes in the 2020 calendar.

Rugby Australia had more exposure to international mobility of players and officials than other Australian sports given the design of the Super-Rugby competition. To their credit, they kept swinging, designing plans for all sorts of circumstances so that they could get competitions back underway to any extent possible. The plan for Super Rugby was to disaggregate and keep the three national divisions separate and conclude those as separate competitions. Thus, Super Rugby AU was born, along with Super Rugby Aotearoa in New Zealand, and Super Rugby Unlocked in South Africa.

Despite these efforts, given international travel mobility and quarantine requirements, on June 1 it was announced that the Sunwolves would withdraw from Super Rugby AU season[40].

On June 11, it was announced that the Super Rugby AU would commence on July 3 and be a five-franchise competition with Western Australian-based franchise Western Force added in place of the Sunwolves, and with each franchise playing all others twice. The finals would be over two rounds, with the franchise finishing the regular rounds in first place going straight through to the grand final and playing the winner of the second-placed franchise against the third-placed franchise[41].

By July 1, Rugby Australia and the Rugby Union Players Association had agreed to an interim pay deal at a flat 70 percent of their contracted wages and match payments until September 30 to cover the Super Rugby AU competition and with the commitment to re-negotiate prior to any test match programs being undertaken[42].

The first good news reflecting a re-engagement of

international competition was on September 11 when SANZAAR nominated Australia as the preferred bubble location for South Africa, New Zealand, Argentina, and Australia to participate in a four nation Rugby Championship[43]. Each nation played each other twice between November 7 and December 12[44].

More good news followed quickly on September 15, when Rugby Australia announced the Wallabies would visit New Zealand to play two test matches against the All Blacks on October 11 and 18 before returning to Australia for the four nation Rugby Championship[45].

Unfortunately, it was a case of two steps forward and one step back, with SANZAAR announcing on October 16 that South Africa would be unable to participate in the Rugby Championship due to South African government travel restrictions and navigating safety, travel, and quarantine for South African players located in various clubs in the United Kingdom and Europe. The Rugby Championship was reverting to a tri-nations series involving Australia, New Zealand, and Argentina[46].

The final piece of the COVID-19 puzzle for Rugby Australia was reaching an in-principal agreement on a new broadcast deal (which required SANZAAR approval). Announced on November 9, the agreement was reached with a new partner, Nine Entertainment Co, for a three-year period commencing from 2021 with a two-year option to extend valued at $100m. In 2020, broadcast rights were shared between pay television provider Foxtel and Channel Ten. The new agreement ended a 25-year relationship with Foxtel.

The new agreement with Nine Entertainment Co included broader coverage through streaming service Stan and the promotion of Australian Rugby across Nine Entertainment Co holdings in radio, newspaper publications, digital media, streaming services, and free-to-air television broadcasting[47]. While COVID-19 had economy-wide impacts including shrinking advertising revenue for broadcasters, Rugby Australia was able to negotiate a slight increase on the previous deal (noting the cash components and contra advertising and audience reach components are not publicly available information).

For the financial year ending June 30, 2020, Rugby Australia had experienced a 40.9 percent drop in revenue of $45.8m compared to the previous financial year, with the profit and loss statement showing an $27.1m loss. The net asset base had entered negative territory.

If there remain storm clouds building on the horizon for Cricket Australia, Rugby Australia was in the middle of a hailstorm that has not yet cleared.

Table 4. Rugby Australia Consolidated Entity Financial Position 2017–2020 (Year Ending December 31)

Profit & Loss ($'000)				
Year	2017	2018	2019	2020
Total Revenue	149,911	119,677	111,742	65,991
Total income/(loss) for the year	17,632	5,204	(9,485)	(27,111)

Balance Sheet ($'000)				
Year	2017	2018	2019	2020
Total Assets	66,660	69,929	59,185	56,524
Total Liabilities	29,541	43,157	40,856	63,893
NET ASSETS	37,119	26,772	18,329	(7,369)

2020 Timeline

January 31   Commencement of the Super Rugby SANZAR competition.

March 3   Australia had confirmed 38 cases of COVID-19 in aggregate with one death.

2020 Timeline

March 15	Super Rugby season postponed with one game left to be completed in round seven.
March 17	Super W semi-finals scheduled for March 21 postponed until May 23/24.
March 31	Rugby Australia announces 75 percent of its workforce would be stood down April 1–June 30.
April 21	Rugby Australia board receive letter signed by eleven former Wallabies expressing their concerns over how the game has been administered in recent years.
April 23	Chief executive officer of Rugby Australia resigns.
May 12	Rugby Australia receives $14.2m from World Rugby emergency relief fund.
June 1	Sunwolves withdraw from Super Rugby AU season.
July 1	Rugby Australia and the Rugby Union Players Association agree to interim pay deal at a flat 70 percent of contracted wages and match payments.
July 3	Super Rugby AU commences.
October 16	Advice that South Africa would be unable to participate in the Rugby Championship.
November 9	In principle agreement on a new broadcast agreement for Rugby Australia.

Sport CEOs tumble during COVID-19

History shows that three of these four major professional codes in Australia experienced turnover in the chief executive officer position during the first six months of COVID-19 becoming a health concern in the country. I make no assertions as to what happened in any of these instances. These are large and complex roles and large and complex organizations. I highlight this only to consider and reflect on the scenarios that each of these organizations were facing.

The CEOs were the meat in the sandwich. They had boards needing to demonstrate to internal and external stakeholders how the sport was going to respond effectively to a once in a lifetime pandemic, the existence of which would be absent in most risk registers, along with their mitigation strategies to demonstrate a board was meeting its governance obligations. There would have been a realization that scheduled games were at risk and that the revenues upon which budgets were built would unlikely be met. There were trickle-down effects of realizing that commitments to commercial partners based on the scheduling of those matches were now also not going to be met, in an environment where those partners were equally facing the financial pressures brought on by COVID-19. At the same time internal stakeholders such as players were experiencing anxiety about what the uncertain future meant for their livelihoods; the potential for short or long periods of time being away from family or with family in bubble environments, and how that impacts other aspects of their lives such as the schooling of children.

As a general rule, financial challenges amplify issues in all other business areas. COVID-19 was unique, however, the impacted finances represented existential threats for these sports. It was a tough first half of 2020 while professional sports in Australia reorganized themselves, and it should be no surprise that issues come to a head and CEOs turnover.

3.3 US sports pivot

The Centers for Disease Control and Prevention (CDC) in the United Stated first alerted clinicians on January 8, 2020, to be aware of, and look for, patients with respiratory symptoms returning recently from Wuhan, China. The first case of COVID-19 infection in the United States was detected in Washington from a traveler returning from visiting Wuhan on the January 15, 2020[48]. The second COVID-19 infection was detected days later in Illinois, although that particular traveler had actually returned earlier to the United States on January 13.

Public health entry screening by the CDC commenced on January 17, 2020, at the New York, Los Angeles, and San Francisco airports, with Atlanta and Chicago airports added one week later. The first person-to-person COVID-19 contagion would occur within the United States before the end of that month.

National Basketball Association (NBA)
The 2019–2020 National Basketball Association season commenced October 22, 2019, with the Toronto Raptors defeating the New Orleans Pelican 130–122. The season motored along, proceeding as normal and as planned through to March 2020 before it came to a screeching halt.

On Wednesday March 11, the Utah Jazz were scheduled to meet Oklahoma City Thunder. Just prior to tip-off, a preliminary positive test result for COVID-19 came in for one of the Utah Jazz players, which caused an initial delay to the game, and eventual postponement. Four other games continued to be played that evening: the Detroit Pistons against the Philadelphia 76ers, the New York Knicks against the Atlanta Hawks, the Charlotte Hornets against Miami Heat, and the

Denver Nuggets against the Dallas Mavericks. A sixth game between the New Orleans Pelicans and the Sacramento Kings was scheduled to be played a little later than these four games and was subsequently cancelled.

Advice filtered out widely on social media channels that the NBA was suspending the season following the completion of games being conducted that night March 11 until further notice.

The Denver Nuggets game against the Dallas Mavericks had not yet been completed when the announcement came through.

In an in-game interview on ESPN, Dallas Mavericks owner Mark Cuban was asked how he assessed the decision of the NBA to call an immediate halt to the season. He responded:

"I mean, I trust Adam*. I mean, you know what, it's really not about basketball or money, I mean literally if this thing is just exploding to the point where you know all of a sudden players and others have had it, you think about your family, you know you want to really make sure you're doing this the right way, you know 'cause it now it's, it's, it's much more personal, and you've seen what's happening in other countries, but just the whole idea that it's come this close and potentially a couple players have it, um just, stunning isn't the right word; I mean it's crazy.".

*Commissioner of the NBA Adam Silver

The potential that a couple of NBA players could have COVID-19 turned into reality the very next day, with Utah Jazz players Rudy Gobert and Donovan Mitchell confirming that they had both tested positive for the coronavirus. Then there was a slow drip of other coronavirus positive player tests, starting with the Detroit Pistons reporting a positive test of one player on March 14, and the Brooklyn Nets confirming four players testing positive to coronavirus March 17.

On March 19, there was a flurry of announcements, with the Los Angeles Lakers advising that two players had tested positive, the Boston Celtics advising one player had tested positive, the Philadelphia 76ers advising that three people from their organization had tested positive, and the Denver Nuggets advising that one member of their organization had tested positive[49].

By March 27, the first two players testing positive, Rudy Gobert and Donovan Mitchell, had been cleared of their coronavirus infections. The Brooklyn Nets similarly advised on April 1 that their four players had now recovered and were symptom free.

More than two months had passed, when on June 5[50] the NBA Board of Governors approved a plan to recommence the season on July 30. The planned restart was contingent on an agreement being reached with the Walt Disney Company to use the Walt Disney World Resort in Florida as a single-bubble environment that would house all players and support staff and host all games and practices for the full duration of the remainder of the season.

With the time lost, the restarted competition would be reduced to 22 teams comprising the eight teams in playoff position in each of the two conferences when the competition was halted in March, and another six teams so that the group of 22 represented the NBA's best records. The playoffs would remain consistent with the traditional playoff format being a best-of-seven series in the first round, conference semi-finals, conference finals, and the NBA finals.

Agreement with the Walt Disney Company was able to be reached, and by June 26, the NBA and the National Basketball Players Association had finalized a plan for the July 30 restart that included stringent health and safety protocols. There would be no fans in attendance in the Walt Disney World Resort bubble including none during the play-offs. By this time, there would be over six million COVID-19 infections occurring in the United States since the middle of January[51].

COVID-19 CASES IN THE UNITED STATES IN THE YEAR 2020

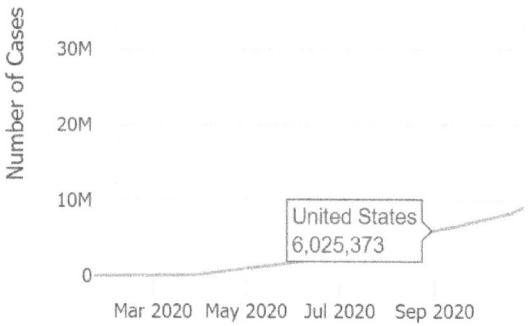

Of the 22 teams participating, nine were from the Eastern Conference: the Milwaukee Bucks, Toronto Raptors, Boston Celtics, Miami Heat, Indiana Pacers, Philadelphia 76ers, Brooklyn Nets, Orlando Magic, and Washington Wizards. They were joined by thirteen teams from the Western Conference: the Los Angeles Lakers, LA Clippers, Denver Nuggets, Utah Jazz, Oklahoma City Thunder, Houston Rockets, Dallas Mavericks, Memphis Grizzlies, Portland Trail Blazers, New Orleans Pelicans, Sacramento Kings, San Antonio Spurs, and Phoenix Suns.

The season was completed under these conditions on October 11, with the Los Angeles Lakers securing their fourth win in the best-of-seven finals series, defeating the Miami Heat 4–2 in the final series.

Timelines

October 22, 2019	Start of the 2019–2020 National Basketball Association season.
January 17, 2020	Public health entry screening for COVID-19 infections by the CDC at New York, Los Angeles and San Francisco airports.
End of January 2020	First person-to-person COVID-19 contagion detected in the United States.
March 11, 2020	NBA suspends season due to COVID-19 concerns until further notice.
June 5, 2020	NBA Board of Governors approve plan to recommence the season July 30.
July 1, 2020	More than 6m COVID-19 infection detected in the United States.
July 30, 2020	NBA season restarts in Walt Disney World Resort bubble, reduced to 22 teams.
October 11, 2020	LA Lakers defeat Miami Heat 4–2 in the best-of-seven finals series.

National Football League (NFL)

Super Bowl LIV of the National Football League took place on February 3, 2020. A crowd of 64,767 attended the Hard Rock Stadium in Miami Gardens Florida, witnessing the Kansas City Chiefs defeat the San Francisco 49ers 31–20.

Unlike other sports covered in this chapter, timing benefited the National Football League with their season concluding at the same time as the onset of the COVID-19 pandemic in the United States. That said, the out of competition period before the next season was to experience massive disruption. Firstly, a new collective bargaining agreement (CBA) was to pass through smoothly in the context of what was to come. The NFL Players Association board endorsed sending the proposed

CBA to all players for a vote on February 26. Official voting ballots were distributed March 5. By March 15, NFL players had voted to approve ratification of the new CBA 1,019 to 959. Following ratification, the NFL Management Council informed teams that the salary cap had been raised by $10m on the previous year to $198.2m per club and represented the seventh consecutive year that the salary cap had been raised by $10m or more[52].

COVID-19 really started to wreak havoc on March 13, with the NFL advising franchises that pre-draft visits were to be halted in response to the growing COVID-19 outbreak. That included both draft-eligible players attending a team facility and club personnel being prohibited to travel to any location to meet a draft-eligible player. NFL teams could conduct interviews via telephone or video conference through to the day before the draft, with interviews restricted to no more than one hour, and no more than three interviews with any specific draft-eligible player per week.

The NFL offices were closed from March 13, and all club facilities were closed from March 26.

In an NFL memo to all 32 clubs on April 6[53], it was shared that government stay at home orders along with the closing of non-essential businesses now covered the home communities of every club and in some cases extended out to June. The NFL draft, which is a signature broadcast event, would now be held as a virtual event April 23–25 rather than attended in person in Las Vegas as planned.

By May 7, the NFL had released protocols for re-opening team facilities provided they were permitted to do so under state and local regulations[54]. These protocols included the prohibition of coaches and players, and a strict limit of no more than 50 percent of non-playing staff, up to a maximum of 75 staff per day. There was one exception on players and coaches, and that was to allow only players that were rehabilitating from injury to attend the facility. Strength and conditioning coaches supporting the rehabilitation program were also able to work at the facility along with the relevant player, but they were, however, otherwise prohibited along with the other coaching staff.

By mid-June, approximately 10 clubs had reported positive COVID-19 tests from their playing groups. As part of COVID-19 risk mitigation, the NFL Players Association were advising players not to work out together in a private capacity[55] prior to team training camps.

Evolving COVID-19 protocols introduced a classification system for people accessing facilities and games. A tier one classification was used for essential and on-field personnel such as players, coaches, team physicians, and equipment managers. Tier two was a classification for other essential personnel who may periodically need to be in close proximity to players and other tier one individuals. Tier three consisted of individuals who perform essential facility, stadium, or event services but who did not require close contact with tier one classified people.

Pre-season training camp started July 28, although meetings were virtual meetings through to the end of July. In-person attendance started at the beginning of August accompanied by daily COVID-19 testing, along with restrictions on who could be present at a facility and when.

The day prior to the commencement of training camp, Roger Goodell, commissioner of the NFL, wrote an open letter to fans setting expectations for the season. This included that the season would look like no other, driven by the need to follow health advice, and needing to be sufficiently agile in order to update protocols based on evolving new information and updated scientific understanding. The open letter also confirmed that all pre-season games had been cancelled[56]. Unlike other major sports that finished seasons within designated bubbles, the NFL was looking like it would have an on-scheduled commencement with regular home and away venues across all 32 teams.

Managing heightened risk[57] with travel and closed spaces involved protocols that limited team travel to tier one and tier two individuals only; wearing masks, physical distancing wherever possible including separate hotel rooms; buses limited to no more than 50 percent capacity; and at least one open seat between airplane passengers. Once at the team hotel, travelling players and coaching staff were not permitted to leave the hotel to eat or use restaurants that were open to the public, nor use shared facilities within the hotel unless the facility had been quarantined by the hotel for the team and had been disinfected.

The public were prohibited from attending facilities during training camps and having any contact with tier one or tier two individuals, while media had limited access to the club facilities and were unable to conduct in-person interviews with players and coaches.

All players, coaches, and staff participated in intake testing July 28–31, as a precondition to in-person contact throughout the remainder of training camp. This involved three tests over these four days. The NFL were very conscious about the potential of a COVID-19 infected person causing an outbreak of contagion across individual facilities.

At a media conference held August 12[58], NFL Chief Medical Officer Dr. Allen Sills shared data from the intake testing as well as monitor testing conducted over the first two weeks of training camps.

Intake testing saw 9,983 players and personnel tested, with new positives being identified in 170 players and personnel

(1.7 percent). Players were 2,840 of the 9,983 group with new positives being returned by 53 players (1.9 percent).

Players and personnel continued to be tested on an ongoing basis as practices and camps progressed. Through August 11, monitoring testing conducted 109,075 total tests returning a positivity rate of 0.46 percent. The player specific positivity rate was 0.81 percent. Not one club exceeded a 1.7 percent positivity rate since testing began. Players would continue to be tested daily for coronavirus through to September 5.

The first major hitch for the NFL occurred late August. Under NFL and NFLPA protocols, any player who tested positive for COVID-19 must have two negative tests before he was allowed to return to practice. This included even if the original test later was found to be a false positive.

On August 22, BioReference Laboratories reported heightened numbers of COVID-19 PCR test results for NFL players and personnel at multiple clubs. The results caused multiple teams to cancel or reschedule practice sessions, bringing to the fore risk mitigation should similar instances occur on game day and with the season start just around the corner. The NFL investigated and retested 77 samples all which subsequently came back negative. An isolated contamination issue during test preparation was determined to be the cause[59].

The season commenced as scheduled on September 10, with the Kansas City Chiefs defeating the Houston Texans 34–20.

The second big hurdle for the NFL occurred in week four. As the season commenced, fines were issued for breaches of COVID-19 protocols, and for the most part they were isolated incidences, along with small numbers of COVID-19 positive tests.

In week four, the Tennessee Titans were the first team to have a significant outbreak. Ten players were already on the

Titans COVID-19 reserve list in the lead up to their Sunday game scheduled against the Pittsburgh Steelers. The day prior to the game, one player and two coaches tested positive. Another player was added to the reserve/COVID-19 list on the Sunday the game was due to be played, which led to the NFL announcing the game with the Pittsburgh Steelers would be postponed until October 25. This particular game would be rescheduled another two times. All up, this outbreak with the Titans totaled 24 confirmed COVID-19 infections.

After investigation, the NFL determined the Tennessee Titans breached COVID-19 protocols, resulting in a $350,000 fine[60] for failing to comply with requirements on wearing masks and insufficient clear communication regarding workouts outside the facility. This was not the last fine of such magnitude to come.

Also in week four, Kansas City Chiefs hosting the New England Patriots was pushed back one day.

Further postponements and reschedules were to occur with one game in week five, three games in week six, four games in week seven, one game in week eight, one game in week 10, two games in week 11, one game in week 12, and three games in week 13.

With the finish of the regular season in sight, Santa Clara County provided the final major hurdle for completing the 2020 season. With COVID-19 infections on the rise, the county announced November 28 that there would be a three-week ban on all sporting activities that involved contact with other people. A mandatory 14-day quarantine was introduced for people travelling into the county from more than 150 miles away.

These changing circumstances led to the San Francisco 49ers relocating to Arizona to play their week 13 and 14 home games from the Arizona Cardinals home State Farm

Stadium. The three weeks ban in Santa Clara was extended and resulted in the 49ers remaining in Arizona for the remainder of their season, finishing week 17 with a 23-26 loss to the Seattle Seahawks.

Super Bowl LV was played on February 7, 2021, at Raymond James Stadium in Tampa, Florida where a COVID-19 safe reduced crowd of 24,835 fans witnessed the Tampa Bay Buccaneers defeat defending champions the Kansas City Chiefs 31–9.

By seasons end, there were 13 teams who did not have fans attend any of their eight home games: Buffalo Bills, Chicago Bears, Detroit Lions, Green Bay Packers, Las Vegas Raiders, Los Angeles Rams, Los Angeles Chargers, New England Patriots, New York Giants, New York Jets, Philadelphia Eagles, San Francisco 49ers, and the Seattle Seahawks.

The Dallas Cowboys had by far and away the best record for fan attendance at home games, achieving almost 200,000 over the eight home games with a crowd average of 28,187[61].

This statistic is eye-watering and reinforces my contrarian view contained in the introductory chapter – sport and politics do mix. The NFL is a national sport and part of the American cultural fabric. Yet federated models of government mean public policy decisions can be made in any one of the 50 states or in one of the 3,243 counties in the United States that end up having a material impact on franchises. From a Santa Clara County instigated ban on contact sports that saw the 49ers move into Arizona to complete their season, to 13 franchises being unable to have any fans attend any of their home games during the season, while the Cowboys were nudging 200,000.

To be fair, elected representatives probably didn't pursue office to battle a pandemic. In the next section, rather than take the lens of general manager of a football fantasy roster, we will consider likely macro-economic factors that influence the thinking of elected officials when being presented with health-policy advice.

2020 Timelines

January 17	Public health entry screening for COVID-19 infections by the CDC at New York, Los Angeles, and San Francisco airports.
January 2020	First person-to-person COVID-19 contagion detected in the United States.
February 3	Super Bowl LIV in front of a crowd of 64,767 at the Hard Rock Stadium in Miami Gardens Florida, witnessing the Kansas City Chiefs defeat the San Francisco 49ers 31–20.
March 15	NFL players approve ratification of new CBA. Salary cap raised $10m on previous year to $198.2m per club.
April 6	NFL memo to all 32 clubs advising the NFL draft would be a virtual event April 23–25.
July 28	Pre-season training camps starting with intake testing.
August 22	Spike in positive test results, resulting in investigation and retesting 77 samples showing original results to be false positives.
September 10	NFL season commences with the Kansas City Chiefs defeating the Houston Texans 34–20.
February 7, 2021	Super Bowl LV played at Raymond James Stadium in Tampa, Florida in front of a COVID-19 safe crowd of 24,835 fans and with Tampa Bay Buccaneers defeat defending champions the Kansas City Chiefs 31–9.

3.4 Australian case study: macroeconomic factors that influence public policy decision-making

Economies in every country are unique. To name but a few, there are material differences in the size and geographical spread of the land mass, the number of people, levels of education attained by the population, the size of both the working and non-working populations, the size of the public sector, the number of companies and size of the private sector, government spending and public debt levels, manufacturing bases as opposed to jobs in the services sectors, areas of concentrated competitive advantage, free market characteristics (as opposed to protectionist policies) and the degree of government intervention, the destination and size of export markets, and the nature of the domestic market.

To look at Australia as a case study and consider the Australian Government's initial response to the onset of COVID-19, it is worthwhile to reflect on some of the unique characteristics of the Australian economy.

The Australian population as at June 30, 2020 was 25,687,041. In terms of the world's largest populations, Australia does not rank in the highest 50 most populous countries. Despite this, the Australian economy is thirteenth largest in the world as measured by nominal Gross Domestic Product (GDP).

As with most developed economies, because of sustained low birth rates and increased life expectancy, Australia has an ageing population. The working age population is defined as 15–64 years of age. The number of Australians aged 65 years and over increased from 14.92 percent of the total population in 2015, to 16.29 percent of the total population in 2020. Over the five years to June 30, 2020, the working-age population in Australia grew by 6.1 percent, compared to 11.4 percent for the remainder of the population.

Table 5. Twenty Largest Economies in the World[62]

Country	Nominal GDP	Population	GDP Per Capita
1. United States	20,936,600.00	329,484.12	63,543.60
2. China	14,722,730.70	1,402,112.00	10,500.40
3. Japan	4,975,415.24	125,836.02	39,538.90
4. Germany	3,846,413.93	83,240.52	46,208.40
5. United Kingdom	2,707,743.78	67,215.29	40,284.60
6. France	2,630,317.73	67,391.58	39,030.40
7. India	2,622,983.73	1,380,004.39	1,900.70
8. Italy	1,886,445.27	59,554.02	31,676.20
9. Canada	1,644,037.29	38,005.24	43,258.20
10. Korea, Rep.	1,630,525.01	51,780.58	31,489.10
11. Russian Federation	1,483,497.78	144,104.08	10,126.70
12. Brazil	1,444,733.26	212,559.41	6,796.80
13. Australia	1,330,900.93	25,687.04	51,812.20
14. Spain	1,281,484.64	47,351.57	27,063.20
15. Mexico	1,076,163.32	128,932.75	8,346.70
16. Indonesia	1,058,423.84	273,523.62	3,869.60
17. Netherlands	913,865.40	17,441.14	52,397.10
18. Switzerland	752,248.05	8,636.90	87,097.00
19. Turkey	720,101.21	84,339.07	8,538.20
20. Saudi Arabia	700,117.87	34,813.87	20,110.30

With GDP per capita of $51,812 USD, Australia is a wealthy nation. Outside of the world's twenty largest economies, there are, however, several countries with smaller populations that have higher GDP per capita than Australia.

Table 6. Economies with smaller populations and higher GDP per capita than Australia[63]

Country	GDP Per Capita	Population
Luxembourg	115,873.60	632,275
Macao SAR, China	86,117.70	649,342
Ireland	85,267.80	4,994,724
Norway	67,389.90	5,379,475
Denmark	61,063.30	5,831,404
Singapore	59,797.80	5,685,807
Iceland	59,270.20	366,425
Sweden	52,259.30	10,353,442

The Australian economy peaked in 2013 with GDP reaching $US1.576 trillion, a high that has not been revisited over the last eight years.

The Global Financial Crisis had a twelve-month impact on the Australian economy where GDP was $US1.054 trillion in 2008 before dropping to $US927.8 billion in 2009, and then rebounding to $US1.146 trillion in 2010.

AUSTRALIA GDP ($US BILLIONS) 1960–2020

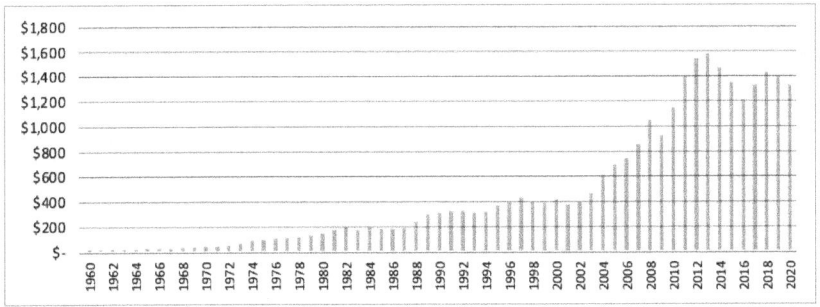

As of June 30, 2020, there were 2,314,448 actively trading businesses in the Australian economy. The public sector accounted for 355 of those businesses. In the private sector there were 240,015 partnerships, 687,569 sole proprietors, and 926,662 companies. Of all trading businesses, 93 percent had turnover of less than $2 million.

Only 2.2 percent of the 2.3 million Australian businesses employed 20 or more staff.

Non-employing businesses	1,441,105
1–4 employees	607,128
5–19 employees	214,435
20–199 employees	47,634
200+ employees	4,146
Total businesses	**2,314,448**

The Australian economy exported goods and services to the value of $475.24 billion for the financial year ending June 30, 2020. The top 10 exports are dominated by the resources and agriculture sectors, with only international education and international inbound tourism outside of these two sectors. The biggest export, iron ores and concentrates, represented 21.6 percent of total exports, while the top 10 exports represent over 67 percent of total exports.

Australia's top 10 Exports, Goods & Services Financial Year Ending June 30, 2020 (A$ million)

1. Iron ore & concentrates	102,864
2. Coal	54,620
3. Natural gas	47,525
4. Education	39,661
5. Gold	24,394
6. Personal travel (excluding education) services	16,368
7. Beef	11,258
8. Aluminum ores & concentrates	8,875
9. Crude petroleum	8,568
10. Copper ores & concentrates	6,854

Recessions are defined by a fall in GDP for two consecutive quarters. Prior to COVID-19, Australia's last recession was in the year of 1991, when there was a fall in GDP for the March and June quarters. From 1992 through 28 years, Australia did not experience another recession.

At the onset of COVID-19, Australia experienced only the slightest of contractions in the March 2020 quarter being -0.3 percent. This was followed by a large contraction in the June quarter of -6.8 percent, hence indicating Australia was in recession and breaking the run of 28 years of consecutive growth.

To contextualize Australia's GDP growth record by way of international comparisons, the graph below charts annual percentage growth across Australia, the United States, China, France, United Kingdom, Germany, and Canada from the year 2006 through to 2020. This provides an easy analysis of the 2009 global contractions bought on by the challenges resulting from the Global Financial Crisis. Due to significant Federal Government stimulus at the time, Australia was able to ward off a recession through the Global Financial Crisis.

GDP GROWTH (ANNUAL %) – AUSTRALIA, UNITED STATES, CHINA, FRANCE, UNITED KINGDOM, GERMANY, CANADA – 2006–2020

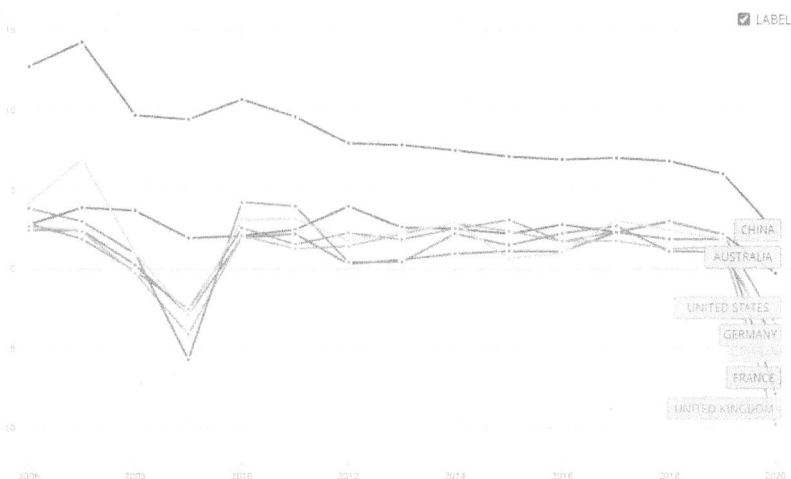

Source: World Bank national accounts data, and OECD national accounts data files.

The unemployment rate in Australia started the 2020 calendar year at 5.3 percent in January, decreasing to 5.1 percent in February, before rising to 5.2 percent in March. It had been stable in the ten months prior to March 2020, varying month to month within a 5.1 percent – 5.3 percent range. Once COVID-19 began to bite, the unemployment rate quickly rose to 6.4 percent in April, 7.1 percent in May and 7.4 percent in June. Over 600,000 jobs were lost from the economy during the month of April in 2020, followed by another 264,000 jobs lost in May 2020.

Underemployment jumped too from 8.8 percent in March 2020 to 13.8 percent in April. Total monthly hours worked in April 2020 revealed a drop of -8.51 percent on the twelve months prior, increasing to a drop of -9.25percent on the twelve months prior in May 2020.

Key Indicators and the initial effects of COVID-19 on the Australian economy

Month	Employed Persons ('000)	Unemployment rate	Participation Rate Seasonally Adjusted	Underemployment Rate Seasonally Adjusted	Monthly Hours Worked (m)
Jun 2019	12,850.80	5.3 percent	66.0	8.2 percent	1,764.5
Jul 2019	12,875.30	5.2 percent	66.0	8.4 percent	1,773.5
Aug 2019	12,917.40	5.2 percent	66.2	8.5 percent	1,777.8
Sep 2019	12,925.50	5.2 percent	66.1	8.3 percent	1,782.2
Oct 2019	12,900.60	5.3 percent	66.0	8.5 percent	1,777.5
Nov 2019	12,930.10	5.1 percent	65.9	8.3 percent	1,779.8
Dec 2019	12,961.50	5.1 percent	66.0	8.2 percent	1,786.9
Jan 2020	12,973.00	5.3 percent	66.1	8.6 percent	1,775.5
Feb 2020	12,992.30	5.1 percent	65.9	8.7 percent	1,771.0
Mar 2020	12,989.20	5.2 percent	65.9	8.8 percent	1,786.5
April 2020	12,381.80	6.4 percent	63.6	13.8 percent	1,616.8
May 2020	12,117.70	7.1 percent	62.7	13.1 percent	1,600.4
Jun 2020	12,328.50	7.4 percent	64.0	11.7 percent	1,664.7

Source: Labour Force, Australia, June 2020 | Australian Bureau of Statistics (abs.gov.au)

The Australian workforce totaled 13,020,500 people in March 2020. The number of workers dropped to 12,328,500 by the end of June 2020[64]. The public sector represented 16.6 percent of the workforce totaling 2,041,200[65] workers. The segmentation of the public sector was 246,000 employees across the Federal Government, 1,609,100 across the eight state and territory governments, and 186,000 in local governments across the country.

There was steady annual growth (2–3.3 percent) in the number of operating businesses in the three years leading up to June 30, 2020. Entry rates of new firms and exits of old firms were similar over this same period.

Australian Businesses 2018-2020[66]

Key Indicators	Year Ending June 30, 2018 – All Industries	Year Ending June 30, 2019 – All Industries	Year Ending June 30, 2020 – All Industries
Operating at start of financial year #	2,137,796	2,208,447	2,268,998
Entries – Total #	343,888	346,946	336,499
Exits – Total #	273,237	286,395	291,049
Operating at end of financial year #	2,208,447	2,268,998	2,314,448
Change #	70,651	60,551	45,450
Percentage change percent	3.3	2.7	2.0
Entry rate percent	16.1	15.7	14.8
Exit rate percent	12.8	13.0	12.8

Australian Government Net Debt

Financial Year Ending	Net Debt $AUD	Percent of GDP
June 30, 2021	$592.2 billion	28.6 percent
June 30, 2020	$491.2 billion	24.8 percent
June 30, 2019	$373.6 billion	19.2 percent
June 30, 2018	$342.0 billion	18.6 percent
June 30, 2017	$322.3 billion	18.4 percent
June 30, 2016	$296.4 billion	18.0 percent
June 30, 2015	$238.7 billion	14.8 percent
June 30, 2014	$202.5 billion	12.8 percent
June 30, 2013	$153.0 billion	10.1 percent
June 30, 2012	$147.3 billion	10.0 percent
June 30, 2011	$84.6 billion	6.1 percent
June 30, 2010	$42.3 billion	3.3 percent

Innovation can sometimes seem a little slower in Australia with highly regulated sectors dominating the largest listed companies by market capitalization. For example, there are five companies from the banking and financial sector in the top 10 largest companies by market capitalization.

The Australian Stock Market had peaked in January 2020 on the previous twelve months, quickly losing 28.2 percent by the time Australia's international borders were closed in March 2020.

Month	All Ords Price Index	Dom. Equity Mkt cap $m
Jun'20	6001.3	1,918,406
May'20	5872.2	1,856,401
Apr'20	5597.7	1,757,205
Mar'20	5110.6	1,594,791
Feb'20	6111.5	2,026,292
Jan'20	7121.2	2,213,451
Dec'19	6802.4	2,118,340
Nov'19	6947.9	2,153,235
Oct'19	6772.9	2,102,358
Sep'19	6800.6	2,109,097
Aug'19	6698.2	2,074,246
Jul'19	6896.7	2,132,177

If politics was a sport, and certainly some argue that it is, a combat sport, then let's put the fantasy league general manager cap back on and think about context and strategic next steps, as if you were an elected representative.

The WHO declared the novel coronavirus outbreak a public health emergency on January 30, 2020. The total value of the Australian stock market dropped 14 percent in February 2020. By March 3, Australia had 38 cases of COVID-19 with one death, while globally there had been 90,846 confirmed cases with 3,115 reported deaths.

Global mobility was the biggest factor of contagion spreading, both by air and by sea. Export markets are at risk; natural resources such as iron ore, coal, natural gas, gold, aluminum, petroleum, and copper. In agriculture, it is beef. What does international trade, shipping and quarantine look like during a global pandemic. How will different countries respond?

What impact will mitigation strategies have on international students coming into the country and Australia's fourth largest export.

Expert health officials advised that COVID-19 is an airborne virus and the best way to minimize contagion is through reducing human to human contact. Lockdowns were war gamed as a principal mitigation strategy.

Australia closed its borders to all non-citizens and non-residents March 20. The Federal Government's department of treasury were considering it plausible that GDP could be 10–12 percent lower in the June quarter than previously forecast and that unemployment could rise to 15 percent. Indeed, Treasury considered it possible that GDP could fall by 24 percent if lockdowns and restrictions mirrored additional sectors as had occurred in Italy and Spain.

By the end of March 2020, the Australian stock market

had lost 28.2 percent of its value over the preceding eight weeks. The unemployment rate rose from 5.2 percent in March, to 6.4 percent in April losing over 600,000 jobs in the process, to 7.1 percent in May losing an additional 264,000 jobs.

Within this context, the conduct of sporting leagues was not part of the thinking. The health and economic crisis were much bigger than that.

Now swap fantasy leagues caps. You are the CEO of a sporting league. What do you do?

4. Talent identification and acquisition: building a championship winning roster

ONE REASON PROFESSIONAL SPORT REPRESENTS the ultimate in accountable business models is because market participants cannot hide from results. In the NFL, you either qualify for the post-season or you do not. The merit order within a division is first place through to fourth place. You have either achieved more than your direct competitors or you have not.

Irrespective of the way the ball bounces, or an incorrect refereeing decision goes against you, or you have more injuries to your key personnel than your competitors, at the end of the season, the ladder is what the ladder is. The order of merit is listed first through to last.

End of season reviews determine what went right and what went wrong. Plans are devised on how to get better. That is the mindset of all competing franchises. If you are not going forwards, you are going backwards. Improvement is not an absolute measure. Even if you do improve, if those behind you have improved more, you may find yourself slipping down the order of merit. The outcomes at all stages are easy to monitor and public.

Talent identification and acquisition

The fastest way to improve is upgrading personnel. How to do that is what this chapter is all about.

The NFL Draft

I started out an earlier chapter by asserting that the NFL was the global sport and league that best represented a metaphor for the perfect market economy. There is, however, one exception to this metaphor, and that is the NFL draft being the principal pathway for attracting new talent. A draft is not reflective of a true market economy.

Why does the draft distort what would otherwise be a free-market economy?

It is a market distortion because the economic principles of supply and demand and the effect on price do not really apply. Every franchise wants the best talent available, but they cannot have it. The order of the draft selection is made from the lowest finishing team selecting first, through to the Super-Bowl winner from the previous season selecting last in each round. This order is replicated over seven rounds (outside of compensatory picks referred to in the second chapter). Any eligible players not selected over these seven rounds are then deemed unrestricted free agents and may negotiate with any franchise in the hope of attending a training camp and ultimately securing a place on a roster.

Now some will argue that this is still reflective of a free-market economy because draft picks are tradeable and where this occurs, the selection order is altered accordingly. While that is true, it comes unstuck in three areas.

Firstly, remuneration included in draft contracts is to a large degree pre-determined by the NFL and on a sliding scale where the first pick earns the most. That is not really a merit system. If your franchise is particularly keen on a specific playing talent, you cannot offer greater remuneration to sway that playing talent to join you, nor can you offer less representing what you feel is true market value. Within that context it is easy to overpay or underpay. A rookie may not influence the result in games as much or be as consistent as some of your other players, but you may be stuck with remunerating them more in the early years if they have been a high draft pick.

Secondly, in any given year there are often suspicions when a bottom-placed team is perceived to perform at a standard even lower than their performances earlier in the season or perceived to make unusual decisions. For example, the final week of the 2021 season saw the Philadelphia Eagles play Washington in the NFC West division. The divisional standings heading into the final game were Washington and Dallas Cowboys each with six wins, the New York Giants with five wins, and Philadelphia with four wins. The Philadelphia Eagles benched quarterback Jalen Hurts while trailing by only three points in the fourth quarter against Washington replacing Hurts with third-string back-up Nate Sudfeld. Philadelphia ended up losing that game. Had they had won, the New York Giants would have taken the division title and qualified for the playoffs, Washington instead took that honor. Philadelphia finished lower in the overall standings thereby improving their draft position to pick no. six overall (if they had won, they would have picked at no. nine).

The season before, it was Miami Dolphins and Cincinnati Bengals experiencing accusations of tanking on social media in order to be able to select at number one and thereby acquire the best quarterback in the draft class. With draft capital so important to future success, opposing fans will always be hard to please if they perceive any variables negatively impact their specific tribe.

Thirdly, talent secured and remunerated through the draft

is a projection of future capability rather than a reflection of achievements to date. Apart from the finance world, where there is the standard disclaimer on financial advice being that 'past performance isn't necessarily an indicator of future performance', in every other field, past performance is used as an indicator of likely future success.

Evaluating talent: the ceiling and the floor

When evaluating talent, NFL commentators refer to a player's ceiling and floor. The ceiling is a perception of future potential. This is based on "tape" (video highlights) from the player's best performances and best plays at college level, along with their physical attributes compared to others in the draft class and assessing the degree to which those attributes are enablers for success at that position in the NFL. It also involves assessing those physical attributes to "comps" (comparisons) to current and former NFL players as an indicator of likely success. This approach is combined with an assessment of intangibles. Intangibles are the harder to measure attributes such as leadership skills both on and off the field, game instincts and decision-making, ability to get on with a diverse group of people both teammates and staff, etc.

Conversely, the 'floor' is the perceived minimum rung on a ladder that a player will achieve. It considers the consistency in outputs put on tape at college, the athlete's weakness in physical attributes compared to others, whether there are red flags on behavior both off the field and on the field and whether these are likely to affect teammate acceptance within the locker room, or red flags on early career injuries which may impact longevity or availability. There is a saying in the NFL – "the best ability is availability". An athlete may have all the talent in the world, but if they are not on the field, there is no return on investment.

To describe some examples of applying the ceiling/floor lens, an athlete may be physically limited compared to others in their position in terms of speed, strength, and mobility, but they anticipate well and are predictable in what they can achieve and consistently deliver. Such an athlete may be described with a higher floor than others but a lower ceiling in terms of how high their play and performance might ascend over time. A physically gifted athlete who may be faster and stronger than most in their playing position, however, demonstrates recklessness with decision-making and proven inconsistent with their performances at college level, may have a lower floor but a higher ceiling in terms of potential to succeed at the NFL level. The assessment recognizes there are areas to work on and develop, and that if that development is successful there will be gains, however, if the development is unsuccessful, the quality of outputs will not be very high.

Apart from the draft, other talent acquisition pathways are through trades or signing free agents (those players coming off contract).

Scouting talent

To look at NFL talent acquisition holistically, let us go back to the months leading to the 2021 NFL draft conducted over two days Friday April 30 and Saturday May 1. The final round of the NFL was held on January 4, meaning 18 franchises began their season reviews while the remaining 14 franchises turned their focus to the playoffs.

The wild-card round, divisional round and Conference Championships were completed by January 25, leaving the Kansas City Chiefs and Tampa Bay Buccaneers to fight out Super Bowl LV on February 8, 2021.

The college season ended on the January 12, 2021, with Alabama Crimson Tide defeating Ohio State Buckeyes 52–24 in the national college championship. Alabama would later have six players selected in the first round of the NFL draft including quarterback Mac Jones, while Ohio State would have just one single player selected in the first round being their quarterback Justin Fields.

With the quarterback position so crucial for success at NFL level, scouting analysis regularly identified five quarterbacks likely to be selected in the first round of the draft. Historically, at the completion of the college season there is a National Invitational Camp, also known as the National Scouting Combine, which is an invitation only four-day event for draft eligible college players to undergo a series of testing across physical attributes, medical and mental, enabling NFL front office and scouts to conduct further deep dive player evaluations. Due to COVID-19, the combine was cancelled in 2021, leaving individual colleges open days for NFL franchises to attend or web calls with individual draft eligible players.

It is during the January through April period that talent identification becomes intense. Anti-tampering rules means franchises cannot speak with free agent players until the start of the new league year. In 2021, this was March 17, 2021.

4.1 Assigning value: not all positions are created equal

Upon the completion of the NFL Super Bowl each year, there is a blackout of about one month before the commencement of the new NFL season. The start of the new season represents the date when trades between franchises can recommence and the free agency period for those players with expiring contracts opens. The trade market and free agent signings become active pretty quickly. Franchises need to know where weaknesses remain in their roster so that they can identify and recruit rookies capable of improving those weaknesses during the April draft, hence there is some urgency.

	2020 Timeline
January 4	End of NFL regular season. Eighteen franchises finished for the year.
January 12	End of college season. Alabama Crimson Tide defeating Ohio State Buckeyes 52–24.
January 25	Wild-card rounds, divisional rounds and Conference Championships completed.
January 30	Los Angeles Rams trade with the Detroit Lions to acquire quarterback Matthew Stafford.
February 8	Super Bowl LV Kansas City Chiefs and Tampa Bay Buccaneers.
March 18	New NFL year.
March 26	San Francisco 49ers trade their pick no.12 for no. three pick from Miami Dolphins. Dolphins then trade No. 12 to Philadelphia Eagles for no. six.
April 30 & May 1	2021 NFL draft.

Competing to secure mature talent – the Rams/Lions, Matthew Stafford/Jarred Goff trade

The first big trade-market domino to fall in 2021 was the contracted quarterback for the Detroit Lions Matthew Stafford. Stafford was the first overall pick in the 2009 draft and had spent his entire career with Detroit having not won a playoff game during his tenure. As happens in all sports, as athletes draw nearer to the end of their careers, the longing to fulfill a title void motivates athletes to consider opportunities elsewhere at a team with a roster capable of challenging for a title.

Stafford had two years remaining on his contract and approached Detroit ownership seeking a trade. The Lions were going to go through a rebuild with a new coach and general manager coming in and given Stafford's respected tenure with the Lions, the trade request was granted.

There was no shortage of interested trade destinations for Stafford. Albert Breer of *Sports Illustrated* reported at the time that among those interested franchises included Washington, Carolina Panthers, Tennessee Colts, San Francisco 49ers, Denver Broncos, New England Patriots, Chicago Bears, New York Jets, and the Los Angeles Rams. While not mandatory, Detroit worked collaboratively with Stafford to understand his destination preferences.

Just like a property auction, as soon as there is competing interest, value goes up. It became public that Detroit was open to trade offers for Stafford on January 23, 2021. Discussions between Stafford and Detroit naturally occurred much earlier, with the potential trade being on the table and discussed as a scenario in coaching and general manager interviews held in early January.

Stafford's availability became officially known on January 23, with the trade negotiated and closed by January 30, despite interest from at least nine franchises representing more than 25 percent of the league. The business lesson the Stafford trade represents is the need for agility in talent identification and acquisition. Talent does not wait for you to get your house in order. This is sometimes colloquially referred to as "snooze you lose" in the business playbook.

Sometimes you need a little luck for cards to fall your way. In this instance, the Rams Coach Sean McVay is buddies with Buffalo Bills receiver coach Chad Hall, and Hall's sister is the wife of Matthew Stafford. Brad Holmes had spent eighteen years in a career with the front office of the Los Angeles Rams and was then appointed as the new general manager of the Detroit Lions. Then during the designated offseason, both McVay and Stafford happened to be holidaying in Cabo, Mexico and were able to find some time together.

That McVay was in Cabo at the same time as Stafford was not a unique or determining fact. A number of NFL players were in the popular vacation destination at the same time including San Francisco 49ers head coach Kyle Shanahan.

Like most things in business, you make your own luck. McVay was determined and hands-on to land his prized new recruit. That didn't involve any shortcuts. He and his team reviewed the tape, determined that the skillset and intangibles were highly desirable, collaborated with ownership to get the green light to go for it, and supported management to make the deal happen. Through the common network, all sides were persistent to close the deal. A deal sooner rather than later minimized the potential for distractions such as other quarterbacks coming onto the trade market, or unknowns and variables impacting draft strategizing. Then the trade offer was strong and indicative of genuine intent, while others were still working through their position of fair market value on a potential trade.

The trade involved Detroit acquiring the Los Angeles Rams quarterback Jarred Goff, a 2021 third-round pick and first-round pick in 2022 and 2023 in exchange for Stafford. This meant that the Rams would not have a first-round draft pick until 2024.

While the trade wouldn't become official until the start of the new NFL year on March 18, the negotiations were completed January 30, just seven days after it became public that Detroit were open to a trade for Stafford.

Competing to secure rookie talent – the 49ers trade up

The next big domino to fall was on March 26, when the San Francisco 49ers traded up from pick no.12 in the draft to secure pick no. three from the Miami Dolphins. This trade meant Miami were to receive the twelfth overall selection from San Francisco, a third-round pick and first-round picks in 2022 and 2023 (Miami later traded pick no. 12 with the Philadelphia Eagles to rise back up the draft order to pick no. six).

The San Francisco 49ers had reached Super Bowl LIV in February 2020 losing to the Kansas City Chiefs 31–20. The 2021 season was marketed as the "revenge tour". Despite the best-laid plans, the 49ers went on to suffer the second-most injuries of any NFL team over the previous 20 years and finished fourth in the NFC West with a 6–10 win-loss record and failing to qualify for the postseason.

At that stage, Kyle Shanahan had been the head coach of the 49ers for four years over the 2017–2020 seasons achieving a regular season win-loss record of 29–35 and qualifying for the post-season just once being the Super-Bowl run in 2019.

Kyle Shanahan Win-Loss Record as head coach of the San Francisco 49ers

Season	Regular Season Record Win-Loss-Draw	Playoff Record Win-Loss-Draw
2020	6–10–0	0–0
2019	13–3–0	2–1
2018	4–12–0	0–0
2017	6–10–0	0–0

In Shanahan's first season, the 49ers acquired quarterback Jimmy Garoppolo from the New England Patriots, with Garoppolo making his 49ers debut in week 14 against the Houston Texans. Over the 2017–2020 seasons, Garoppolo achieved a 24–8 win-loss record with the 49ers. The disconnect between Shanahan's win-loss record and that of Garoppolo is due to injuries; Garoppolo missed 13 games in 2018 and 10 games in 2020. When Garoppolo played, the 49ers performed well. When he was not available, the 49ers had a losing record.

Having made the playoffs just once in four seasons, the quarterback position was identified as the key enabler and an area that needed strengthening. Like most teams, the 49ers were not planning for ongoing poor results, and at pick 12, didn't feel they would be that close to the top of the draft order again in the foreseeable future.

Having missed out on Stafford, trading up and securing a quarterback on a rookie contract was determined to be the best option rather than bringing in mature talent via trade or free agency. A good business lesson here is about holding a belief in a scheme and philosophy but being flexible and fluid in achieving that vision. What does the perfect world look like? And if the universe conspires to prevent that perfect world immediately coming to life, what does plan B and plan C look like as steppingstones to the perfect world?

An example of assigning value: the Jimmy Johnson NFL draft chart

In chess, each playing piece has a different value. Pawns are worth one point, knights and bishops are worth three points, a rook (castle) is worth five points, and the queen piece is worth nine points. The king piece is not assigned a value as the purpose of the game is to capture the opposing players' king otherwise known as check mate.

In the NFL draft, there is no formally designated value for picks by position in the draft order. In terms of strategy, franchises either select based on need, that is addressing a weakness in their playing squad evident from the results of the previous season or due to player exits from their roster during free agency, or they select based on best player available. That said, because pick positions are tradeable between franchises, notional values are always calculated by teams when developing their trade and list management strategies. Not dissimilar to having a point system in chess.

One of the storied examples of creating a draft methodology and evaluation framework was developed by Hall of Fame coach Jimmy Johnson. Johnson was head coach of the Dallas Cowboys for five seasons between 1989–1993 winning Super Bowls in each of his final two seasons, and later going on to coach the Miami Dolphins for four seasons (1996–1999).

As draft picks are tradeable Johnson's draft chart assigns a numerical value per draft pick order. Table 7 provides an example of this chart using the 2021 draft order.

Table 7. Jimmy Johnson Draft Chart

ROUND 1		ROUND 2		ROUND 3		ROUND 4		ROUND 5		ROUND 6		ROUND 7	
Pick	Value	Pick	Value	Pick	Value	Pick	Value	Pick	Value	Pick	Value	Pick	Value
1	3000	33	580	65	265	96	116	128	44	161	27	193	14
2	2600	34	560	66	260	97	112	129	43	162	27	194	14
3	2200	35	550	67	255	98	108	130	42	163	26	195	13
4	1800	36	540	68	250	99	104	131	41	164	26	196	13
5	1700	37	530	69	245	100	100	132	40	165	25	197	13
6	1600	38	520	70	240	101	96	133	40	166	25	198	12
7	1500	39	510	71	235	102	92	134	39	167	25	199	12
8	1400	40	500	72	230	103	88	135	39	168	24	200	11
9	1350	41	490	73	225	104	86	136	38	169	24	201	11
10	1300	42	480	74	220	105	84	137	38	170	23	202	11
11	1250	43	470	75	215	106	82	138	37	171	23	203	10
12	1200	44	460	76	210	107	80	139	37	172	23	204	10
13	1150	45	450	77	205	108	78	140	36	173	22	205	9
14	1100	46	440	78	200	109	76	141	36	174	22	206	9
15	1050	47	430	79	195	110	74	142	35	175	21	207	9
16	1000	48	420	80	190	111	72	143	35	176	21	208	8
17	950	49	410	81	185	112	70	144	34	177	21	209	8
18	900	50	400	82	180	113	68	145	34	178	20	210	7
19	875	51	390	83	175	114	66	146	33	179	20	211	7
20	850	52	380	84	170	115	64	147	33	180	19	212	7
21	800	53	370	85	165	116	62	148	32	181	19	213	6
22	780	54	360	86	160	117	60	149	32	182	19	214	6
23	760	55	350	87	155	118	58	150	31	183	18	215	5
24	740	56	340	88	150	119	56	151	31	184	18	216	5
25	720	57	330	89	145	120	54	152	31	185	17	217	5
26	700	58	320	90	140	121	52	153	30	186	17	218	4
27	680	59	310	91	136	122	50	154	30	187	17	219	4
28	660	60	300	92	132	123	49	155	29	188	16	220	3
29	640	61	292	93	128	124	48	156	29	189	16	221	3
30	620	62	284	94	124	125	47	157	29	190	15	222	3
31	600	63	276	95	120	126	46	158	28	191	15	223	2
32	590	64	270			127	45	159	28	192	15	224	2
								160	27				

Using this chart, one player at pick no. six (1,000 points) is the equivalent value of two players at pick no. 26 (700 points) and pick no. 60 (300 points).

If we apply this valuation mechanism for the Los Angeles Rams and Detroit Lions trade, they swapped quarterbacks, and Detroit received a 2021 third-round pick and first-round picks in 2022 and 2023. If the Rams were to win the next two

Super Bowls, this value would be pick 32 in the first round at 590 points each year and pick 95 in 2021 at 95 points, for a total of 1,275 points. It is a sizeable investment. Where this becomes problematic for the Rams, in the highly competitive NFC West, is if they fail to qualify for the wild-card play-offs meaning a pick order of 18 or higher (900 points x two years plus the third-round pick from 2021). We will discuss roster management in another chapter, however, here you can see an early challenge, and that is your investment is also a sunken cost. If the investment fails to deliver superior results, it ties your hands and makes it harder to climb the results ladder later because of those sunken costs.

This is no different to any business. You might open up a new location. The premises, if purchased, will be an asset that increases in value or decreases in value over time. Alternatively, you may take out a lease for the building which may be over three, five, seven, or ten years with contracted options for extension. Once that lease is committed to, the new operation needs to deliver as per the business plan for that new site otherwise you are playing catch up and losses amortized across the rest of the business.

In the instance of the 49ers trading up from pick no. 12 to pick no. three, the Johnson valuation methodology translates this to an upgrade of 1,000 points. If the 49ers finish in the top eight in each of the next two seasons by qualifying for the divisional playoff, it would be a maximum pick no. 25 at 720 points x two years for a total 1,420 plus one round three at pick no. 89 valued at 145 points for a total 1,595. Subtracting the 1,000 points upside in trading up from pick no. 12 to pick no. three, the total differential is 595 points and equivalent to the final pick from the first round in future drafts. The trade has the same sunken cost risks as showcased with the Rams and Stafford investment should the 49ers finish lower on the end of year table; they would have thereby forgone higher valued assets come draft time.

Naturally, this is not a straight-line exercise. Lower rookie salaries help meet salary-cap restrictions and franchises need to balance capabilities within the salary cap. Or if franchises trade away too many draft picks, they will need to rely on free agents to fill vacancies on the roster. In instances where these are veterans accepting the minimum salary as contained in the CBA, the veteran's ceiling may be limited compared to a rookie who has yet to be realized potential.

Assigning value in a broader business context

The main point here is that leaders are always making assessments on asset value whether this is infrastructure or your human capital. This is not just in sport, but in any business.

As humans, we can get really uncomfortable assigning value to human capital in our businesses. This is irrespective of whether you are the board setting executive remuneration, executives undertaking end of year performance reviews and assessing incentive payments of team members, business unit leaders developing proposed budgets for the next financial year, or any team member looking to achieve a pay rise. Every person wants and deserves to be valued by their employer.

For a business to be sustainable, however, let alone excel, assigning value to positions and people is a reality and needs to be a discipline. If you go too high on salaries, you mortgage your future. If carefully considered, this may be a legitimate business tactic particularly if you are going all in taking an early market leader approach and wanting to hoover up market share before others follow and compete. Or if there are competitors active in the market that may solicit key resources away from your operations which if removed will inhibit the ability for the business to achieve its goals.

Conversely, if you go too low on salaries, your capabilities won't deliver the desired business performance. Salary benchmarking products and services assist businesses to understand the competitive labor market. They are but a tool. If you decide to meet medians for specific roles, then the question becomes intangibles and why would a prospective employee join your business over others. The benchmarking products are retrospective using data collected from the previous twelve months, hence looking in the rearview mirror means that they do not pre-empt changes that have already started in the market.

Salaries are subject to the laws of supply and demand just like every other input and output in business. If the skills and expertise of a role can be easily replaced with comparable skills and experience readily found in market, a salary will be low. If skills and expertise are hard to replace and hard to find for critical business functions, salaries will be high. Not all positions in a business organization chart are created equal. There may be roles supporting commoditized products and services, which means there will always be pressure on keeping wages low. If there are greenfield areas which hold the promise of much upside for the business, required skills and expertise will be well remunerated. If you are a team member in a commoditized area of the business, looking to secure that pay rise, you would be well placed to demonstrate how your productivity has been enhanced relative to other parts of the operations that would justify the pay rise or demonstrate how your role has taken on more responsibility or complexity in response to market trends.

Valuations and creating a winning formula in the NFL

In any team sport, not all positions contribute equally to achieve a winning formula. In the NFL, rosters are limited to 53, with an additional 16-man practice squad. The offense is the playing group that has control of the football and the objective of moving the ball into the opposition's end zone scoring a touchdown or scoring a field goal by kicking the ball through the posts. The quarterback position is unequivocally the most important position in any team and is the 'general' responsible for moving the ball around the offense in order to exploit opposition weaknesses. Defense looks to protect field position and cause a changeover either by securing a turnover from the offense or having the offense punt the ball down field.

Franchises will have two to three quarterbacks on their 53-man roster to account for form and injuries. That said if the capability of two quarterbacks on any squad is at a similar level, to the extent that they compete for the starting position on the team or share snaps during practice, there is a saying in the US that "if you have two quarterbacks, you have none". The intent of this colloquialism is to say that if there isn't a clear-cut superior resource in the quarterback position on your franchise's roster, you don't have sufficient quality in the quarterback position to consistently beat out your competition.

After the quarterback position, the next two positions of most importance and hence higher salaries are left tackle and defensive end, both specifically because of their relevance to the quarterback position. The left tackle protects the blind spot of the quarterback. If the quarterback is hit from the left without seeing the defense, the ball may be unprotected, and a turnover can result. Minimizing unexpected tackles also minimizes opportunities for the quarterback to be injured.

The defensive end is on the other side of the scrimmage line, and they are the ones responsible for pass rushing – that is pressuring the opposing quarterback and looking to affect a tackle before the quarterback passes the ball so that the offence loses field position, or delivers a poorly executed pass, or loses the ball altogether which is then ideally secured by the defense.

Within the confines of a salary cap, each franchise will determine the importance of each position to their football philosophy and system, whether that be positions of guard, tight end, wide receiver or running back on the offense, or linebacker, corner back or safety on the defense.

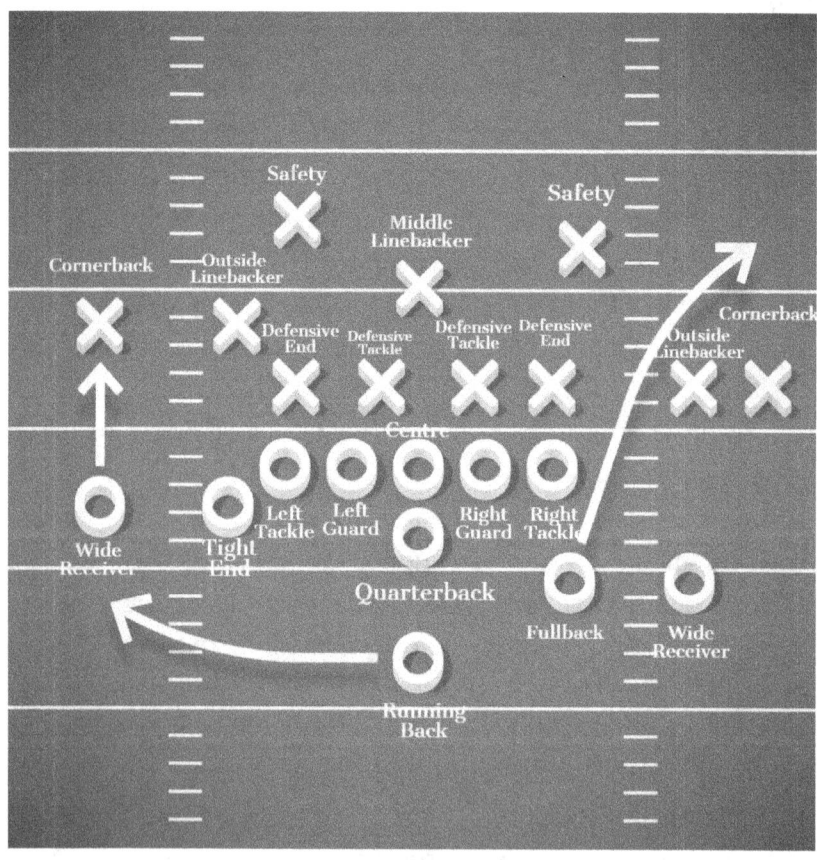

Then, just like all positions are not created equal, neither are all players. At any given time, personnel departments would have an evaluation of each quarterback in the league and be able to list them one through 32 in terms of strongest capabilities through to the weakest. The same can be evaluated across all positions. Within the confines of capabilities and market value, personnel departments and coaches make assessments of the value of players coming off contract in terms of remuneration being offered in new contracts or attracting players from other rosters to join their franchise. At all times this is a balancing act. What value one specific quarterback is to one team will be different to the value for this same player to another team.

Just like any business, value in the NFL is affected by market downturns. As it became apparent that COVID-19 would impact revenues, the NFL salary cap was reduced for the 2021 season. Contract durations are different from player to player, and those with expiring contracts were faced with reduced bargaining power. The best players coming off contract were still able to negotiate high remuneration because there was high competition for their services. The mid-tier players were the ones that experienced the most squeeze. Some elected to pursue new deals of just 12 months in duration in the hope that society learned to live with COVID-19 to the extent that revenues rebounded, and that the salary cap would too, thereby affording increased capacity for franchises to pay in future seasons.

NFL Salary Cap by Year

2021: $182.5 million	2018: $177.2 million	2015: $143.3 million	2012: $120.6 million
2020: $198.2 million	2017: $167.0 million	2014: $133.0 million	2011: $120.0 million
2019: $188.2 million	2016: $155.3 million	2013: $123.0 million	

Source: Pro Football Network[67]

4.2 Evaluating potential

> *Consistency is the truest measurement of performance*[68]
> Sean McVay, head coach Los Angeles Rams

When trading up from pick no.12 in the 2021 draft to secure pick no. three from the Miami Dolphins, the San Francisco 49ers gave themselves five weeks to undertake additional and deep dive due diligence on how they would use that selection to best set themselves up for future success.

Given the size of the future draft capital forgone to invest in securing pick three by the 49ers, there really was only one position that would justify the size of that investment: the quarterback position.

There were five draft eligible quarterbacks that analysts regularly identified as likely first rounders: Trevor Lawrence from Clemson University, Zach Wilson Brigham Young University, Trey Lance North Dakota State University, Justin Fields Ohio State University, and Mac Jones from University of Alabama.

Even if you know nothing about football and the NFL, let's take a moment to envision the 49ers scenario, and war game some criteria that you might use to determine the order of priority of who you would like to select with the no. three pick. It needs to be a prioritized order, because if you just identified your number-one preference, the teams with pick no. one and pick no. two might select your preferred option leaving you with no plan b when it came time for your selection. You may have a preferred running back or tight end in mind for later selections, but you would not simply move that selection up because the opportunity cost is too high (see Johnson value chart).

This is no different to any recruitment exercise within any business. Interviewers are not aware of whether candidates have other options. If your first preference does not accept the job offer, are other candidates also suitable? What is the order of second and third preferred candidates? Even if there are internal candidates, interviewers do not know if or where external opportunities are also being pursued.

Thus, you need to plan for various scenarios, and complete a deep dive on the best available talent. What criteria would you choose?

In the case of selecting a quarterback, how about criteria such as the following:

1.) Arm strength? In the accompanying table, Mac Jones has the longest successfully completed throw at 94 yards, followed by Trey Lance at 88 yards, Trevor Lawrence at 87 yards, Zach Wilson at 78 yards, and Justin Fields at 65 yards.

2.) Passing touchdowns? Fields had 67, Lawrence had 66, Wilson and Jones both had 56, while Lance had half that at 28.

3.) Rushing touchdowns as indicator of the best dual-threat capability with both throws and feet? Fields had 19, Lance 16, Wilson 15, Lawrence 10, and Jones 2.

4.) Rushing from general field position? Lawrence's longest college run was 67 yards, Lance's longest rush was 61 yards, Fields 51 yards, Wilson 36 yards, and Jones 18 yards.

5.) Consistency and efficiency with passing? Lawrence with 10,098 yards at 66.6 percent completion rate, Wilson with 7,652 yards at 67.6 percent, Jones with

Talent identification and acquisition

    6,126 yards at 74.3 percent, Fields with 5,701 yards at 68.4 percent, and Lance with 2,947 yards at 65.4 percent.

6.) Resilience and longevity? What type of injuries has the athlete suffered prior to nominating for the draft? How likely are those injuries to affect future longevity? How has the athlete been able to bounce back after being sacked? Lawrence played 40 games at college level and was sacked 43 times, Fields played 34 games and was sacked 56 times, Wilson and Jones both played 30 college games with Wilson sacked 53 times and Jones sacked 16 times, while Lance played 19 games and was sacked 15 times.

Then, what does the data not tell you? There are so many possible criteria such as a quarterback's vision on the playing field, their touch with the pass, ability to anticipate, ability to get on with teammates, respect with which the athlete is held by teammates and coaches, decision-making when the pressure is on, consistency in execution, the players ability to maximize the performance of their teammates; the list goes on.

Other variables might include track record in winning championships, the quality of the opposition in games, and the quality of your teammates. Accuracy in completions is not just the pass of the quarterback but the quality and performance of the receiver, and the quality of the opposing defense.

For example, Mac Jones' Alabama Crimson Tide had six players selected in the first round of the 2021 NFL draft, Trevor Lawrences' Clemson had two players selected in the first round, while Zach Wilson was the sole selection in the first round from BYU, Lance the sole selection in the first round from North Dakota State, and Justin Fields the sole selection in the first round from Ohio State.

When the 49ers traded up to pick no. three, there was a lot of noise in public commentary that Coach Shanahan had Mac Jones in mind.

Lawrence had been widely considered to be a generational talent and was the presumptive number one pick ever since his freshman year when he led Clemson to a national title.

Evaluating quarterbacks – insights from coaches

Urban Meyer has one of the strongest coaching records at college level having coached three teams to national championships, the Florida Gators to the national championship in 2006 and 2008, and the Ohio State Buckeyes in 2014. Myer went into an analyst role with ESPN after finishing his stint at Ohio State in 2018 and was coaxed into the NFL for the first time accepting the head coach role at the Jacksonville Jaguars for the 2021 season.

Meyer was asked on *Good Morning Football*, what makes Trevor Lawrence special, responding:

> "… number one is his competitive spirit, he's a competitor, is 34 and two as a starter, he's an extreme competitor, all the homework we've done on him, when I talk to him on zoom calls and you know I don't have to really do much more zoom 'cause I know so much about Trevor, but he's been great in our conversations, that's number one. He's a tough guy. I witnessed that live when I watched him play against Ohio State in a playoffs not this past year, year ago, and that his intelligence, football intellect, his leadership, and then his ability to adapt in the spread offense … he can do it all. He's five from five in those areas".

It was clear that, for a first time NFL coach with an outstanding record of winning at college level, Meyer and the Jacksonville Jaguars were not going to blindside with an unexpected number one pick. Lawrence was their man.

It was also clear over the March–April 2021 period that the New York Jets with pick no. two were going to select Zach Wilson. New York is the NFL's biggest market, and it is also the largest media market in the United States. There are lots of eyes and ears everywhere watching every move providing confidence that Wilson was going number two.

That left the 49ers with three quarterbacks to choose from being Mac Jones, Justin Fields, and Trey Lance. Shanahan shared his thoughts on evaluating the quarterback position on the *Flying Coach Podcast*[69] with Sean McVay and Peter Schrager. To paraphrase Shanahan:

> There is so much that goes into evaluating the quarterback position, you've got to be smart, you've got to be able to process it, but you can't go in there and overthink it, otherwise you have no chance to play. You have to be in the zone, have a clear mind, have low blood pressure and heart rate, just to play the right way. The biggest thing is to have the right arm. If you can't make the throws in this league, it will catch up with you. And there are many variants of that. You can have the strongest arm in the world, but guys that have the strongest arm usually don't throw with anticipation because they have never had to.
>
> My biggest thing is, can you play in the pocket and keep your eyes down the field. And that's hard for guys who have been running around their whole life. I don't feel Peyton Manning and Tom Brady ever ran around. They sat in the pocket at every age and learnt how to dissect people, get rid of it, and make plays.

Then you have got people who have never played that way because they haven't had too because they are good athletes.

I can go so many different directions with the quarterback, but if you don't bring in the running element, you have got to be one of those rare people that can sit in the pocket and keep your eyes down field and not let that rush affect you. And the way you don't do that is you're either smart and it comes fast to you, or you're smart enough to where you can study the playbook and you are automatic with where everyone is going to be, that you could do it in a dark room at any moment without hesitating.

Ultimately, the 49ers would go on to select Trey Lance with the third pick in the 2021 NFL draft. We will never know the final criteria Shanahan and 49ers General Manager John Lynch used, and how they weighted each of the key drivers of their decision. What we do know, is that by trading up early and trading up that high, they permitted themselves time to accurately target the available talent pool, at the position they deemed most in need, and then deep dive to evaluate the potential of the available talent.

Shanahan would later say[70]:

You're not moving up if you don't feel good about both of those [Jones and Lance], and if, it would have just been one, then we would have said – no, well we probably wouldn't have said no 'cause it's too risky – but we would like, we really would've, either one of those players would have been a great pick in my opinion, and the third guy with Justin, like he would have been a great pick. So it's just what direction do you want to go, and there's so many things that play into it, you gotta make that decision but ... I didn't blame people all for thinking it would be Mac Jones 'cause Mac Jones deserves that, like he's that good of a player and he put it on tape for a whole year ... but Trey brought another element, and it doesn't mean that he's better or worse, it just means he brought another element, that over the course of us studying it really intrigued us, and that's the direction that I would love to go and would always wanted to go, but the guy has got to be able to do it all, and Trey sold us that he could, and that's why I'm excited to work with him and it's up to us to get him to do it.

COLLEGE STATS FOR THE FIVE QUARTERBACKS SELECTED IN THE FIRST ROUND OF THE 2021 NFL DRAFT

		TREVOR LAWRENCE			
		SEASON / TEAM	SEASON / TEAM	SEASON / TEAM	
		2018 / CLEM	2019 / CLEM	2020 / CLEM	Career
PASSING	GAMES	15	15	10	40
	CMP	259	268	231	758
	ATT	397	407	334	1138
	CMP percent	65.2	65.8	69.2	66.6
	YDS	3,280	3,665	3,153	10,098
	AVG	8.3	9.0	9.4	8.9
	TD	30	36	24	90
	INT	4	8	5	17
	LNG	74	87	83	87
	SACK	11	17	15	43
	RTG	157.6	166.7	169.2	164.3
RUSHING	ATT	60	103	68	231
	YDS	177	563	203	943
	AVG	3.0	5.5	3.0	4.1
	TD	1	9	8	18
	LNG	32	67	34	67
SCORING	PASS	30	36	24	66
	RUSH	1	9	8	10
	TD	1	9	8	10
	PTS	6	54	48	60

ZACH WILSON

		SEASON / TEAM 2018 / BYU	SEASON / TEAM 2019 / BYU	SEASON / TEAM 2020 / BYU	Career
PASSING	GAMES	9	9	12	30
	CMP	120	199	247	566
	ATT	182	319	336	837
	CMP percent	65.9	62.4	73.5	67.6
	YDS	1,578	2,382	3,692	7,652
	AVG	8.7	7.5	11.0	9.1
	TD	12	11	33	56
	INT	3	9	3	15
	LNG	70	75	78	78
	SACK	23	19	11	53
	RTG	157.2	130.8	196.4	162.9
RUSHING	ATT	75	67	70	212
	YDS	221	167	254	642
	AVG	2.9	2.5	3.6	3.0
	TD	2	3	10	15
	LNG	36	26	33	36
SCORING	PASS	12	11	33	56
	RUSH	2	3	10	15
	TD	2	3	10	15
	PTS	12	20	60	92

TREY LANCE

		SEASON / TEAM 2018 / NDSU	SEASON / TEAM 2019 / NDSU	SEASON / TEAM 2020 / NDSU	Career
PASSING	GAMES	2	16	1	19
	CMP	1	192	15	208
	ATT	1	287	30	318
	CMP percent	100.0	66.9	50.0	65.4
	YDS	12	2,786	149	2,947
	AVG	12.0	9.7	5.0	9.3
	TD	0	28	2	30
	INT	0	0	1	1
	LNG	12	88	23	88
	SACK	0	12	3	15
	RTG	200.8	180.6	107.1	173.8
RUSHING	ATT	8	169	15	192
	YDS	82	1,100	143	1,325
	AVG	10.3	6.5	9.5	6.9
	TD	2	14	2	18
	LNG	44	61	54	51
SCORING	PASS	0	28	2	28
	RUSH	2	14	2	16
	TD	2	14	2	16
	PTS	12	84	12	96

JUSTIN FIELDS

		SEASON / TEAM	SEASON / TEAM	SEASON / TEAM	
		2018 / UGA	2019 / OSU	2020 / OSU	Career
PASSING	GAMES	12	14	8	34
	CMP	27	238	354	423
	ATT	39	354	225	618
	CMP percent	69.2	67.2	70.2	68.4
	YDS	328	3,273	2,100	5,701
	AVG	8.4	9.2	9.3	9.2
	TD	4	41	22	67
	INT	0	3	6	9
	LNG	57	60	65	65
	SACK	4	31	21	56
	RTG	173.7	181.4	175.6	178.8
RUSHING	ATT	42	137	81	260
	YDS	266	484	383	1,133
	AVG	6.3	3.5	4.7	4.4
	TD	4	10	5	19
	LNG	47	54	44	51
SCORING	PASS	4	41	22	67
	RUSH	4	10	5	19
	TD	4	10	5	19
	PTS	24	60	30	114

MAC JONES

		SEASON / TEAM	SEASON / TEAM	SEASON / TEAM	
		2018 / ALA	2019 / ALA	2020 / ALA	Career
PASSING	GAMES	6	11	13	30
	CMP	5	97	311	413
	ATT	13	141	402	556
	CMP percent	38.5	68.8	77.4	74.3
	YDS	123	1,503	4,500	6,126
	AVG	9.5	10.7	11.2	11.0
	TD	1	14	41	56
	INT	0	3	4	7
	LNG	94	85	90	94
	SACK	1	2	13	16
	RTG	143.3	186.8	203.1	197.6
RUSHING	ATT	3	16	35	54
	YDS	-8	36	14	42
	AVG	-2.7	2.3	0.4	0.8
	TD	0	1	1	2
	LNG	1	18	14	18
SCORING	PASS	1	14	41	56
	RUSH	0	1	1	2
	TD	0	1	1	2
	PTS	0	6	6	12

GLOSSARY

ATT: Passing Attempts
AVG: Yards Per Pass Attempt
CMP: Completions
CMP percent: Completion percentage
INT: Interceptions
LNG: Longest Pass
PASS: Passing Touchdowns
PTS: Total Points
RTG: Passer Rating
RUSH: Rushing Touchdowns
SACK: Total Sacks
TD: Passing Touchdowns
YDS: Passing Yards

Source: https://www.espn.com/nfl/player/stats

In this section on evaluating talent, we have looked at a small window of only four months in 2021 (January through to the NFL draft at the end of April) focusing on the instances of the Los Angeles Rams securing quarterback Matthew Stafford via a trade with the Detroit Lions, and the San Francisco 49ers trading up to pick three in the NFL draft eventually securing quarterback Trey Lance.

The framework for identifying and evaluating talent for the NFL runs over years ensuring a dynamic talent pipeline. All franchises have staffing roles dedicated to scouting, that is, experienced evaluators travelling across the country to observe and evaluate college playing talent, and monitoring college player development over time.

Remembering that to be eligible to nominate for the NFL draft, players must have been out of high school for at least three years and are only draft-eligible in the year after the end of their college eligibility, scouting departments have three years of opportunity to observe, monitor, and evaluate talent. It is not a consistent opportunity. Few NFL draftees get to start in their first year of college, increasing their game time as those in their final year of college leave.

Talent identification and acquisition

Prior to this, colleges themselves are evaluating talent, actively acquiring high-school talent, to ensure their programs are best placed to succeed.

Every business wants to attract the best possible talent it can at a price it can afford. The battle for talent means that the labor market across all sectors is incredibly competitive. Despite this, for most businesses, evaluating potential is limited to advertisements when vacancies become available within your operations, curating applications and resumes, selecting the four to six candidates who on paper best meet the role requirements, and undertaking interviews with those curated candidates to determine the talent most likely to succeed. It is limited to a specific time and place availability scenario, relying on a bell curve to provide sufficient skills and expertise to choose from. For mid-level to senior roles, a recruitment agency might be engaged to undertake some targeted head-hunting in lieu of, or in addition to, the public advertising.

Bigger brands and businesses invest far more heavily into evaluating potential. They will have a presence at university orientation weeks, meeting new and returning students through the lens of future potential employees as students move into their preferred courses of study and enter the top of their talent funnel pipelines. These bigger brands and businesses will sponsor university awards and provide internship placements. They will host meetups on specific topics of interest relevant to their industry and profession areas, building a community of contacts with relevant skills and capabilities likely needed to meet future business needs. They will host hackathons to provide opportunities for out of the box thinking, collaborating with peers, and designing solutions to complex problems, investing in winners, and building their brand recognition.

There has been an explosion of incubators and accelerators designed to give talent an opportunity to pursue a business idea and gain traction in the market. These cater for students leaving university, young teams that have been in market for a short period of talent and need assistance scaling, or talent exiting consulting firms who have seen a gap in the market and determined the time is right to go out on their own. Venture capital and angel networks are a mature component of this ecosystem providing mentoring and education to assist founders to grow and develop, getting an early insight into talent and capability of the startup team, understanding the size of the total addressable market of the business problem the startup is looking to solve, understanding where the strengths and weaknesses are of the founding team, and gaining an early insight into possible investment opportunities.

Technology's not the disruptor, people are.
Steve Vamos, former CEO Xero

If the capability of your people is crucial to your future success, your human capital pipeline needs to be a disciplined funnel approach, and your evaluation of talent needs to be a science.

4.3 Chip on your shoulder

The colloquial use of the phrase "chip on your shoulder" refers to someone who is aggrieved about some perceived past mistreatment, causing that person to hold a grudge, and perhaps even lashing out now and then. In the NFL, the

Talent identification and acquisition

phrase is also commonly used, however, without the negative connotations.

Yes, it can mean holding a grudge, and yes it means responding to a perceived slight, but it also means a player using that chip as motivation in a positive way to drive personal and team improvement, lift standards, pursue excellence, and overachieve.

When evaluating talent, how do you know a person will be successful? A chip on their shoulder means that talent has a higher level of drive to disprove the doubters and is driven to invalidate perceptions.

Examples of elite players displaying a chip on the shoulder: Aaron Rodgers and Tom Brady

In the weeks leading up to the 2005 NFL Draft, there were two quarterbacks being spoken about as having the potential to go number one. A quarterback had gone first in the draft in the previous four years. In 2005, there was Aaron Rodgers from the University of California and Alex Smith from the University of Utah. Rodgers had finished ninth in Heisman voting with a pass completion percentage that season of 66.1 percent, while Smith had a pass completion percentage of 67.5 percent and finished fourth in Heisman voting.

The San Francisco 49ers held the first pick and had a need in the quarterback area. Rodgers was a 49ers childhood fan and had dreamed of playing for the franchise one day. However, when the commissioner called out the 49ers first pick of the 2005 draft, it was Alex Smith.

Asked by a reporter after the draft how disappointed Rodgers was about not becoming a 49er, Rodgers replied, "Not as disappointed as the 49ers will be that they didn't draft me."

Aaron Rodgers was 21 years old. Despite being widely

touted as a potential number-one pick, he had to wait nearly five hours before his name was called, going to the Green Bay Packers with pick 24. Reflecting on the draft day experience in NFL Films production *Caught in the Draft 2005*[71], Rodgers said:

> On the inside there was a lot of disappointment, embarrassment, just thinking about, you know, the hard work I put in, and the disappointment of it not paying off in my mind at the time, as I saw, you know, team's pass on me that I know I had talked to and thought were interested, and had players drafted who I felt like I was better than.
> ... You start questioning everything from where you worked out, to how hard you worked, to the people you surround yourself with, to leaving college. [It was] very humbling.

How did Rodger's prediction go that the 49ers would end up more disappointed that they didn't pick him than he would be for not drafting him?

Rodger's first three seasons in Green Bay were played behind Hall of Famer Brett Favre. Rodger played three games, two games, and two games across those first three seasons. In his seventeen seasons to 2022, Rodgers has played in 213 games passing for over 55,000 yards with a completion rate of 65.3 percent, throwing for 449 touchdowns, and being intercepted 93 times. By way of comparison, Alex Smith who was the number one draft pick and taken by the 49ers in 2005 played nine games in his rookie season, followed by the full sixteen games in year two. Smith was with the 49ers for seven seasons before being traded to the Kansas City Chiefs for the 2013 season. Overall, Smith's career was 14 seasons for 35,650 passing yards at a completion rate of 62.6 percent,

Talent identification and acquisition

throwing for 199 touchdowns and being intercepted 109 times.

49ers fans would point to Rodgers being 0–3 against the 49ers in postseason games. Perhaps the more persuasive position would be that since the 2005 NFL draft, Green Bay has appeared once in a Super Bowl with Rodgers starting as quarterback and winning a ring by beating the Pittsburgh Steelers 31–25. The 49ers over the same period have appeared in three Super Bowls, losing in 2013 to the Baltimore Ravens 31-34, losing in 2020 to the Kansas City Chiefs 20-31, and losing in 2024 again to the Chiefs 22-25. While the 49ers have won five Super Bowls, their last was in 1995 beating the San Diego Chargers 49–26. Would having Rodgers on the 49ers team have turned the tide in either of those most recent 49ers appearances in a Super Bowl? And would the 49ers have qualified for more Super Bowls had Rogers steered the ship over the last seventeen seasons? Many would argue yes.

Another legendary NFL player commonly viewed as having excelled due to a chip on their shoulder is Tom Brady. Brady has won more Super Bowls as quarterback than any other (seven in total: six with the New England Patriots and one with the Tampa Bay Buccaneers). The next most successful are Joe Montana and Terry Bradshaw both with four Super-Bowl wins each. Montana won his four with the San Francisco 49ers and Bradshaw his four with the Pittsburgh Steelers.

So how is it possible for Brady, the Greatest of All Time (GOAT) in the quarterback position, to have a chip on his shoulder? It all comes from the path taken, the trials and tribulations of overcoming adversity, experiencing an elongated pathway towards success, and hearing doubters along the way of his ability to achieve his aspirations.

When Brady joined Michigan University for his college

career, there were seven players on the positional depth chart. He went on to play 29 college games that resulted in an overall passing completion rate of 61.9 percent, with 30 touchdowns and 17 interceptions[72]. His college career ended on a high with Michigan playing Alabama Crimson Tide in the Orange Bowl. He had already started earning the moniker of the Comeback Kid. In the Orange Bowl final, Michigan led by Brady, came back twice from 14-point deficits to tie the scores. A scoreless fourth quarter saw the game tied at 28–28, and the teams went into overtime. Michigan scored first through a Brady touchdown pass with the extra point successful. Alabama's reply also earned a touchdown; however, the extra point was missed, and Michigan won 35–34.

Brady entered the 2000 NFL draft, and despite his college record, was taken in the sixth round and pick 199 by the New England Patriots. Six other quarterbacks were selected in the draft before Brady. Adding to the emotional slight, Brady was a lifelong 49ers fan, with his father holding season tickets for 25 years. The 49ers overlooked Brady in the third round of the draft and took a different quarterback. Further salt was added into the wounds when the Cleveland Browns took quarterback Spergon Wynn with pick 183 in the sixth round. In his final year of college, Wynn had a completion rate 47.8 percent with 13 interceptions and only 12 touchdown passes[73].

Tom Brady's father, Tom Brady Sr, would later be interviewed in an NFL Films production *The Brady 6: Journey of the Legend No One Wanted* saying:

> We couldn't believe it 47 percent! I mean, Tommy had thrown it better than 62 percent his senior year, had thrown twice as many TDs as interceptions, had come back in games and the biggest stage with 100,000 people in the stands and he didn't get any respect.

Since the time of the 2000 NFL draft a draft report on Brady has been shared widely on the internet which says poor build, skinny, lacks great physical stature and strength, lacks mobility and ability to avoid the rush, lacks a really strong arm, can't drive the ball downfield, does not throw a really tight spiral, system-type player who can get exposed if forced to ad-lib, gets knocked down easily.

Steve Sabol of NFL Films interviewed Brady in 2002 after he won his first Super Bowl with the Patriots and read Brady his draft report. Brady replied:

> That kind of gets me fired up because I'm thinking *What the hell do these people know?* That sounds like Joe Montana right there ... When people tell you "Hey you can't do this. You can't do this," and you keep overcoming that, you build this confidence in yourself and this belief in yourself that even when nobody else believes in you, that I'm still gonna do it. Because I don't give a s--t what you say. I know what I can do, and I've done it.

The doubters resurfaced when after 20 seasons and six Super-Bowl rings with the New England Patriots, Brady signed with the Tampa Bay Buccaneers. There was much speculation in the fan bases and across media as to whether New England Patriots coach Bill Belichick was the principal architect for the Patriots success, or whether it was Tom Brady.

In his first season with the Buccaneers, Brady went on to secure his seventh Super-Bowl ring. Despite all the success, even twenty years later, the chip remains as evidenced in a Brady interview on the *Dax Shepard Armchair Expert* podcast[74]:

> I think there's always been doubt around what I could achieve. And I think that's what it was. There's always

heard the people say, "He'll never do that. He'll never be the starting quarterback in high school." My senior year: "He'll never go to a real good division one school and play football. He should just stick around and play at a local school. And then, he'll never be a pro quarterback, certainly never be a starting quarterback." I'd say I'm very motivated. I have a real strong fire that burns based on me never wanting to let myself down. You know, giving less than my best effort is probably a real hard thing for me.

A chip on a team's shoulder: cricket's West Indies

A chip on the shoulder need not be limited to an individual, but rather can also apply to teams. Let me focus on an example from the cricket arena.

International test matches are played over five days, with three two-hour sessions per day. There is a 40-minute break after the first session, and a 20-minute break after the second session. There are 90 overs mandated per day. This doesn't always happen. If the number of overs is reduced due to inclement weather, the remaining days are extended to try to make up those overs lost. If there is general tardiness and a couple of overs are lost on any day, the offending team receives a monetary fine and those overs are lost.

In countries where cricket is not played, sports fans are often amazed that a match can go for five days and 450 overs, yet at the end of that time, there may not be a winner declared, rather the game ends in a draw.

Cricket was not initially designed this way. The first ever test match was played between England and Australia March 15–19, 1877 at the Melbourne Cricket Ground. Test cricket matches were timeless from the inaugural game through to

1939 so that a winner was assured, and so that inclement weather did not inhibit a result.

The final timeless test was the fifth test played on England's tour of South Africa in Durban March 3–14, 1939. The match was abandoned as a draw after 10 days of play (spread over 11 days because of weather). Batting first, South Africa scored 530 and England 316. South Africa were then dismissed for 481 in their second innings leaving England a target of 696 to win. England had progressed to 654/5 in their second innings needing only 42 runs[75] to win when the match was abandoned. To have gone further would mean that England missed their scheduled boat home. World War II was impending meaning the English team were particularly keen not to miss their boat.

Test matches were changed to five days from 1939 onwards thus removing future scheduling barriers.

In cricket, a pitch for playing on is 66 feet (22 yards) bowling stumps to batting stumps. In front of each set of stumps there is a line indicating where the bowler must land behind to register a legal delivery. A batsman can stand in front, on top or behind this line at the other end of the pitch. The distance between these two lines is 58 feet.

In baseball, the pitcher's plate is 60 feet, six inches away from the back point of the home plate.

In both cricket and Major League Baseball, there is the fabled 100 miles per hour club. In 2015, Major League Baseball stadiums introduced Statcast technology to accurately measure speed and player movements. Since the introduction of Statcast, 10 pitchers have thrown 37 or more fastballs over 100mph in games they have started.

In cricket, the current technology has been available since the early 2000s. The 100mph club is really measured in kilometers per hour (exceeding 160 kilometers per hour which is not quite 100mph). There have been five bowlers who have exceeded 160kph in test matches:[76] Shoaib Akhtar from Pakistan at 161.3 kph (100.2mph), Shaun Tait from Australia at 161.1kph (100.1mph), Brett Lee from Australia at 160.8kph (99.9 mph), Jeff Thomson from Australia at 160.6kph (99.8 mph), and Mitchell Starc from Australia at 160.4kph (99.7mph).

Just behind this group was Andy Roberts from the West Indies (Windies) and the Leeward Islands who was timed at 159.5kph (99.1 mph). Both Roberts and Thomson were timed with different technology back in 1975. The 60s and 70s were a different era in terms of the ability to protect a pitch and outfield from inclement weather and the range of protective equipment available to batters. It made for some unique environments where the bravery of batters was constantly tested.

From the mid-sixties through to the mid-nineties, the Caribbean Islands was a production line of rapid fast bowlers and courageous attacking batsman. The bowlers were lithe and athletic and intent on terrorizing batters. It started in the sixties with Wes Hall and Charlie Griffith. Analysis of film footage suggests Hall bowled as fast as 103mph. Then the procession of Andy Roberts, Joel Garner, Michael Holding, Curtly Ambrose, Courtney Walsh, and Ian Bishop.

My personal favorite was the uber athletic Michael Holding, nicknamed 'Whispering Death' because he was so light footed on his approach to the bowling crease that umpires allegedly found it difficult to hear him running in. He ran in fast but was poetry in motion, ending by spearing the ball with great pace and accuracy. Ambrose and Bishop would later have similar bowling motions to Holding, however, as larger physiques would not emulate Holding's stealth-like style.

The West Indies had a golden run not losing an international test series for 15 years between 1980 and 1995. The start of the golden run can be traced back to a series lost to

Australia in 1975 and wonderfully chronicled in the documentary *Fire in Babylon*.

Australia's great fast bowling pairing of Dennis Lillee and Jeff Thompson took 56 wickets between them of the 110 West Indies wickets to fall. The 1975 series started evenly, being 1–1 after the first two matches and ended in a bruising 5–1 defeat[77] for the Windies.

"Injuries, broken fingers, broken shoulders, cracks on the head and it was humiliating; it was like a military assault on West Indies cricket."
– Historian Professor Hilary Beckles on the 1975/76 test series lost to Australia, *Fire in Bablyon*

The West Indies regrouped in 1976. The hurt from the 5–1 loss in Australia created a steely resolve and a new mindset, with the Windies actively seeking to replicate Australia's advantage in the fast-bowling stocks. A refreshed squad hosted a visit from India winning the series 2–1, before travelling to England. While the first two matches against England in the five-match series ended in draws, the West Indies won the remaining three tests to win the series 3–0.

The West Indies and Australia had a tremendous rivalry and certainly the test series loss to Australia in 1975 added to the chip on the West Indies shoulder. The chip, however, existed before that and was much deeper, with England representing the greater rivalry.

The chip stemmed from colonization and lived experiences of racism. The cricket field was an opportunity to achieve equality.

To give some insight into the depth and breadth of the chip, below are some quotes from Windies legends as contained in the *Fire in Bablyon* documentary.

"People didn't feel the West Indies players had the fight in them, this Calypso cricket stigma stuck with us; we weren't willing to go there and fight to the end; we just gave up."

– Gordon Greenidge (7,558 runs at an average of 44.72 in 108 test matches)

"It was representing a region, representing something more significant than just cricket. It was a matter of feeling of worth.

"We wanted to show Englishman you brought the game to us, and now that we are better than you."

– Michael Holding (249 wickets at an average of 23.68 in 60 test matches)

"Aggression meets aggression and that's how I look at life. You fight; I'm going to fight. We had a mission, and a mission that we believe in ourselves, and we believe we were just as good as anyone, equal for that matter.

"We stepped beyond the sport, where a whole lot of things needed defending, rather than the cricket ball itself."

– Sir Vivian Richards (8,540 runs at an average of 50.23 in 121 test matches, plus 32 wickets)

Chip on the shoulder and the broader business context

So how does a chip on the shoulder evidenced in professional sport relate to a broader business context?

It is evidently true that a team member carrying a chip on their shoulder can negatively impact both their own performance and the performance of others. It may be simply a case of distracting other team members from their areas of required focus, or by deflecting from the business' core mission.

There is no science on how to channel the energy of someone's chip in a constructive manner. That said, it cannot be ignored that there are simply too many instances in professional sport where a chip on a player's shoulder or a chip on a team's shoulder has led to excellence.

As a general principle, businesses will seek to allocate their best talent towards those areas with the potential for the biggest returns. The opportunity is to augment this approach by creating an environment where those with a chip, who might not be viewed as being within the current cohort of best available in-house talent, are provided with opportunities to work on new scopes of work to extend themselves and test how far their drive may take them and the business.

It won't always be apparent why a chip exists, and the cause may not rise to the surface no matter how deep a business leader delves. The chip is often innate and personal, driving that person to overachieve. It may involve matters outside of the workplace which they simply do not wish to share. It could be a single parent who is driven to provide better opportunities for their children. It could be an older worker who due to personal circumstances had to curtail opportunities earlier in their career and now feels driven to prove something to themselves. Or the impetus may have been built within the workplace, causing reluctance within the team member to share due to the risk of offending others or being ostracized.

Ultimately, it does not matter what the driver is. People are different. The question is whether the business can recognize the chip and funnel the energy into constructive outcomes. If you accept that recognizing a chip on the shoulder can provide business advantage, the question for leaders is how to delve into past experiences during recruitment processes. A process might be designed that extends past skills, aptitude, and cultural fit, to find ways to identify talent who may have a chip that can be harnessed for good.

A chip on the shoulder is not limited to individuals. It can exist for a business unit or a business as a whole. A business-wide chip may have developed because of negative press or negative customer sentiment over an extended period, or the business went to the precipice faced with an existential threat, developing the chip and the hardened commitment to turn things around.

Just as in sport, chips for businesses can also be created simply to garner effort – the siege-mentality strategy of creating a competitor in the minds of the team is a way of galvanizing effort and driving continuous improvement.

4.4 Transferrable skills

What do we mean by transferrable skills? In any job role, a team member will be applying both hard skills and professional skills. Hard skills are areas that require technical know-how and training. You may pick these up at college or university and apply them in a specific industry context. For example, programming and coding skills working in product development at a technology company. Another example would be hard skills in a healthcare setting such as a surgeon, chiropractor, physiotherapist, anesthetist, or radiologist. There is a base level of education undertaken at university followed by specialization training and then master-apprentice support in practice, along with observation in the workplace prior to autonomous professional practice. A trades setting is not too dissimilar, whether it be electrical trades, mechanical trades, or construction. Hard skills are often the types of skills that require a license or registration as a prerequisite to practice and are the ones you just can't pick up through life experience because there is too much at risk for your client or consumer.

Professional skills (sometimes called soft skills) on the other hand are harder to quantify. You can certainly enhance these skills through professional development, but there is an element where these skills are built over time through life experience. Areas such as problem solving, communication, interpersonal skills, and leadership.

Whether hard or professional skills, some skills are more easily transferred between professions than others. Indeed, in some instances, they may be so closely aligned that development in one area contributes to mastery that can be applied in another.

In their desperation for talent, businesses can sometimes advertise for new hires with the longest of laundry lists both skills and experience, knowing that they will take the candidate that can best fit 75 percent of the criteria in the critical areas. Understanding job design is crucial for all business leaders. It is not something that can be handballed to human resources otherwise you run the risk of sunk costs in a recruitment exercise because the initial curation of applications and preliminary screening fails to match the 75 percent of critical criteria.

Position descriptions are often seen as an administrative

task to be delegated (or ignored). In fact, how often do you see position descriptions remain stagnant for two to three years within a business and end up not reflecting the actual expectation of the role in an operating environment that has evolved?

Earlier in this chapter, we touched on the strategies big business adopts to embed themselves into university ecosystems as a means for identifying and securing up and coming talent. If a business is mid-sized and unable to adopt such an approach, or can't meet market salary expectations of top graduates, seeking broader pathways into their talent pipelines affords an opportunity to uncover new talent at a market rate below those of their big-business competitors.

How do you know whether skills are transferrable from one industry sector to your business? Firstly, their needs to be an intimate knowledge of job design and job functions contained in your current roles. What skills do you utilize? Where are the gaps? And what skills do you need to meet your ambitions over the next two to five years. Then you need to be able to research and identify what those skills look like in other industry settings. Once you have determined what transferrable skills look like and decide to bring those skills in from outside your industry, there needs to be an organization commitment and infrastructure to support the new hire upskill in those business specific and industry specific areas they do not hold.

Let's frame transferrable skills by looking at examples in professional sport.

To establish our baseline, we will consider some examples of superhuman feats in professional sports, that while inspiring, do not represent deeply transferrable skills. Then we will look at some examples where skills have clearly been transferrable across sports.

Sportspeople succeeding in more than one sport, but not because of transferrable skills

Many sportspeople have played multiple sports in their youth. It is common for young people who have an affinity with exercise and competition to compete in a sport for the winter season and a sport for the summer season. When you are an athlete going through college in the US, you might combine football with basketball. In Australia, it has historically been common to combine cricket in summer with one of the football codes during winter.

For some naturally gifted individuals, it is possible to excel as an athlete in multiple sports. When entering sport as a profession, athletes eventually come to a fork in the road where they need to choose between their two passions. Scheduling is one of the reasons for the fork in the road with sporting seasons overlapping and internationalization impacting mobility and logistics. Then as an athlete there is the time required to achieve your potential. There is an expectation that you make a full commitment to your craft and to your team using the off-season to improve your conditioning and skills specific to the role you are best remunerated to perform.

Sometimes athletes choose to pursue their second sport after retiring from their first. Boxing is a prime example where an athlete may have pursued a sport professionally from the range of 18–32 years of age, and then pursued a second career in boxing from their early thirties through to the start of their forties.

As athletes age, agility, and speed will decline, faster for some than others. However, strength can be maintained over a longer period, coinciding with an athletes' optimized game smarts and mental conditioning in preparing for battle.

In addition to boxing, another example is motor racing.

Grand Prix racing on motorcycles is for the super elite and comes with significant risk. There have been several examples where professionals in motorcycle classes turn their attention to four-wheel racing after a career where their peak athleticism has tapered off or injuries prevent continued racing on motorcycles to the level of excellence of which they were accustomed.

In Australia, Wayne Gardner (1987 500cc World Champion, 18 Grand-Prix victories), Michael Doohan (five times 500cc World Champion, 54 Grand-Prix wins), Casey Stoner (two times MotoGP World Champion, 38 MotoGP Grand-Prix wins, 5 250cc Grand-Prix wins and two 125cc Grand-Prix wins), Troy Bayliss (one MotoGP Grand-Prix win), and Darryl Beattie (three 500cc Grand-Prix wins) all tried their hands at four wheels for various tenures following successful motorcycle careers. In the US, motorcycle legend Kevin Schwantz (1993 500cc World Champion, 25 500cc Grand-Prix wins) tried his hand at NASCAR, Auscar, and Super Touring in Australia.

An example in tennis is Australian sports superstar Ash Barty, who shocked the world in 2022 by retiring at the age of 25 while currently ranked the number-one player in women's tennis and being the reigning Wimbledon and Australian Open champion. Barty won three Grand-Slam titles and 15 titles in total with career prize money nearing $US24m[78].

Barty had previously walked away from tennis in 2014 for a short period, turning her sporting interests to cricket. There Barty earned a professional contract with the Brisbane Heat for the 2015/16 season in Australia's national T20 women's competition. Barty played nine games with a top score of 39, before returning to tennis and winning the French Open singles in 2019.

These examples in boxing, motor racing, and tennis are all linear. Focus on training and playing one sport, and then take a break to focus on training and playing another. It must be noted that there are numerous examples of footballers undertaking boxing matches in between seasons, none, however, were at the pinnacle of the boxing sport.

There are a select few who have managed to juggle elite-level participation concurrently in two different sports.

Ellyse Perry is one of Australia's most decorated professional sports people. She was selected in the Australian national teams for both cricket and football at the age of 16. Perry is the only athlete to have played for Australia in both the cricket and football World Cups.

Perry was capped 16 times for Australia's national football team the Matildas and is fondly remembered for a goal scored in Australia's 3–1 loss to Sweden in a quarterfinal of the 2011 World Cup. Receiving the ball along the ground from a corner kick ten meters outside the 18-yard penalty box, Perry had one touch leaving the ball a yard from the 18-yard box and located outside the right-hand post of the goals. Perry's strike with her left foot was angled across the goals and went into the top left corner.

The inevitable clash between the two sports came to a head in 2014. Perry was overlooked for both football's Cyprus Women's Cup and the AFC Women's Asian Cup. Then Matildas coach Hesterine de Reus put this down to the growth of the women's game in Australia[79]:

> It's not a concern to play two sports – I think in Australia it's very common to do that – but when you play at the highest level you need to invest a lot of time to become a world-class player. To do that with two sports at the same time is a bit harder. It's a good sign for the development of women's football that it's harder to earn a spot in the team.

Perry's international cricket career continues to this day and she was a member of Australia's victorious 50-over World Cup team who defeated England by 71 runs April 3, 2022, and with Perry scoring 17 not out.

As of March 2022, Perry's international cricket career[80] includes 10 test matches scoring 752 runs at an average of 75.20 and taking 37 wickets at 19.97; 127 one-day internationals scoring 3,352 runs at 50.02 and taking 161 wickets at 24.9; and 126 T20 internationals scoring 1,253 runs at an average of 27.84 and taking 115 wickets at 19.45.

At one level, there are many common attributes across professional athletes that can be applied to any number of other sports. Athletes have bigger motors than the average person and greater aerobic capacity. Same too with speed, muscle mass, and agility. But this is not quite what I mean by transferrable skills. My use of "transferrable" relates to a niche aspect of a job role. People, the same as professional athletes, have certain skills for which you attract your market rates, and these skills, in some instances, are equally desirable in other professional capacities.

A motorcycle racer does not use the same skills and physical techniques in a four-wheeler. A boxer does not use football skills or techniques in the ring. Neither Perry nor Barty are strong examples of transferrable skills between sports. In the case of Perry, there would be some level of transferability of a sliding tackle in football that could be applied in the outfield of a cricket oval diving to make saves. Fielding in cricket, however, is not the skill that earns the professional contracts. Batting and bowling are the clear differentiators and playing football does not assist in batting or bowling. In the instance of Barty, undoubtedly good hand/eye co-ordination developed in tennis supports batting in cricket, and a strong right arm developed through forehands in tennis would assist in playing some cricket shots like those over mid-wicket and potentially through cover point. Again though, not strong transferability of tennis skills and techniques to cricket.

To test the assumption, simply ask whether other top athletes could cross over from football to cricket and succeed the very next season? If the answer is no, there is not strong transferability of skills. The same between tennis and cricket. The technique needed for hitting the ball in tennis is dissimilar to batting in cricket.

In the US, college athletes will often participate across multiple sports: gridiron, athletics, basketball, baseball, swimming, lacrosse, or any other number of sports. When it comes to graduation time, athletes need to decide between sports which to pursue professionally. Only a select few have been able to juggle competing demands across the topflight of two sports.

Top of the list in the US have been Bo Jackson and Deion Sanders. They were both incredible football players in the NFL, and both have great records as baseballers.

Bo Jackson is the only athlete to have been named as an All-Star in baseball and a Pro Bowler in football. He was selected in the fourth round of the 1986 Major League Baseball draft with overall pick 105 by the Kansas City Royals. He played 694 regular season games over eight seasons with three franchises having 598 regular season hits with 141 home runs at an average of .250 and Runs Batted In (RBI) of 451[81].

Jackson played five seasons and 38 games in the NFL with the Los Angeles Raiders. Playing as a running back, he scored 18 touchdowns rushing for 2,782 yards at an average of 5.4 yards and receiving for 352 yards at an average 8.8 yards.

From 1989, Deion Sanders played 641 games across 11 seasons of Major League Baseball that included playing stints with the New York Yankees, Atlanta Braves, Cincinnati Reds, and the San Francisco Giants[82]. He had 558 hits with 39 home runs and held a career batting average of .263 and an RBI of 168[83].

In the NFL, Sanders was the fifth pick overall in the 1989 NFL Draft, taken by the Atlanta Falcons. He played 14 seasons in total, his first five with Atlanta, followed by a single season with the San Francisco 49ers, five seasons with the Dallas Cowboys, and one with Washington. Sanders took three seasons off from 2001, returning for two more seasons with the Baltimore Ravens. He played 188 games in total as a cornerback making 270 tackles and 53 interceptions and scoring 22 touchdowns. He is the only athlete to have played in a World Series in baseball and a Super Bowl. He won two Super Bowls in consecutive years, the first with the Niners, and the second with the Cowboys. He played in the 1992 World Series for the Atlanta Braves, going down 4–3 to the Toronto Blue Jays.

Despite the incredible athleticism of both Jackson and Saunders, skills from one professional sport were not transferrable to the other. Yes, athletes need to run fast in both baseball and football whether that is making an outfield catch or running around the bases in baseball or running for offensive yards as a running back in football or spoiling a pass or making a tackle as a cornerback in football. That said, running in the outfield in baseball is not the same as making a cut at speed and in traffic as a running back in the NFL, or making yards after contact or after catch. No point being a cornerback in the NFL running fast, if you cannot read the play, minimize separation from the receivers, spoil the pass, and make the tackle.

Sportspeople succeeding in more than one sport because of transferrable skills

So what would be examples of transferrable skills?

Kyler Murray was the number-one draft pick in the 2019 NFL draft selected by the Arizona Cardinals. He was thrown in as starter in his very first season playing the full 16 games. In his first three seasons, Murray totaled 46 games, passing for 11,480 yards with a completion rate of 66.9 percent. One of Murray's key attributes was his speed and agility and had rushed for an additional 1,786 yards.

Murray was the first player selected in the first rounds of both the NFL and MLB. He was selected with the ninth overall pick by the Oakland Athletics in the 2018 MB draft that had an assigned value of US$4,761,500[84]. In his final season of college baseball Murray played 50 games, having 62 hits for 10 homeruns, an RBI of 47, and an average of .296.

While selected in the 2018 MLB draft, Murray continued on to play his final season of college football thereafter, before being selected as the number-one pick of the 2019 NFL draft.

There are two strong examples of transferrable skills that Murray holds which are niche, specializations, and benefit play in both the NFL and baseball. First are arm mechanics and throwing distances. While a baseball and a football have little that is similar in term of size and shape of the ball, the single-hand arm motion for throwing the ball is replicable. It is possible for athletes to have strong power over shorter distance by aiming a throw downwards. Naturally, with the laws of gravity, there is only so much distance that can be achieved throwing downward. To achieve longer distances requires an upwards aim and arc motion. Some basic mechanics to achieve distance involve a side-on stance and planting weight on the backfoot of the throwing arm to maximize power. The follow-through after releasing the ball is also important for distance and accuracy.

Secondly, for quarterbacks, mastery of rounding the bases in baseball and sliding into a base is also a transferrable skill to football. In the chess match that football is, every inch and every yard counts, as does protecting the football given turnovers prove costly. For fleet of foot quarterbacks such as Kyler Murray, being able to run through or around the line of scrimmage when opportunities present can produce easy yards. The challenge is once those yards have been made and the quarterback runs into a 245-pound linebacker intent on causing a turnover. Easy and efficient sliding allows the quarterback to end a down prior to contact, protecting the team's key asset from possible injury and ensuring the protection of the ball to continue time in possession.

The baseball slide represents a clear transferability of skills when you review the NFL quarterbacks. Not all quarterbacks slide the same, some even struggle to do it at all. Those who have played baseball in their youth and those who have played at a high level during their youth are highly efficient sliders to end a down in football. Russell Wilson, the recently acquired quarterback for the Denver Broncos, formerly of the Seattle Seahawks, played high-level college baseball in his youth, and is a very proficient slider in picking up rushing yards in the NFL. Jameis Winston, quarterback from the New Orleans Saints, is another who can rush at speed and efficiently find the knee sliding before reaching a tackler. Tom Brady is another, while not a frequent rusher, who can slide to find the knee and end the down efficiently well before a defender can attack the ball.

AFL skills transferrable to the NFL

Another example of transferrable skills in the NFL is easily identifiable by looking at Australians who have successfully made the transition to the gridiron. There is no Pop Warner youth football in Australia and kids grow up playing a variety of other sports. It is almost unfathomable that an Australian could compete for a roster spot in the NFL with an American youth who has grown up with Pop Warner, played high school football followed by college football. The population of the United States is 332 million while the population of Australia is less than one tenth of the United States at 26 million.

The first Australian punter to have sustained success in the NFL was Darren Bennett. Bennett landed in the NFL in 1995 going on to play 11 consecutive seasons. The first nine seasons were with the San Diego Chargers and the last two with the Minnesota Vikings. He played 160 games, punting 836 times for 36,316 yards at an average of 43.4 yards. His longest punt was 66 yards which he managed in four seasons. His inside 20 percentage average was 31.34.

Bennett had a seven-year career in the AFL playing 78 games. He joined the West Coast Eagles in 1987 for their inaugural season in the national competition. His first two seasons were with West Coast playing four games in his first season and none in his second due to injury. The following season he was drafted by the Melbourne Demons playing five seasons through to 1993. He kicked 215 career goals and was Melbourne's leading goal kicker in both the 1989 and 1990 seasons.

Ben Graham was soon to emulate Bennett.

Ben Graham's professional sporting career started off in the AFL as a forward for the Geelong Football Club (Victoria, Australia). He debuted in 1993 playing 219 games across 12 consecutive seasons, kicking 145 goals and 113 behinds[85]. He played in the 1995 AFL Grand Final where Geelong lost to Carlton by 61 points.

In 2005 he travelled to the US earning a contract as a punter with the New York Jets and becoming the oldest rookie in the NFL at 31 years old in his debut against the Kansas City Chiefs.

Ben Graham played 10 seasons in the NFL from 2005–2012 across four franchises (New York Jets 2005–2006, New Orleans Saints 2008, Arizona Cardinals 2008–2011, Detroit Lions 2011–2012). He played 99 games in total, punting for 20,661 yards for an average distance of 44.1 yards and longest punt of 69 yards. He has a career punts inside 20 percentage of 34.62. Career highlights included being the first Australian to captain an American professional sporting team. Unfortunately, history would repeat itself for Graham in the main show, when Arizona won through to Super Bowl XLIII only to lose to the Pittsburgh Steelers 27–23.

Sav Rocca soon followed in Bennett's and Graham's footsteps. Rocca was the most accomplished athlete from the AFL successfully transitioning to the NFL. Rocca played 257 games of AFL across 15 seasons 1992–2006 (nine seasons with the Collingwood Magpies 1992–2000 and six seasons with the North Melbourne Kangaroos). He kicked a total of 748 goals with 411 behinds.

Rocca then became the oldest player in NFL history to be rookie listed by the Philadelphia Eagles. He played four seasons with Philadelphia and a final three seasons with Washington for a total of seven consecutive seasons 2007 through 2013. He managed to play all sixteen games in each of his seasons for a total of 112 games, making 517 punts totaling 22,169 yards at an average of 42.9 yards per punt. His longest punt was 65 yards in each of his first two seasons and finished with an inside 20 percentage of 34.43.

The examples of Bennett, Graham, and Rocca are clear examples of transferrable skills. None had a background of playing on the gridiron their youth. Yet they could use their skills and knowledge of kicking the ball in AFL and apply those skills successfully in a game on the gridiron.

A ball in the NFL is of a slightly different shape to that used in the AFL. That said, the dimensions are very similar. An AFL ball has a long circumference of 28.5 inches and 21.7 inches for the short circumference. An American football has the same long circumference of 28-28.5 inches, and just a slightly smaller short circumference of 21–21.25 inches.

Bennett, Graham, and Rocca were all goal scorers in the AFL. The purpose of kicking in the AFL is to transition play at a faster rate, finding the best route to have a player take a shot on goal. To score means threading the ball through goals posts from any possible scoring position. It is not uncommon for AFL players to take shots at goal from outside of 50 meters meaning distance and accuracy are highly desirable.

Punting does not have the same purpose in the NFL. The primary purpose for punters in the NFL is to pin the opposition as far back as possible while giving time for special teams to run down field and tackle the catcher. If a punter kicks the ball too far and it touches the ground in the end zone of the opposition, the result is a touchback with possession given to the opposition and the ball spotted at the 25-yard line. The ideal is to punt the ball high hoping for a fumbled catch and maximizing hang time to allow your team the most time to run down the field, close open field opportunities, and effect a tackle. Should the ball find the ground, then the ideal is for the ball to finish its momentum as close to the opposition end zone as possible without going into the end zone. The result for the punting team is that the ball will be spotted at the point it stops. Hence, there is plus or minus 25 yards at stake. If the punting team has no real field position, it may be okay to reach the end zone and have the play restarted at the opposition's 25-yard line. It is quite the skill to minimize balls ending up in the end zone and yet as close as possible.

Evidence of skills transferability is that there have been three Australian punters to make this transition successfully. All had longest kicks in the 65–69 yard range. All three had career average yards per punt around 43–44 (only a 1.2 yard punt difference across the three of them). The inside 20 percentage were almost identical for two of them and a small range across the three of 31.34 to 34.62.

Transferability is replicable and repeatable.

Thanks to the pioneering feats of these three punters, the transition from AFL to the NFL does not happen as much nowadays. That is not to say it cannot, but rather than the NFL actively targets transferable skills from earlier in career trajectories. Australian athletes know of the opportunities and will search them out earlier. There is great attraction for Australian athletes to obtain an education from American colleges and experience American culture as part of a professional sports dream.

In today's NFL, Australian punters will still have played AFL in their youth but leave Australian shores in the pursuit of an NFL dream prior to achieving the elite AFL level.

Examples include Michael Dickson who played one season of reserves for the Sydney Swans in the AFL before heading to the NFL. Dickson is an active punter with the Seattle Seahawks having notched up six seasons 2018–2023 for 99 games, 428 punts for 20,525 yards at an average of 48.0 yards per punt, and an impressive inside 20 percentage of 42.29.

Jordan Berry kicked the AFL ball around as a junior and has completed seven seasons in the NFL 2015–2021, the first six with the Pittsburgh Steelers before going to the Minnesota Vikings. He has played 108 games in the NFL punting 463 times for 20,728 yards at an average of 44.8 and an inside 20 percentage of 38.88.

Mitch Wishnowsky played junior AFL football up to the age of 18. He has five seasons under his belt 2019–2023 in the NFL as a punter with the San Francisco 49ers, playing 83 games and punting 288 times for 13,148 yards at an average of 45.7 and with an inside 20 percentage of 44.10.

Cameron Johnston was drafted as an AFL rookie with the Melbourne Demons but did not play senior ball. He has played six seasons in the NFL 2018–2023, the first three with the Philadelphia Eagles followed by three seasons with the Houston Texans. He has 95 career games punting 445 times for 21,029 yards at an average of 47.3 and an in 20 percentage of 40.90.

Lachlan Edwards played Australian Rules at junior and senior level, however, did not play games at the top level in the AFL. In the NFL, he has five active seasons 2016–2021, playing the first four with the New York Jets followed by one with the Carolina Panthers playing 74 games in total and making 376 punts for 17,189 yards at an average of 45.7 and with an in 20 percentage of 30.85.

Today the production line of Australians in the US college system seeking a career in the NFL as a punter is extensive.

AFL players are expected to run 7.5–12.5 miles in an AFL game at an elite level. There may still be opportunities to attract older AFL players to the NFL when their careers can no longer maintain this level of running. A player's kicking leg strength remains and is transferable. Arryn Siposs is one such example playing 28 senior AFL games with St Kilda across four seasons 2010–2014. Siposs joined Auburn University as a punter for the 2018 and 2019 seasons, before becoming a member of the Detroit Lions practice squad in 2020 and then making the Philadelphia Eagles 53-man roster across the 2021-2023 seasons. Across that time, he played in 32 games, punting 107 times for 4,768 yards at an average of 44.6 and a longest punt of 68. His inside 20 percentage was 32.71.

Rugby League and Rugby Union transferable skills to the NFL

Punting may not be the last example of transferrable skills from Australian sports to the NFL. Jordan Mailata is the left tackle for the Philadelphia Eagles and in 2021 completed his fourth season in the NFL. Originally drafted with pick 233 in round seven of the 2018 draft, Mailata debuted in the 2020 season playing 15 games and followed with another 15 games in 2021 including his first postseason game. Mailata is almost six foot seven inches tall and 360 pounds. For a big-frame man, he is very mobile with quick feet and quick hands.

Just prior to the start of the 2021 NFL season, Mailata signed a four-year contract extension with the Eagles for $64m with a max of $80m and $40.85m guaranteed[86]. The value of the contract indicated he had beaten out Andre Dillard for the starting left tackle position. Dillard was a 2019 first rounder in the NFL draft and had played three college seasons with Washington State in the Pac-12 conference. While Mailata has benefited from the NFL's International Pathways Program, this was still a significant achievement and an example of transferrable skills.

Mailata played junior Rugby League for the Canterbury Bankstown Bulldogs in the Under 18 SG Ball Cup and the South Sydney Rabbitohs in the Under 20s. At the elite NRL level, games are played over two halves of 40 minutes each for a total of eighty minutes, with a 10-minute halftime break. While stoppages do occur during the game, the rules are designed to ensure the 40-minute halves are played as quickly as possible.

Each team has 17 players, with only 13 on the field at any one time and four players on the interchange bench. While it is never evenly split (the bigger players tend to play for shorter periods), as a rule of thumb you can multiply the 80 minutes by the 13 players on the field, and divide it by 17 players in total, and you would need a capability of all players being able to play at their elite best for more than 60 minutes. All players have a role in offense and defense. Size is important for a power game to be able to gain extra yards in offense with time in possession tiring the opposition, however, there is clearly a minimum aerobic capacity required to play at the elite level.

Rugby Union is slightly different to Rugby League. Rugby Union involves 15 players on the field for each team with the availability of seven or eight substitutes. Both Rugby League and Rugby Union are played on a rectangular field the same as the NFL gridiron. A Rugby League field try line to try line is 109 yards long (100 meters) and 74.4 yards (68 meters) wide, while a Rugby-Union pitch is the same length of 109 yards long and no more than 76.6 yards wide (70 meters). NFL games, too, are played on a rectangular field with dimensions of 100 yards in length goal line to goal line and 53.3 yards in width (48.7 meters). While the width of the NFL gridiron is smaller, there is also fewer players on the field, each team comprising 11 players.

Big-frame athletes above 340 pounds in Rugby League and Rugby Union have skills that are transferrable to the NFL of speed and agility for humans of unique size. To demonstrate that Mailata is not a one-off and that skills transferability is replicable and repeatable take the example of Daniel Faalele, an Australian who played Rugby Union as a junior (along with basketball). Faalele stands at six foot eight inches and weighing 380 pounds. He played three college seasons with the University of Minnesota before nominating for the 2022 NFL draft. Faalele was selected with pick 110 in the fourth round going to the Baltimore Ravens.

An example of transferable skills outside of sport

Let's finish with an example of transferrable skills for businesses outside of professional sports, by taking the profession of accounting. As a general guide, accountants are highly numerate, have a strong eye for detail, are good at identifying patterns and trends, have strong skills in mathematical modelling, and experience in interpreting business risk and legislation. These are the sorts of skills that are also highly desirable in the role of an actuary or statistician. While not as obvious, they are also skills highly desirable in cyber security or quality controllers, or systems management.

Understanding job design and skill transferability is an important tool for businesses that may be struggling to find sufficient talent to meet their objectives or in instances where demand from big business is also high making it difficult to compete on market rate expectations of available talent.

5. Talent development

THERE ARE TWO ENDS OF the talent-development spectrum. At one end, businesses acquire talent who are market leading and ready to roll without any hand holding. Targets are assigned, systems and processes in place, and talent are empowered to go out and make it happen.

At the other end of the spectrum, rookies are brought in knowing there is no underpinning knowledge for the job role and that the business will need to develop this knowledge and hone the appropriate skills on the job.

For any team member to achieve their career aspirations, they will need to undertake their own learning outside of the workplace. This may be formal or informal. It may involve the business co-investing in the development, or it may require total self-funding.

Within any business, the priorities for learning and development may be specific to the business unit or business wide. These learning and development plans may or may not align with the career aspirations of team members. It may be compliance training or training to overcome identified organizational risks.

There has been much written on the value of annual or bi-annual performance reviews or, alternatively, ignoring such processes altogether believing that feedback is of greater effectiveness when given immediately at the point of reference rather than at a later date of review.

For new entrants to the workforce, the notion of being assessed by your direct manager or by your peers can be quite uncomfortable. Indeed, discomfort on being assessed is not limited to new entrants. Professionals at any level can experience anxiety in relation to receiving feedback no matter how constructive or well-intended the feedback may be.

To expedite career opportunities, coming to terms with being assessed is a must. In a sporting context, the analogy is to worry about only those things you can control. The reality is everyone is always assessed: by managers, by senior executives, by peers, by competitors, by customers, or by indirect customers such as relevant government representatives and industry bodies.

Consider the NFL context. The 2021 draft was held April 29, 2021, to May 1, 2021. After the draft is completed, rookies sign their playing contracts and join an extended squad of 90 players to train during the preseason. As the new season got closer, franchises were required to reduce the size of their squads three times, finalizing a 53-man roster by August 31, 2021, with an additional 16 players on a practice squad.

Hence upon entering the initial training camp, all players know that 21 players will fail to secure a position to participate in the forthcoming season.

It is not quite that straight forward – some players move between franchises both during the preseason and the regular season, while others will be promoted from the practice squad when players are injured and placed on the Physically Unable to Perform (PUP) list with practice squads backfilled with a player outside of the roster. It may or may not be a player who was cut during the initial roster finalization process.

Talent development

The important point here, however, is that all players enter training camp knowing that they will be constantly evaluated, and that 21 places will be removed before the regular season starts. This reduction occurs over a four-month period and makes for a complicated relationship-building process for any newcomer.

Shaun O'Hara, Super Bowl XLII world champion with New York Giants in 2008, is a football analyst with the NFL network and was asked what kind of advice he would give rookie players heading into their first training camp[87].

> Be on time. Clearly. You can't be late, and you got to get on the field. You can't make the club in the tub. So look, for rookies, I think the one thing you have to realize is that this is a job. So you have got to act as if, [and] always know that you are being evaluated. Every single thing you do, from the minute you walk into the building, where you eat lunch, how you conduct yourself with the people in the building, the training room, the weight room, every single thing, you are being evaluated, and you have got to find a way to provide value, not just on the field, but as a part of the team. Then the other thing I will say to the rookies is don't cut yourself. You can't make mental mistakes. Physically, there is going to be days where you get beat or you don't make the catch, you don't make the throw, you don't make the block, but mentally you can never cut yourself by not knowing what you got to do.

The sentiments expressed by O'Hara apply to any business setting. When joining a new business irrespective of your seniority, it is important to be on time respecting the time of your peers and line managers, show that you are eager to contribute, be open to meeting new people while being situationally aware and respecting the time of colleagues, and treat all people equally and with respect. When settling into the new role, have the mindset O'Hara outlines of finding ways to add value.

If you can accept that at all times you are being evaluated by someone, then it is easier to not be distracted by things outside of your control and outside your sphere of influence. You will find yourself empowered to be proactive and at your most efficient to deliver the value and solve the problems for which you were hired.

Strengthening the roster through proven talent acquisition

Of the two ends of the talent-development spectrum, in recent times the LA Rams have been found at one end of the spectrum acquiring proven talent as opposed to securing unproven talent who will require developmental support.

Every year in the NFL draft, each franchise has one selection per round. Some franchises can gain additional selections under the compensatory formula for losing minority coaches and executives or losing free agents, nonetheless, the standard draft is one pick per franchise per round over the seven rounds. This draft capital is tradeable.

In 2016, the LA Rams traded with the Tennessee Titans to move up from pick 15 to the number-one spot. The trade involved swapping the 2016 first-round picks, and the Titans also getting the Rams two second-round picks and third-round pick in 2016, and a first-round pick and third-round pick in 2017. In exchange the Rams also received the Titans fourth and sixth round picks from 2016.

With the number-one pick in 2016, the Rams selected quarterback Jared Goff. Trading first-round picks continued for the next six years, with the Rams trading their 2018 first-round pick to New England for receiver Brandin Cooks, their 2019 first-round pick to move down for the second and third round picks from Atlanta, their 2020 and 2021 first round picks trading for safety Jalen Ramsey from the Jacksonville Jaguars, and then even though Goff and the Rams went to the 2019 Super Bowl losing to the New England Patriots 13–3, Goff was traded for Matthew Stafford in a deal that included the Rams 2022 and 2023 first-round picks.

This all produced seven consecutive years without a first-round pick for the Rams. Their desire to win now has been clearly driven by an ethos of acquiring proven talent to strengthen key areas as the highest priority, and forgo the investment required to bring rookie talent up to speed.

The Stafford-Goff trade epitomizes this ethos. Goff was the number-one pick in 2016, and in only his third season led the Rams on a charge to the Super Bowl which was ultimately unsuccessful. Rather than continue to develop this quarterback asset, a decision was made to trade for a twelve-season veteran in Stafford even though Stafford had only three playoff appearances and no postseason victories during his Detroit Lions tenure. The assessment had been made that Stafford's attributes enhanced the Rams chances for future success in preference to the ongoing development of Goff.

There are many lessons to learn from a talent development lens in the NFL. Imagine being at the top of the talent tree in college, the best in your position, then being thrown into the deep end by being drafted by the worst possible team. Yet that is exactly what happens in the NFL. The best player in the draft is generally selected by the worst performing team of the previous year (unless they trade down to collect more picks because their talent pool is really shallow). From the player's perspective, yes, they have pride in being recognized as the number-one pick, and they secure generational wealth through a four-year contract (with fifth year option) that is worth close to US$40 million.

However, in going to the worst-performing team from the previous year, you get a four-month window to train with your new teammates, and no period to acclimate by shadowing and learning from a veteran. Come round one, the coach points to the deep end and says jump on in and lift the performance of your teammates.

Depending on the talent of the first-round pick, the talent level of the supporting cast, and the capability of the coaching unit, you may successfully learn on the job and achieve some success, or it could be a long season with few wins.

Benefits of rookies building T-shaped skills

Unlike the NFL, young professionals do have freedom of labor mobility. As such, access to development opportunities should be a key criterion when considering landing spots in your formative years. As you apply your skills and knowledge in the workplace, building T-shaped skills will be vital for achieving your career aspirations. T-shaped skills is a model where the horizontal line of the "T" represents breadth in cross-discipline expertise, while the vertical line of the "T" represents depth of discipline and subject matter.

If you join an employer that is going to expose you to a breadth of disciplines, you will have greater opportunity to find your passion and a better understanding of where gaps in the market exist that will likely lead to better remunerated opportunities, rather than joining an alternative employer that is offering the ability for depth immediately in a narrow, specialized area. You won't know that the specific discipline is your passion until you give it a go, or that the business is a cultural and values fit. The opportunity-cost equation needs to be considered. Remuneration is always important, however, development opportunities throughout a career and in the early years will maximize remuneration opportunities over the lifetime of the career.

An example of T-shaped skills in the NFL world is the offensive line and its five positions of left tackle, right tackle, left guard, right guard, and center. At college, it is natural that the largest physical specimens find themselves in the left or right tackle position particularly outside the big schools where player depth isn't as prominent. However, at the elite level, such size is no longer unique. Through draft-grading processes, franchises can be attracted to a rookie with attributes that afford versatility across offensive-line positions. Even if a rookie's natural fit is at left or right tackle, it may take several years of continued strength and conditioning to maximize output in those positions. In the meantime, if a rookie can cover left or right guard, or center on rotations as well in their starting years at NFL level, that immediately adds value to the franchise.

There will come a time during the rookie contract when a specific position needs to be the focus (i.e. the vertical line of the T shape) so that franchise can get the best return from the rookie's talents. Mastery comes from dedicated and deliberate practice, again an opportunity cost equation. The more time spent broadly inhibits extending the depth of the vertical line. As an evolution, this specialization represents a win-win for both franchise and player and will maximize remuneration proceeding the rookie contract, by showcasing a specialist skillset that is highly desired by both the current franchise and other teams. The alternative is to be a jack-of-all-trades, master of none, which is more common and therefore under standard supply and demand market forces will attract less remuneration.

5.1 The insights of teammates matter: you cannot fool the players

"You cannot fool the players" is a phrase that I first heard Colin Cowherd from Fox Sports use to describe competition in the locker room and is one that I find profound and applies across all contexts within a business. Cowherd uses it to describe players observing each other's capabilities and having a view, expressed or otherwise, as to which teammates should hold starting positions.

In the competitive world of the NFL, the season starts with extended squads of 90 players that are whittled down to 53 before the season starts, which is just the beginning of the ruthless business cycle. Players on contract years (i.e. their contracts finish at season end) are highly motivated to deliver eye-catching performances and consistently big seasons so there is a continued market for their services heading into the next season, and hopefully competition for their services to maximize their remuneration. The converse also happens should seasons go badly.

Ultimately, play on the gridiron is a team sport. While you may have prepared yourself to perform at the highest level, there are some variables outside your control, such as broader team performance and how that impacts on the win-loss record. As such, there is a vested interest in the outcomes of team selection. One player coming off contract at seasons end may have a different view to the coach as to who should hold the quarterback keys particularly if the coach is looking at the team's best interests over the coming two to three seasons.

Heading into the 2021 NFL draft, there were five quarterbacks broadly being tipped to be selected in the first round. Trevor Lawrence (Clemson University) had been the presumptive number-one pick for several years, leaving Zach Wilson

(Brigham Young University), Trey Lance (North Dakota State University), Justin Fields (Ohio State University), and Mac Jones (University of Alabama).

The last time the Jacksonville Jaguars made the postseason was 2017, where they won their first two playoff games before losing to the New England Patriots in the Conference Championship. They followed this with three straight losing seasons 5–11 (2018), 6–10 (2019), and 1–15 (2020).

Lawrence did go first pick to Jacksonville, who then traded incumbent starting quarterback Gardner Minshew to the Philadelphia Eagles prior to season commencement.

A tougher time had been had in New York as 2010 was the last time the Jets made the postseason. Sam Darnold was selected with pick three by the Jets in 2018 and was starting quarterback for three seasons that ended with losing records of 4–12 (2018), 7–9 (2019) and 2–14 (2020). The Jets selected quarterback Zach Wilson with the second overall pick in the 2021 draft, and then traded Sam Darnold to the Carolina Panthers prior to the commencement of the season.

In both instances, it was clear that the selections for Jacksonville and the Jets would result in Lawrence and Wilson being the starting quarterbacks in 2021 for their respective teams. They were not going to allow their rookie time to sit and improve behind the incumbent.

It was unclear how much development time would be needed for Trey Lance (third overall pick by the San Francisco 49ers), Justin Fields (eleventh overall pick by the Chicago Bears), and Mac Jones (fifteenth overall pick by the New England Patriots). Quarterback incumbents were Jimmy Garoppolo for the 49ers (who held a 24–8 win-loss record with the 49ers), recently signed 10-year and 144-game veteran Andy Dalton for the Bears, and another 10-year veteran with 140-games Cam Newtown with the New England Patriots.

For teams that have performed poorly in previous seasons, a high draft selection pick creates a lot of excitement. Not just for the fans, but also for team ownership. Excitement and improved results provide enhanced business opportunities. Hence there is a lot of external pressure and media focused on how long rookies sit behind an incumbent when results remain sub-optimal.

An often-quoted example of the perfect scenario is that of Kansas City Chiefs quarterback Patrick Mahomes. Mahomes was drafted with the tenth pick in the 2017 draft and played just the one game in his rookie season sitting behind veteran Alex Smith. Smith was the Chiefs starting quarterback from 2013 through to 2017 missing the postseason just once in that time and leading the charge to winning records of 11–5 (2013), 9–7 (2014), 11–5 (2015), 12–4 (2016) and 10–6 (2017). Mahomes had the opportunity to acclimate for a full season behind Smith before taking over in 2018 inheriting a winning record and culture which Mahomes seamlessly continued and built upon securing a winning record of 12–4 (2018) and 12–4 in 2019 that culminated in a Super-Bowl ring.

Few are able to come into a starting role in such a strong position. The 49ers (6–10), Bears (8–8) and Patriots (7–9) all failed to achieve winning records and qualify for the post-season in the 2020 season leading into the 2021 draft.

During the preseason, players develop their own sense and views as to what the roster is likely to look like and which specific players give the franchise the best chance of winning – *You cannot fool the players.*

Following a practice session early in the preseason (August 3, 2021), San Francisco 49ers head coach Kyle Shanahan was asked during a media conference as to when Trey Lance would become the 49ers starting quarterback. Shanahan's response was "When I think he gives us the best chance to win"[88]. This was a consistent response repeated throughout the preseason.

The Patriots conversely acted decisively cutting veteran Cam Newton before the season started, going all in on their rookie Mac Jones. Despite blowing out to an initial losing record of 3–5, the 49ers remained stoic and kept Jimmy Garoppolo as their starting quarterback for the entire season. Due to injury, Lance did start two games winning one and losing one, while also playing snaps in three others. The Bears started Dalton for the first two games of the season before injury provided an opportunity to Fields. An injury to Fields late in the season saw Dalton back to starter for the last two games of the year. All told, Fields played snaps in 12 games and Dalton played snaps in eight games.

By seasons end, the Patriots and 49ers qualified for the postseason and the Bears did not.

"You cannot fool the players" in a broader business context

How does "You cannot fool the players" apply in a broader business context?

Firstly, it can be easy to identify an under-performing member of the team. It is much more complex to understand if there are barriers that can be removed or whether there is support that can be provided to lift performance to the desired level.

The quarterback examples showcased in this book, however, have an added layer of complexity. Your business may have a performing "vet", but there may also be a younger talent behind them who have a greater ceiling. If progression is too slow for the younger talent, their development may be hindered. Moving away from the vet may sound easy enough to do, but in practice, particularly if they have been performing, this can cause tension in the "locker room".

Over time that may be manageable, or conversely it could snowball and magnify. Players coming off contract at season's end can have their values impacted by a reduction in team achievement. There is no right or wrong way to manage such situations, however, that does not mean the best interests of the business can be shirked, or otherwise you risk losing valuable assets to "free agency". It is a competitive labor market, and professionals will seek out opportunities that best realize their value.

Secondly, on the gridiron a "gunner" is a special team's player who lines up on the sideline when your team is going to punt the ball. Their job is to beat the blockers of the opposing team and to get to the punt returner as fast as possible to make a tackle and minimize yards gained.

In Aussie parlance, a "gunna" is slang for 'going to'. Whether it be at executive level, managerial level, or business unit level, a gunna represents the stereotype of a team member who continues to make commitments and fails to follow through or fails to deliver. Something always gets in the way of delivering their commitment.

Another gunna stereotype is a member of a team who demonstrates privilege and a sense of entitlement. They may be a newer member coming into a successful team and has not been part of the grind to date. Nonetheless, they see the success and are slow to deliver and not a contributor to the broader team. Their purpose is self as opposed to being part of something bigger. There is a saying in baseball that reflects such privilege and entitlement "some people are born on third base thinking they hit a triple". It reflects unearned arrogance.

No-one outside of group-meeting environments has observed or appreciated the commitments made by the gunna, nor that there is a pattern of gunna behaviour over time. It may be a situation where the team member gives textbook management responses or business rhetoric which gives line managers and executives the sense of being a contributor, but in reality, they spend their time busy being busy without focusing and delivering on core objectives.

Another stereotype would be a team member who consistently requests additional support, lamenting that they will only be successful once the business removes this one barrier or another. Or it could be a case of lots of activity invested in the wrong areas, again a case of too busy being busy to focus on critical business areas.

"The problem with doing nothing is not knowing when you are finished."

– Benjamin Franklin

It can happen at board and executive level too. Board members develop relationships with key executives and take what business information is provided at face value, not aware of the accuracy or unplanned additional support provided, or priorities triaged to get business progress over the line. A strong board understands that their main job is to hire and fire the chief executive, approve the strategy, and resource the budget, and then oversee the governance of company risks. A weak governance model has board directors seeking to influence executive retention and acquisition, neither of which assure business outcomes but rather may alienate and negatively impact the business culture. Only those meeting at the table know when team members are performing or not – *You cannot fool the players.*

6. The secret sauce of success: grit

When you think of professional sports and grit, what comes to mind? A player being injured during a game and seeing out the clock despite the injury. A team securing the win despite losing a key player during the game. A player returning to competition after a potentially career-ending injury. A perceived less talented team beating a perceived higher talented team. A traditional underperforming team making the postseason. A team experiencing season-ending injuries to key players, yet still making the postseason. A team coming back from a large points differential to ultimately win the game. A player's commitment to achieving their full potential, undertaking the grind day in day out, year in year out?

Grit is all these things, and much more. Passion, persistence, determination, perseverance. Central to grit is mindset. Demonstrating a strength of character and having the courage and resolve to overcome adversity.

"Everyone has a plan until they get punched in the mouth."

– Mike Tyson, former heavy weight boxing champion

The secret sauce of success: grit

Let us look at some examples of grit that have inspired sports fans.

Grit: Players injured during a game, seeing out the clock, and inspiring success

Matthew Stafford – Detroit Lions v Cleveland Browns 2009
Rams quarterback Matthew Stafford is one such player in the NFL, developing a reputation for being tough and resilient stemming back to his rookie season.

In 2008, the Detroit Lions became the first NFL team to finish a season with a 0–16 record. They went the entire league season of sixteen games without a win. (The Cleveland Browns went on to emulate the feat in 2017.) Detroit then select Stafford with their number-one draft pick in 2009.

Going into week 11, Detroit had managed to win two games in 2009 and were facing the Cleveland Browns who at that point had won just a single game in that season. With eight seconds of game time left,[89] Detroit was down 37–31.

Stafford took the snap receiving the football 38 yards away from the Cleveland end zone and rolled left beating one Browns tackle on the 40-yard line. With no options, Stafford then ran it back to his right, throwing the ball from the 38-yard marker. He experienced a devastating hit while completing his throw. The throw sailed into the Browns end zone, and a pass interference call was made on the Browns, meaning the next snap would be taken from just one yard out.

Meanwhile Stafford was writhing in considerable pain on the ground. Stafford left the field to be assessed with what looked like a major injury to his left shoulder. The Browns took a timeout to regroup and prepare for the final snap of the game to come from one yard out. Given the timeout, Stafford was allowed to re-enter the game under the rules. Despite the obvious and immense pain, Stafford came back in, and passed the ball for a touchdown, immediately running back to the sideline. Broadcast microphones picked up Stafford saying his shoulder went out and back in during that final play. With Stafford watching from the sidelines, Detroit's attempt at point after touchdown (PAT) was successful resulting in a 38–37 win.

Justin Fields – Ohio State v Clemson Tiger 2021 Allstate Sugar Bowl Playoff Semifinal

Chicago Bears quarterback Justin Fields demonstrated similar grit in his final college season before entering the 2021 draft. Fields was playing for the Ohio State Buckeyes against the Clemson Tigers in the 2021 College Football Playoff Semifinal at the Allstate Sugar Bowl. At stake was a place in the 2021 College Football National Championship.

Having worked their way back from a 7–14 deficit, Ohio was leading Clemson 21–14 at the 6:12 minute mark of the second quarter when Fields took a snap 30 yards out from the Clemson end zone. Rather than pass, Fields scooted off for a run making it to the 19-yard marker before being hit in the back of the rib cage by a Clemson linebacker and going down injured. Fields stayed down for several minutes before heading to the sideline. Upon review, the linebacker was ejected from the game for targeting[90]. (Targeting in the college game is any hit where the defender leads with the crown of their helmet regardless of where contact occurs.)

Backup quarterback CJ Stroud came on to substitute for Fields and was active for just one play before Fields came back in. The very next snap Fields threw 17 yards for a touchdown, which along with the successful point after touchdown took the scores to 28–14. Ohio State went on to beat Clemson

49–28 securing their place in the 2021 National championship game against Alabama Crimson Tide.

Grit and examples of playing through the pain barrier in Rugby League

In Rugby League, there are many examples of players playing through injury, particularly in the championship game. John Sattler had his reputation for being a tough player celebrated when as captain of the South Sydney Rabbitohs he managed to play through the 1970 Grand Final having broken his jaw in three places in the opening minutes. Broken jaws are difficult to navigate in Rugby League. Even though there has been much done to protect the head in recent times given a greater understanding of head injuries and concussions (Chronic Traumatic Encephalopathy – CTE), Rugby League is still played without a helmet unlike the NFL. With natural differences in player heights from six foot six to five foot eight, there is an inevitability of encountering a shoulder or swinging arm to the head at various stages throughout the game.

Sattler led South Sydney to a grand-final win over the Manly Sea Eagles 23–12 making 20 tackles and touching the ball 29 times with one offload in traffic[91] despite his broken jaw.

History repeated itself 44 years later with South Sydney captain Sam Burgess breaking his cheekbone in the very first tackle of the 2014 grand final against the Canterbury Bankstown Bulldogs. Burgess played the entire eighty minutes of the game making 39 tackles and making 22 runs for 218 meters[92], ultimately leading the Rabbitohs to a 30–6 win.

Example of grit are not limited to injuries suffered during a game; they also include playing when injuries have not yet healed. The 2018 NRL grand final saw the Sydney Roosters going up against the Melbourne Storm. The Roosters qualified having beaten the South Sydney Rabbitohs 12–4 in a preliminary final the week before. Rooster's halfback Cooper Cronk was injured in the game against the Rabbitohs and was in doubt for the grand final. As is often the case, teams can become coy around the status of injuries to minimize the opportunity for opposing teams to target the weakness.

Much of the media in the lead-up to the grand final was suggesting Cronk was experiencing a rotator-cuff injury. Despite being in doubt all week Cronk plays 78 of the 80 minutes in the grand final. Throughout the entire grand final Cronk did not make one run, focusing instead on organizing the team's attack through passes and field position through his kicking game. Even then his involvement was not high, making 14 passes, nine tackles, and four kicks[93]. He was, however, the general guiding his team around the paddock to lock up field position and time in possession, ultimately leading the Roosters to 21–6 win.

After the game it was revealed that Cronk played with pain killing injections both before the game and at halftime. He had in fact played with a broken scapula right through the bone.

Players grinding to return to competition after a potentially career-ending injury

Defensive end Dee Ford was an eight-year veteran in the NFL having started with the Kansas City Chiefs in 2014 before joining the San Francisco 49ers in 2019. Ford played 11 games in 2019 and was part of the 49ers team that made a Super-Bowl run ultimately losing to Ford's former team the Chiefs 31–20.

The following season Ford was limited to just one game due to back and neck injuries.

At one 49ers press conference during the 2021 preseason[94], Ford was asked how his rehab was going, replying:

"We're stacking days; we're getting better you know, [it's] been a long process but, you know we got a great team of people, so, I am feeling good, but I'm not where I need to be, but we're working every day ... I've been here three times before, so I kind of knew the flow of things, and what I should be expecting, and it's always frustrating in the beginning, but as you keep pushing, keep rehabbing every day, you know you'll breakthrough a wall and you know everything [will] start feeling better; you'll feel more functional; it's all it's just a feel thing."

Ford referred to having had surgery twice before and not really being able to have a third. When asked if had considered retiring at any stage, his replies included:

"Hell no ... I put in too much work. I haven't put my best ball on tape, yet. So, you know this is my life; it's what I do.

"If you love the game ... I love what I do ... you know, I got a great support team, my family is great, I had no excuses, as long as I can keep doing it, as long as I wasn't risking anything, I was going to give it a shot; that's how I roll."

Despite Ford's best efforts of rehabilitation, he was released by the 49ers in July 2022 and has not returned to the gridiron.

Alex Smith was a quarterback in the NFL whose rookie season was with the San Francisco 49ers in 2005. Smith played 14 seasons, the first seven of which were with the 49ers, the next five seasons with the Kansas City Chiefs, and the last two seasons with Washington. Smith was the starting quarterback when Patrick Mahomes red shirted his first season with the Kansas City Chiefs back in 2017.

Smith's career statistics were 174 games for 35,650 passing yards at a career completion rate of 62.6 percent for 199 touchdowns and 109 interceptions.

A week 11 clash on November 18, 2018, saw Smith and Washington facing the Houston Texans. Smith was taking a snap on the 24-yard marker from Houston's end zone. The Houston pass rush was able to quickly move past the Washington offensive line with Smith scrambling back to the 40-yard line before being sacked. Smith's right foot got caught in the turf as two defenders rolled over the top of him, sending his weight backward while the foot was temporarily stuck beneath a defender. The result was a broken fibula and tibia in his right leg.

Smith appeared on ESPN's *Outside the Lines*[95] the day before Super Bowl LIV between the San Francisco 49ers and Kansas City Chiefs (February 3, 2020), sharing insights into his injuries and the challenges he faced and continued to face:

> "You hear about broken bones all the time in sports and life … I greatly underestimated the complexity of, first of all a broken tibia and fibula, and how hard they are to heal … [I] had some unforeseen things happen: I had a pretty serious infection that had a lot of complications with it. [I had] a bunch of surgeries that ended up leading to, you know, basically a limb-salvage surgery for my leg to save my leg. [I was] faced with the decision to amputate or limb salvage and [I] elected obviously to try to save my leg and [I'm] thankful for the doctors that that did so."

The initial surgery went well with Smith having several plates inserted into the leg, before later an infection was identified that resulted in sepsis. In Smith's words, he was "very much lucky to be alive, very lucky to still have my leg."

After 17 surgeries, the near leg amputation and almost two years, Smith did make it back onto the gridiron in the week five game against the LA Rams October 11, 2020. He spent the next four weeks in backup roles before starting in a loss against the Detroit Lions on November 15. With Smith in the starter role, Washington was able to win its next four games, before a calf injury sidelined Smith until the final game of the year against divisional rival the Philadelphia Eagles.

In that final round, all four teams in the NFC East were playing each other. Washington and the Dallas Cowboys were tied at the top of the division with six wins each, and the New York Giants were back one game with five wins. (The Philadelphia Eagles were on four wins and out of contention for the postseason) In the must-win game, Washington, guided by Smith, beat the Eagles 20–14, while the Dallas Cowboys lost to the New York Giants. Washington won the NFC East division title and secured a place in the postseason for the first time since 2015.

Washington went on to lose in the wild-card round of the playoffs, and Smith was cut by season's end, retiring some weeks later.

Smith was awarded the 2020 NFL Comeback Player of the Year, and his comeback journey exuding grit is preserved in the ESPN documentary *Project 11: Alex Smith's Final Drive*.

Grit: Teams grinding and overcoming adversity

Las Vegas Raiders NFL season 2021-2022

We have looked at some individual players exhibiting grit above and beyond, however grit also applies to teams as a collective. Two teams stood out in the NFL 2021–22 season.

Firstly, the Las Vegas Raiders. There was much excitement

for the Raiders heading into the 2021–22 season, with the opening of their new facility Allegiant Stadium, nicknamed the Death Star from Star Wars fame, because of the predominately black exterior, external fluorescent lights when on at night, and spaceship shape. Allegiant Stadium was a $1.9billion construction. The Raiders hosted the Baltimore Ravens in week one of the 2021–22 season christening their new stadium with a 33–27 overtime win with 61,756 fans in attendance.

Since losing to the Tampa Bay Buccaneers at Super Bowl XXXVII back in 2003, the Raiders had only a sole winning season and visit to the postseason (2016). The 3–2 winning start to the 2021–22 season was showing much promise until the first hurdle for the year struck – coach Jon Gruden resigned with immediate effect.

Gruden had been appointed head coach for the Raiders in 2018 signing a 10-year contract worth a reported $100m. Several emails had surfaced from Gruden through an investigation into the Washington Football team which occurred while Gruden was a football analyst with ESPN.

There were then reports that emails Gruden wrote over a 10-year period included racist, misogynistic, and anti-gay language. Assistant coach Rich Bisaccia was appointed as interim head coach following Gruden's resignation.

After week seven, the Raiders had moved to a winning record of 5–2 heading into their bye in week eight.

Henry Ruggs III was a wide receiver from the University of Alabama and selected by the Las Vegas Raiders with draft pick number 12 in the 2020 NFL draft. In his first season in the NFL, Ruggs played 13 games for 26 receptions and 452 yards at an average of 17.4 yards per reception for two touchdowns.

His 2021 season was showing great progress. In the first

seven games of the season, Ruggs had 24 receptions for 489 yards at an average of 19.5 yards per reception and another two touchdowns. His statistics were on target to double those of the previous season.

Around 3.30am Tuesday November 3, 2021, Ruggs was the driver of a vehicle that collided with another car, and the incident killed a 23-year old women and her dog. Ruggs was later arrested and charged with alleged driving over 150 miles per hour just prior to the impact and having a blood alcohol level twice the legal limit. The Raiders cut Ruggs immediately, and the case against Ruggs is being progressed through the courts at the time of writing.

Just weeks later, the Raiders cut cornerback Damon Arnette who had also been a first-round pick (pick 19) along with Ruggs in the 2020 NFL draft. A social-media post by Arnette had gone viral, one in which he was brandishing a gun and threatening to take a life.

For the Las Vegas Raiders, all this upheaval occurred before week 10 of the season. Teams lose coaches and players mid-season all the time. These circumstances, however, were highly unique and carried a huge emotional weight for their impact on others, which was felt not just by the locker room, by the broader Raiders institution and fans, the NFL and its fans, and broader society.

The Raiders faced AFC West divisional opponents the LA Chargers in week 17 the final game of the season. Both had 9–7 win-loss records. The Kansas City Chiefs had already secured the divisional title, with the Raiders and Chargers competing for a wild-card position in the postseason. The Raiders won 35–32 in overtime, securing their place in the postseason for the first time since 2016. While they would eventually go on to lose to Cincinnati Bengals in the wild card round of the postseason, the difficulties they faced in getting that far showed an incredible amount of character and grit.

"The tough times are really when people separate themselves."[96]
– Sean McVay, Head Coach Los Angeles Rams 2017–2022+

San Franscisco 49ers NFL season 2021-2022

Another example of a team showing grit throughout the 2021–22 NFL season was the San Francisco 49ers. The season started out well enough with their first two games on the road resulting in a win against the Detroit Lions (44–37 in week one), and then beating the Philadelphia Eagles (17–9 in week 2). There weren't too many red flags indicating what was about to come. Yes, the 49ers were leading the Lions 38–17 going into the final quarter before a strong Lions comeback outscoring the Niners 16 to 3 in the final quarter. Yes, the Niners were only up 7–3 going into the final quarter against the Eagles; they did win, however, in a game that could have gone either way. It was the beginning of the season though, and no team would yet be at their best.

The 49ers went on to lose five of their next six games, including two games against NFC West divisional rival the Arizona Cardinals, and one game against another divisional rival the Seattle Seahawks. It also included a 30–28 loss to the Green Bay Packers when the 49ers took the lead 28–27 with just 37 seconds of play remaining. The Packers started a final drive at the Green Bay 25. Two Aaron Rodgers pass completions of 25 yards and 17 yards, along with an incompletion and two spiked balls, led to a 49ers timeout that left just three seconds on the clock and 51 yards to go. Enter

Mason Crosby for the Packers, successfully kicking a field goal with the 49ers going down 30–28.

Quarterback Jimmy Garoppolo was injured in the first quarter of the week four game against the Seattle Seahawks and was replaced by rookie Trey Lance for the remainder of the game. Lance started week five against the Arizona Cardinals. The 49ers bye was in week six, and Garoppolo returned for the next game against the Indianapolis Colts in week seven.

Going into week 10, the 49ers record was 3–5, and they were scheduled to meet another NFC West divisional opponent, the LA Rams. The Rams at this stage had a winning record of 7–2. Against the trend, the 49ers produced an old-style smashmouth game of football, rushing the ball 44 times. The 49ers end up winning 31–10 with the Rams never really in the contest at any stage.

The 49ers extended this victory to go on a 5–2 winning run beating the Jacksonville Jaguars, Minnesota Vikings, Cincinnati Bengals, and Atlanta Falcons, while recording a second loss to NFC West divisional opponent the Seattle Seahawks and losing in very wet and windy conditions against the Tennessee Titans in week 16. Quarterback Jimmy Garoppolo's thumb was jammed in the turf during the second quarter against the Titans. While Garoppolo toughed it out and played the remainder of the game, tests would later revel a chipped bone and ligament tear that sidelined him for the game against the Houston Texans.

Going into week 17 there were only two games left in the regular season. Despite now having a winning record of 8–7, the 49ers needed to win both their final games to qualify for the postseason.

Week 17 saw rookie quarterback Trey Lance stand in for Garoppolo for the 49ers game against the Houston Texans, the first in two must-win games. The 49ers were down 7–3 at halftime. There was a lone touchdown in the third quarter seeing the 49ers leading 10–7 going into the final quarter. An early 49ers touchdown in the fourth and a couple of field goals eventually saw a comfortable 49ers win 23–7.

The final game of the regular season was against NFC West divisional opponent the LA Rams. The only intra-division game the 49ers had won this season had been the first match-up against the LA Rams. The 49ers had lost both regular season games to both the Arizona Cardinals and the Seattle Seahawks, even though the Seahawks finished comfortably fourth in the division.

A win by the Rams would guarantee the NFC West Divisional title. The Cardinals were one game back and playing the Seahawks. A win by the 49ers would guarantee their place in the postseason.

A sole field goal separated the teams at quarter time, with the Rams leading. Two touchdowns in the second quarter, and the score at halftime had the Rams leading 17–3. The 49ers were able to score two touchdowns of their own in the third quarter to take the scores level at 17 all. Then a touchdown each in the fourth quarter had the game tied 24 all at the end of regulation time.

In overtime, the 49ers received the ball making 12 plays for 69 yards, eventually taking a field goal to take the lead by three points. The Rams final drive, as it turned out to be, went 20 yards from four plays, before a deep pass from Rams quarterback Matthew Stafford was intercepted by 49ers cornerback Ambry Thomas, thus ending the game. The 49ers qualified for the postseason, despite finishing third in the NFC West division.

The secret sauce of success: grit

> *"When you go through tough times with people, it makes you stronger."*[97]
> – Kyle Shanahan, Head Coach San Francisco 49ers
> 2017-2024+

Despite the uphill battle and needing to navigate two must-win games, the 49ers roll did not stop there. In the wild-card round of the postseason, the 49ers went on the road beating Dallas in Dallas 23–17, followed by a road trip to Lambeau Field to take on the number-one seed in the NFC Conference the Green Bay Packers. As the number-one seed, the Packers had had the previous week off. Going into Lambeau on a snowy evening, the 49ers trailed 7–3 at the end of the third quarter. The 49ers were fortunate to be this close, due to a special teams block of a Packers field goal attempt at the end of the second quarter.

This wasn't the end of the clutch plays by the 49ers special teams' unit. With four minutes 41 seconds left in the fourth quarter, and the Packers leading 10–3, a Packers punt was blocked by the 49ers and recovered by 49er Talanoa Hufanga taking the ball into the end zone for a touchdown. Kicking the extra point good left the scores at 10–all. The Packers were not able to score with their next drive, leaving the 49ers final drive securing field position for 49ers kicker Robbie Gould to take a 45-yard field goal attempt with just four seconds remaining. The kick was successful, and the 49ers were through to the NFC Championship game.

The 49ers went on to lose the NFC Championship to the LA Rams 20–17, with the Rams going on to win the Super Bowl. Nonetheless, the 49ers stared down and were able to overcome adversity on at least five occasions. Firstly, starting the season with a win-loss record of 3–5. Then beating the LA Rams to go on a win-loss run of 7–2. Then winning must-win games in weeks 17 and 18. Week 17 with a rookie quarterback in just his second start, in week 18, beating the NFC West front runner. Then going on the road to win two playoff games. All this was achieved with their regular starting quarterback nursing thumb and shoulder injuries. It was a season of classic grit.

Examples of grit in cricket

Let us look at some different examples of grit in international test match cricket with a focus on the West Indies, English, and Australian teams. In chapter four, we looked at the origins of the chip on the shoulder of the West Indies cricket team and how that chip provided the impetus for sustained success.

The 1976 test match series with the West Indies beating England 3–0 really emphasized three examples of grit.

Firstly, the West Indies as a team led by captain Clive Lloyd demonstrated grit to lift standards and improve the results over a 12-month period following the bruising 5–1 series defeat to Australia. This improvement was not linear, but a line of best fit, constantly on the upswing. After losing to Australia in Australia, the West Indies hosted India in the West Indies taking a 1–0 advantage after the first test. The second test was drawn, and India won the third, leaving the fourth and final test as winner take all. The West Indies prevailed. In the series against England in 1976, the first two tests were drawn, before the West Indies motored home winning the last three test matches.

Improvement is rarely linear, however, momentum matters.

The second example of grit is Michael Holding coming of

age over three consecutive series against Australia, India, and England to help anchor the lifting of standards within West Indies cricket. In the series against Australia, Holding had taken just ten wickets in playing five of the six test matches. Against India, Holding went on to take 19 wickets over the four-match series. Then in England, not having played the first test, Holding captured 28 wickets in the final four test matches including in the last test, a haul of eight wickets in the first innings and six wickets in the second innings.

The final example of grit I wish to highlight didn't come from the West Indies team in the series against England.

Grit is not limited to receiving any actual injury and battling on anyway. Grit includes staring down the challenge in the face of an onslaught. It isn't limited to a David and Goliath battle. Grit is not limited to winning. Grit involves having a crack even when you are outgunned.

In the West Indies series against England, at 46 years old Brian Close returned to the England team after a near nine-year absence. Close had played 19 test matches during the years of 1949–1967 and had a reputation as a no-nonsense hard man.

In the third test at Manchester, the West Indies batted first and were dismissed for 211. England followed and were dismissed cheaply in their first innings for 71. The West Indies batted a second time and declared one hour before stumps on the third day with their second innings at five wickets for 411 leaving England a target of 552 with 75 minutes of play left in the day.

As is often the case, with a short stint available at batsmen before stumps and plenty of rest available overnight before the next day's play, bowlers are emboldened, and let rip holding nothing back. Michael Holding and his colleagues were lethal that evening and worked over Close and his opening partner

John Edrich. There were lots of near misses with the cricket ball whistling past heads without the protection of helmets. And lots of balls to the rib cage that didn't miss. It is well worth looking up the digital archives[98] to see Close's bruised torso with at least five clear balls careening directly into his rib cage. Despite the intensity and the physical battering, Close and Edrich saw the session through to the close of play without loss. After more than an hour, Close would start the next day undefeated on one. Grit.

Some more contemporary examples of grit in cricket. In the summer of 1995–96 South Africa hosted England for a five match test series. The first test was drawn at Centurion Park, with the second test moving to Johannesburg. South Africa batted first and were dismissed for 332. England's first innings reply was 200. South Africa's second innings went better than their first, eventually declaring nine wickets down for 346. This declaration left England needing 479 runs to win with more than five sessions of play remaining.

The South Africans had a highly respected pace bowling attack led by Allan Donald (330 career test wickets) and Shaun Pollock (421 career test wickets). England captain Mike Atherton opened the batting, and in an incredible display of concentration and grit, would go on to remain undefeated scoring 185 runs having faced 492 balls in an innings that last for 10 hours and 43 minutes staving off defeat and securing a draw for England (England ended the day at 351/5).

Winning is not always the outcome of a display of grit. In the instances of both Brian Close and Michael Atherton, grit is staring down the challenge in the face of an onslaught.

The late Dean Jones was one of Australia's finest test cricketers from 1984 through to 1992. Jones played 52 test matches scoring 3,631 runs at an average of 46.55 and with a highest score of 216 against the West Indies. His career-defining moment came in only his third test match, which was against India held in Madras September 18–22, 1986 (Madras was later renamed Chennai in 1986).

Jones had made his debut almost two years earlier, playing two tests in March and April 1984 against the West Indies before being dropped. His four scores across those two games were 48, five, one, and 11.

All five days of the first test between Australia and India in 1986 had weather forecast to be around 40° Celsius (104° Fahrenheit) with 80 percent humidity. Australia won the toss and batted with Jones earning a recall for the first time since April 1984. Jones came to the crease at the fall of the first wicked with the score at 1–48. He went on to post a 158-run partnership with David Boon before Boon was dismissed for 122 with the score at 2–206. Australia moved to 2–211 at stumps on the first day.

Jones would later share that he did not know much about hydration at that time and did not drink much water that night before heading into day two. As day two proceeded with temperatures again stifling, Jones started feeling unwell leading to vomiting and an inability to control urination. Jones batted with Australian captain Allan Border and reached 170 before telling Border that he couldn't go on.

Playing to competitive spirit across Australian states, it is now legend that Border said to Jones, "We'll get someone tough out here; we'll get a Queenslander," which cajoled Jones (a Victorian) into more action. Ultimately Jones was dismissed just after the tea break on the second day for 210. In the dressing rooms, Jones collapsed and was taken to hospital to be placed on an intravenous drip having lost seven kilograms over that day.

Years later, reflecting on his innings, Jones would say[99]:

"I don't find that courageous; that nearly so-called dying or putting yourself in the grave, being gravely ill and sick and dehydrated [is not] a courageous thing. I expect that from any person wearing a baggy green cap or to wear the Australian colors whether it be in any other sport. I don't find that courageous. I think that's what's expected."

Australia declared early on day three scoring 574 with seven wickets down. India was dismissed in its first innings for 397. Australia declared its second innings closed at 170 runs for the loss of five wickets leaving India 348 runs needed to win. The match finished in a historic tie with India bowled out for 347. This was only the second tied match in test-cricket history.

Clarity of vision as an enabler of grit – Tom Brady

Professor Angela Duckworth has devoted her career to understanding personal attributes as a predictor of success. In her book *Grit: The Power of Passion and Perseverance*, she writes that some of the common attributes across successful people are having a very deep understanding of what they want and being unusually resilient and hard working.

We have all seen athletes in our favored sports who look like they hold elite attributes yet fail to live up to expectations, while other less-talented athletes excel. Yes, particularly in team sports, context has an impact, but nonetheless why is it that some athletes overachieve?

Duckworth theorizes that if you consider individuals in identical circumstances, what each achieves depends on talent and effort. Talent and effort results in skill. Achievement, however, is the practical application of skill meaning that effort is factored into calculations twice. Effort builds skill and effort makes skill productive.

The secret sauce of success: grit

We looked at Tom Brady the greatest of all time NFL quarterback in an earlier chapter and the evident chip Brady carries on his shoulder. Now we will look at how that chip has played out in terms of achievement over his career.

There have been only a dozen players to have played more than 300 games. At the completion of the 2022 season, Tom Brady was one of those with 335 games. This made him sixth highest in the number of games played of all players.

Over a career, you would expect a player's statistics to be like any bell curve. As they enter a league, they would improve and get better. The progress would not be linear, but the line of best fit would be on an upslope. Then as a player reaches their prime having optimized physical conditioning and game smarts (learnings from winning and losing optimizing situational awareness), there is a plateau of peak performance before physical capabilities start to degrade. Each player's upslope, plateau, and downslope will be different, but there is a natural circle of life to any sporting career.

Injury histories in sports will expedite the decline in performance and shorten careers, or in worse-case scenarios, result in immediate cessation of playing.

Tom Brady is the GOAT because he has more Super-Bowl rings (seven) than any other player. The next highest is five Super-Bowl rings won by linebacker Charles Haley (two with the San Francisco 49ers, and three with the Dallas Cowboys). There is a large group of thirty players who have won four Super Bowls including Hall of Fame quarterbacks Joe Montana (all with the San Francisco 49ers) and Terry Bradshaw (all with the Pittsburgh Steelers).

Even more remarkable is that Brady's first 19 seasons were spent with the same franchise, the New England Patriots, where he won six Super Bowls, and not one other player on the Patriots roster joined Brady for four or more of those six

Super Bowl wins. Kicker Adam Vinatieri won four Super Bowls, joining Brady for three Patriot wins in 2002, 2003, and 2005 before securing his fourth ring with the Indianapolis Colts. The inimitable Rob Gronkowski tight end did achieve four Super-Bowl rings with Brady; the first three with the New England Patriots in (20015, 2017, 2019) before gaining the fourth at the Tampa Bay Buccaneers in 2021.

Thus, another key attribute in Brady achieving GOAT status has been longevity – the best ability is availability. There was only one season that was wholly disrupted through injury being 2008 when Brady tore his left Anterior Cruciate Ligament (ACL) and Medial Collateral Ligament (MCL) in the first quarter of week one. This required surgery resulting in the rest of the season being missed. Brady hasn't been without any other injuries; however, he has generally been able to manage those while continuing to play.

Brady has been a dedicated student of maximizing peak performance, and in 2013 co-founded TB12 along with his long-time body coach Alex Guerrero positioned as a holistic approach to health and wellness centered on muscle pliability, balanced nutrition, optimal hydration, mental fitness, and functional strength and conditioning.

Brady's personal results cannot be disputed. The standard bell curve was not evident in his case and is more of an s curve where the top of the s is elongated and a plateau of peak results, with virtually no drop off in his final season of 2022.

Table 8 below breaks Brady's career statistics down over three decades: those seasons in his twenties, those seasons in his thirties, and those seasons in his forties.

Brady has won more Super Bowls over fewer seasons in his forties. In his thirties where you might expect the peak of mental strength, game strategy and management, and the ability to execute was the decade with the fewest Super Bowls yet the most seasons.

The bell-curve trend is evident in average yards per attempt in passing with his thirties (7.8 yards per attempt) higher than his twenties (7 yards per attempt) and declining in his forties (7.2 yards per attempt). However, there is next to no decline in his forties across interceptions per game and passing touchdowns per game. In fact, in some statistical categories, he continued to show improvement such as pass completion percentage and sacks per game. The trends in the rushing component of a quarterback's game are evident too, with Brady scoring rushing touchdowns at a higher rate in his forties, and fewer fumbles per game. It is quite an extraordinary feat.

Table 8. Tom Brady's NFL career statistics segmented in three decades

Age	23–29 years old	30–39 years old	40–45 years old
Years	2000–2006	2007–2016	2017–2022
Number of Seasons	7	10	6
Super Bowl Wins	3	1	3
Teams	New England	New England	6 (3 New England, 3 Tampa Bay)
Games Played	96	141	98
Passing			
Completions	1,896	3,348	2,509
Attempts	3,064	5,160	3,826
Completion percent	61.9	64.9	65.6
Yards	21,564	40,018	27,632
Average Yards per Attempt	7	7.8	7.2
Passing Touchdowns	147	309	193
Passing Touchdowns per game	1.5	2.2	2.0
Interceptions	78	74	60
Interceptions per game	0.8	0.5	0.6
Total Sacks	182	235	148
Sacks per game	1.9	1.7	1.5
Rushing			
Attempts	239	293	161
Attempts per game	2.49	2.08	1.64
Yards	435	505	183
Yards Per Attempt Average	1.82	1.72	1.14
Rushing Touchdowns	3	14	11
Rushing Touchdowns per game	0.03	0.10	0.11
Rushing First Downs	79	103	47
Rushing First Downs Per Game	0.8	0.7	0.5
Fumbles	59	46	27
Fumbles Per Game	0.61	0.33	0.28
Rushing Fumbles Lost	8	2	5
Rushing Fumbles Lost Per Game	0.083	0.014	0.051

Now some might argue that his decision to leave the New England Patriots to join to the Tampa Bay Buccaneers after nineteen seasons was an indication that he saw the writing on the wall at the Patriots, that a team decline was coming, and by joining a stronger roster he was able to pad the results in his forties. An alternative lens is to recognize Brady's commitment to continue to improve and his incredible drive to take things to the next level. Ultimately, he was taking a risk by leaving what he had known for twenty years to go and find his desired next stop and continue to move forward.

Duckworth's research on grit finds that those people who identify with their work as a calling are grittier than those who consider their occupation a career or a job. There is no doubt that Brady displays the highest epitome of grit and that for him, the game of football has been a calling.

"Realizing my potential is what my career has been all about. Things that I've dreamed about have actually come true. Things have happened in my life as I kind of hoped they would happen. It's been, I mean, just a complete evolution, you know, how I just kind of kept fighting and clawing to power forward. You just keep putting one foot in front of the other, and you just keep trying to make progress, so when I look at over 20 years, I look at how far I've come."

–"Man in the Arena: Tom Brady" nine-episode series, ESPN

---

7. Roster management: where fluidity and proactivity are business enablers

RUGBY LEAGUE IS ONE OF the few professional sports without a national draft. The talent pipeline is funneled from junior nurseries, that is, junior-age competitions played within a specific geography. The Penrith Panthers have the largest junior nursery of registered players. The Parramatta Eels and Brisbane Broncos also have large junior nurseries.

Given the size of these nurseries, it is not possible to funnel all elite young talent through to the professional franchise. Competitors can see the available talent in the local competitions, undertake a program of monitoring and assessing talent, and are ready to pounce once players are nearing a time to turn professional. Regional franchises can benefit here such as the Newcastle Knights. The Knights represent a large geography in the Hunter region of Northern New South Wales and are roughly a two-hour drive to Sydney where the bulk of the franchises are located. It isn't possible to jump in a car and travel two hours each way and train to a professional level, so emerging elite talent either need to sign with the local franchise or move.

Roster management: where fluidity and proactivity are business enablers

In the Knights instance, do players with professional aspirations 16–18 years of age really want to leave home and reside in the pathway development programs in city centers? It would need to be a very enticing opportunity to forgo the local pathway.

What would make such an opportunity enticing?

If you are a junior in the Penrith Panthers catchment area, you can see the strength and depth of your competition. The Panthers were runners-up in the 2020 NRL title, before going on to three-peat in 2021, 2022 and 2023. The competition to forge a pathway to the elite level in Penrith is very difficult. Signing with an alternative club may provide earlier opportunities and expedite experiences and player development.

The counter argument for the emerging talent would be to articulate and quantify the risks of going to a poorer-performing franchise. What has been holding that franchise back? Is it the coaching? Is it the infrastructure? Is it a perennial poor supporting cast? Did they lose key players at similar times through retirement or to other franchises when contracts expired and are now in reset mode?

While likely to receive earlier opportunities, if those opportunities are with a losing team, will that hold development back? Will those experiences inhibit a longer and successful career?

And then of course is remuneration. Players have a short shelf-life and need to maximize their earning capacity while a professional player. A bird in hand, that is a greater dollar-value contract, in the earlier years heavily influences the decision-making processes.

In the NFL and AFL, where drafts exist, the player entering the league has little ability to influence their initial landing spot. After that, a rookie's contract expires and is open for negotiation.

Heading into the 2023 season there were two teams in the National Rugby League with the longest active streaks for failing to make the playoffs: the Wests Tigers and the Auckland Warriors. Both last made the playoffs in 2011. In the Australian Football League, the Gold Coast Suns stand solo with the longest absence in finals football not having made the playoffs since their inception into the league, also in 2011.

In the NFL, the New York Jets have the longest streak, last appearing in the playoffs in the 2010 season where they won two playoff games before losing to the Pittsburgh Steelers in the Conference Championship 13–6.

Imagine failing to make the playoffs for over a decade. How do you bridge the gap?

An immediate injection of elite talent is the only way to make an instantaneous improvement. This doesn't always mean a player or players who have reached their ceiling; it could mean younger players who are clearly on an upward trajectory and yet to hit their peak.

Why would an elite player, one who can instantly uplift the playing capability of a roster, leave their current franchise to go to a cellar dweller that has no record of recent success?

Money becomes the major lever. Even in salary cap restricted leagues. Teams are either getting better or getting worse; there is no sitting on the fence.

Imagine being a member of the Penrith Panthers premiership winning team in 2021. When you come off contract, you know you are part of loaded squad. Talent is everywhere, and all talent must be remunerated. If an offer comes in from the West Tigers, a franchise that has not made the playoffs in over ten years, what are the factors influencing the decision to stay, or to go?

A player's age comes into it also. If a player is younger

and yet to reach their ceiling, deciding whether the current environment best places them on a continued growth trajectory, or whether a new environment would aid or hinder that trajectory is an important consideration. If a player is older and one who has reached their ceiling, it may be a case of wanting to optimize earnings in the few years left before retirement. Or if a player has competed for a decade and not yet won a competition, there may be a burning desire to accomplish that feat, deciding to forgo maximizing earning capacity in order to re-sign with their current team or a new roster that affords the greater possibility of winning a competition.

Partners and children are factors, and the accompanying support network. If the player has younger children yet to reach school age, this may mean they have more geographical mobility. Even if a new contract offer affords a salary increase, is it material considering the cost-of-living factors in some geographical areas?

In Australia, income tax is administered federally and hence is consistent across all states and territories. It is a progressive tax system, meaning the more one earns, the more that individual can contribute to society via the tax system.

All is not equal, however, as cost of living varies from state to state, and capital city to capital city. Sydney in NSW has the highest cost of living, followed by Melbourne in Victoria. Brisbane in Queensland is cheaper, while Adelaide in South Australia is cheaper again.

The highest income tax bracket is 45 cents in the dollar over $180,000 per annum. If there is a difference of $100,000 between competing contract offers, and knowing it involves an interstate move to a higher cost of living center, and that 45c in the dollar will be lost to income tax, how material is that $100k for a player to make that move?

In the US, cost-of-living variances are significantly higher. There are states that do not levy any income tax such as Florida, Nevada, Tennessee, and Texas. This makes the Jacksonville Jaguars, Miami Dolphins, Tampa Bay Buccaneers (Florida), Las Vegas Raiders (Nevada), Tennessee Titans (Tennessee), Dallas Cowboys, and Houston Texans (Texas) franchises that are very attractive from an expense-reduction perspective. There are combinations of flat income tax rates and progressive tax systems in other states. California has the highest marginal tax rate at 13.3 percent impacting the attractiveness of three franchises being the Los Angeles Rams, Los Angeles Chargers, and San Francisco 49ers. New Jersey has a similarly high rate at 10.75 percent affecting the attractiveness of the New York Jets and New York Giants.

The biggest markets and populations centers in the US are California, Texas, Florida, and New York/New Jersey.

The bigger the market, the greater the commercial opportunities outside of the playing contract. When you combine the biggest markets to maximize revenue, while lowering the cost base via the absence of income tax, there is quite the advantage for those franchises in Florida and Texas.

For the West Tigers to convince a player from a team that regularly qualifies for the postseason to join them, it really needs to be either a better playing opportunity or significantly higher remuneration. A better opportunity might mean more playing time or the ability to start in a preferred position. Significantly higher remuneration is an individual decision where the negatives of leaving a high-performing team are outweighed by the financial rewards. Acquiring talent based on providing a better opportunity is important so that there is a pipeline of younger talent on the roster to ensure sustainability over the medium term.

For a franchise that has failed to make the playoffs for more than a decade, however, bridging the gap means attracting a talent who can lift the performance of the supporting cast. And the head office and coach are going to need to take a punt on that, projecting the current performance of a player with a weaker support cast and paying over market rate for that privilege.

Roster management is the application of microeconomics as it is for any business. There are scarce resources and trade-offs occur in allocating those scarce resources based on the best available information, as imperfect as that information is, and influenced by social, cultural, and political factors.

Over the odds remuneration may be needed for both attracting a new player or keeping a current star playing who is coming off contract and who is attracting interest from rival clubs.

"The truth is most anything that I've ever been involved in that ended up being special, I overpaid for, every time, to the end. Anytime I've tried to get a bargain, I got just that; it was a bargain in a lot of ways and not up to standard."
— Jerry Jones owner of the Dallas Cowboys reflecting on the 2021 re-signing of quarterback Dak Prescott

---

All-star talents can have the multiplier effect by enhancing the ability to attract others to the roster, but when you pay over the odds in a salary-cap restricted league, something will eventually give in that scarce resource allocation. It could be that contracts are back ended to maximize the ability to compete in the here and now, or depth is lost to accommodate the salary of an all-star who now represents a higher portion of the salary cap than any other. Back ended means that salary is not paid pro-rata over the life of the contract, but rather lower amounts are paid in the early years of the contract and higher amounts paid in the last years of the contract. Sometimes salary-cap increases can avoid an inevitable crash. If timing sees multiple players' contracts expiring at the same time with back-ended contacts, salary-cap casualties result.

For teams that have failed to perform for several years, paying over the odds is a legitimate business strategy. If you are not moving forwards, you are going backwards. It is preferable that new talent is acquired in positions that can most influence the outcome of a game. In Rugby League, that is what is colloquially known as the spine: fullback, five-eighth, halfback, and hooker. The trade-off is that what is being paid to the newly acquired all-star talent puts downward pressure on the remuneration of all others on your list.

Of course, teams do not really have any influence on the number of players coming off contact at the end of season, and there is always pressure on coaches and the front office to improve performance. So, whether there is a player available as part of the spine or not, teams will make a pitch for the best players available.

An alternative approach is to go for youth. A team may accept that the ability to make the playoffs with the current squad is highly unlikely, and that time is better spent on developing the next generation to expedite a return to success. This means moving on older players, or sometimes even good players who have higher aspirations and do not want to lose career years being part of a rebuild.

With pressure on coaches to deliver results by year three, rolling the dice on a youth and development strategy happens less and less these days. When a new coach is brought in to address team underperformance, very rarely are they let go after one season. It can happen, but that is more the exception than the rule, and often due to some off-field issue(s) more so than the team performances during year one.

Bringing in a new coach generally provides two opportunities even if contracts are for longer durations. The first season allows the new coach to evaluate the current roster and articulate the playing ethos and identity to start building the culture. Then the second season is an opportunity to manage an initial on-boarding and off-boarding to continue to entrench the desired ethos, identity, and culture. If results remain poor after the second season, there may not be a third. If improvement has been shown, then year three is the time when the coach is accountable for the roster they have put in place.

Nowadays, as building youth pathways into the professional program goes hand in hand with active roster management, coaches are just not going to get four-plus seasons to develop young talent in the hope to reach the postseason. Indeed, a consideration often in hiring a new coach is the perceived ability of the new coach to attract mature talent.

At the other end of the spectrum, there is going all in on mature talent forgoing up and comers. That is, preferring talent acquisition as a tactic rather than investing in upskilling.

Sean McVay signed with the Los Angeles Rams in January 2017 becoming the youngest coach in the modern NFL at 30 years of age. At that stage, the Rams had experienced twelve consecutive losing seasons and had not appeared in the postseason since 2004. In McVay's very first year, the Rams posted a winning record of 11–5. In his first five seasons, the Rams qualified for the postseason four times appearing in two Super Bowls and winning one ring. Even in the year the Rams missed the postseason with McVay, it was a winning season with a 9–7 record.

McVay has cultivated an ethos and culture that focuses on winning now by acquiring proven talent in exchange for future Ram's draft picks. This meant that 2023 was the seventh consecutive year that the Rams went without a first-round pick in the draft.

Heading into the 2021 season, the Rams already had a strong roster. Their win-now mentality, however, meant they were always cognizant of opportunities to get stronger. The pursuit of quarterback Matthew Stafford pre-season was not a case of back and forth between ownership, coach, and front office. There was open and constant communication, and a collective mindset of getting the job done. By operating swiftly, potential competitors had limited opportunity to make their pitch, and the Ram's prized new quarterback was secured.

Injuries in the NFL are part and parcel of the game. Speed, size, and collisions create an environment for the body to twist and bang in ways it is not designed for. The Rams experienced injuries to key players in the early stages of the 2021 season, however, not to a level higher than many other teams. There is the tenet in the NFL of "next man up" across all teams.

After week seven, the Rams were sitting pretty with a winning record of 6–1. The Denver Broncos had started the season with three consecutive wins, however, followed this with four consecutive losses to sit with a losing record of 3–4 at the conclusion of week seven. However, the Broncos were not out of postseason contention by any stretch of the imagination with still 10 regular season games remaining.

Bronco's outside linebacker Von Miller was concussed in

the week seven game against Washington, leaving the field early, and remained out for the week eight game. Miller was the Most Valuable Player (MVP) in the Broncos Super-Bowl win in 2016. Miller was in the final year of a playing contract in 2021 where he would become a free agent at season's end. We can only speculate on the war gaming that led to the Broncos front office and coach deciding to trade one of their best players before the trade deadline and particularly with postseason aspirations still alive.

Nonetheless, the LA Rams pounced and landed Von Miller in a trade executed on the Monday preceding the 4pm Tuesday, November 2 trading deadline. The NFL[100] reported that the Rams acquired Von Miller in exchange for their 2022 second and third round draft picks, with the Broncos paying $9 million of the $9.7 million that Miller was owed for the remainder of the 2021 season.

In essence the Broncos had decided to forgo the availability of one of their best players for the remainder of the season while still paying his salary, in exchange for two rookie players the following year. From the Rams perspective, they were securing a quality asset for an intended Super-Bowl run, forgoing the ability to draft two young players the following season, and knowing that as a free agent, there were no guarantees Von Miller would re-sign with the Rams for future seasons.

One week after the Von Miller trade, the Cleveland Browns placed wide receiver Odell Beckham Junior on waivers having come to a mutual agreement to part ways. The agreement included a settlement of $4.25 million if Beckham passed through waivers, becoming a free agent. If he was claimed on waivers by another team, that franchise would be required to meet $7.25 million salary for Beckham for the remainder of the season.

The waivers period passed at 4pm on Tuesday November 8 with Beckham becoming a free agent. By the Thursday, just two days later, Beckham signed a deal with the LA Rams for the remainder of the 2021 season. Beckham played six games with the Cleveland Browns in the 2021 season, and eight with the Rams including the Super Bowl.

That was not the end of acquisitions by the Rams during 2021. Following the completion of week 18 and the regular season, the Rams added Eric Waddle to the practice squad. Waddle was a safety who had last played for the Rams in the 2019 season before retiring. Waddle had missed the 2020 and 2021 regular seasons in their entirety. By the end of that week, Waddle was promoted from the practice squad to the active roster and played in all four of the Rams postseason games including the Super Bowl making 10 solo tackles and eight assisted tackles.

In the 2021 Super Bowl the Rams defeated the Cincinnati Bengals 23–20. Von Miller sacked the Bengals quarterback Joe Burrow twice. Odell Beckham Junior was injured in the second quarter and did not return after a suspected Anterior Cruciate Ligament (ACL) tear. Despite missing more than half the game, Beckham had two receptions for 52 yards including one touchdown. Weddle had four tackles, three of which were solo ones.

None of these players were in the Rams thinking heading into the season yet were integral to the Rams success.

The Rams won the Super Bowl by just three points 23–20 over the Cincinnati Bengals. They won the NFC Conference title game beating the San Francisco 49ers also by three points (20–17). They won the divisional title by beating the Tampa Bay Buccaneers also by three points (30–27).

Would the Rams have won the Super-Bowl ring had they not acquired these three players? Hypotheticals can never be known. What we do know is that these three players played meaningful snaps contributing to the Super-Bowl win. We also know that the Rams had the mindset of always looking to make their roster stronger, and that with this mindset, they defeated all comers to take the Super-Bowl ring.

List management also requires a playbook for talent-exit strategies. In the LA Rams instance, wide receiver Odell Beckham Junior became available because of discontentment with the Cleveland Brown franchise. It was mid-way through the season, all franchises had full rosters with only a select few having salary-cap space. In any given season, and across all sports, players can become available mid-season through disenchantment, disillusionment, or discontentment. If the talent is desirable, it will mean freeing up salary-cap space and moving other players on to make room. These are difficult decisions and emotionally felt by the player directly affected and those players that remain in the locker room. Movements handled badly will impact the brand, affect the fan base, and create distractions the roster does not need for the remainder of the season.

Of course, disenchantment, disillusionment, or discontentment is a two-way street. There will be instances where players reach the end of their chances whether that be due to form, off-field incidences, or personality clashes with coaches or other team members. What makes this particularly tricky is that any assessment is subjective, and some players may be perceived to be given greater leniency than others, with any variances affecting overall locker-room chemistry. Either way, the objective is the same. Each situation needs to be handled sensitively, and in a way that best positions the impacted person to succeed in a new environment. When it is not handled sensitively it can look petty, overly judgmental, or unfair. When the brand is impacted, it affects both on-field and off-field. On-field, it creates barriers to attracting talent in future. Off-field it creates barriers to attracting corporate partnerships and growing the fan base.

"Let's dive into Baker Mayfield and the Cleveland Browns and Doc Rivers said something along time ago in an interview or maybe in a press conference and has stuck with me forever: that your talent has to exceed your problems and the moment your talent doesn't exceed your problems and your problems are bigger and worse than what you bring to the table, in pro sports you're gone, they're done with you; it's easy to deal with the diva if he's LeBron James or Aaron Rogers. It's another thing if you're a middle of the road quarterback."
– *Three and Out with John Middelkauff* podcast[101]
March 17, 2020

Roster management take-aways for business

All businesses have an environmental context to their decision-making; strategy and tactics cannot take a cookie-cutter approach. Within that environmental context, there will be investment-capability constrictions. That said, sometimes boards or executive management can get too rigid around staffing establishments, particularly in a difficult economic climate. More so for businesses with staffing establishments below 200 rather than mid to large enterprises. Good governance does require checks and balances. However, if people and capability are your number-one asset and the main input for achieving great outcomes, then businesses need flexibility to acquire great talent at the time they become available.

There are four key takeaways for business when considering roster management in professional sport:
1. Talent is the critical input for a business to succeed. Acquisition or upskill needs to be a conscious decision in workforce planning in order to successfully execute.
2. To fulfil a business's potential, exits will need to occur. Having mature systems in place that enable a dignified exit for the departing team member is not just about brand protection, it is the right thing to do. Businesses evolve, and what was once needed for the business is not always going to be needed for the business. Support structures to allow for separation that allow the team member to land well is beneficial to all. An example in the NFL is when a franchise works with player and their representation to find a desirable landing place in a trade.
3. Always be looking to improve the roster irrespective of the budget and resource-allocation cycles. Have some flexibility built into governance systems and processes so that you can move fast and successfully in instances where desirable talent becomes unexpectedly available. Anytime there is organic turnover have the goal to always get better at the position. Do not settle for going backwards at the position unless it allows an upgrade in a higher-priority area or provides a development opportunity for current talent who has not yet reached their ceiling.
4. If you are behind the competition, it is okay to pay over. Yes, it does need to be managed in terms of expectations of new recruits and the relevant business unit, and yes it may create some challenges around equity and performance expectations with the current

roster, but if you need to bridge the gap and make the leap to be in postseason contention, then you need to be aggressive and have a crack. If you want to achieve something meaningful, your team must be resourced. Whether that is capital, infrastructure or … talent.

8. Scheme and philosophy (aka your north star)

For centuries, the celebrated North Star has been the almost mystical beacon, shining the path for marine vessels to navigate the oceans during the hours of darkness. The North Star is a guiding light that keeps vessels safe and on the path towards success, while also providing the early warning system should the vessel be veering off into the wrong direction.

In business, there are a variety of ways that North-Star metrics have been used to galvanize teams and focus energies on the right direction. Some businesses tie measures to revenue, while others use a metric of active customers; common, however, is that the North-Star metric leads to growth. North-Star metrics can be companywide or product specific. For tech startups, it is often the one and the same. The company is the product for which it has been founded, focused on solving a specific problem and satisfying a specific gap in the market.

In business we start with vision, followed by strategy and then tactics implemented to achieve the strategy. Who we are, what do we do, why we do what we do, and how do we do it? It all starts with the vision.

The Collins-Porras vision framework has three components. The first component is core values and beliefs which is a system of guiding principles that cannot be altered and a philosophy on life and business. The second component is purpose. Purpose being the guiding star on why you exist, and while you are always worked towards it, it is never fully attainable. The third component is the mission which includes a Big Hairy Audacious Goal (BHAG) to be achieved within a specific timeframe, and one where a new mission is set once the current mission is achieved.

Using the NFL as an example, every franchise in essence holds the same mission: to win a Super Bowl. There are thirty-two franchises competing each year, and there can only be one winner. Thus, the BHAG will vary depending on where the franchises perceive themselves to be, as will the specific timeframe.

For some NFL franchises, they would consider their Super-Bowl window as open, and a goal within reach in a 12-month timeframe, as well as on a rolling basis for however long that window is open. The Los Angeles Rams certainly did in 2021. They were all in. And they may have that same mission each and every year while their Super-Bowl window remains open.

For other franchises, the mission may be to put themselves in a situation where they can compete in the postseason each and every year. For others, the desired state may be making the postseason for the first time after a long absence has been experienced; while for others again, the mission may be to climb the ladder within their division and show improvement to ownership and the fan base whereby creating confidence that they are heading in the right direction.

As mentioned in the opening chapter, the NFL league itself has a mission[102] of:

Scheme and philosophy (aka your north star)

"We are all stewards of football.

We unite people and inspire communities in the joy of the game by delivering the world's most exciting sports and entertainment experience."

This mission is driven by a core belief that

"every member of the NFL community embraces our unique leadership role in society, and assumes the trust, character, and responsibility that comes with that role. We bring fans and communities from all walks of life together to celebrate a game that is constantly evolving, balancing the authenticity of tradition with the power of innovation".

This core belief is supported by values of respect, integrity, responsibility to team, and resiliency.

Well before the first of their six Super-Bowl titles, the New England Patriots committed to a mission that was documented on the bottom of their scouting manuals[103] from the year 2000 onwards: "We are building a big, strong, fast, smart, tough, and disciplined football team that consistently competes for championships." From a standing start, and in just over two decades, by 2022 the New England Patriots held the honor of most Super-Bowl wins at six, tied with the Pittsburgh Steelers.

Just behind these two franchises are the Dallas Cowboys and the San Francisco 49ers, each with five Super-Bowl wins a piece.

John Lynch joined the San Francisco 49ers as general manager in 2017 to form new leadership alongside head coach Kyle Shanahan. While having a fabled history in the NFL, the last of the 49ers Super-Bowl victories was in 1995. Upon joining the franchise, Lynch crafted a new mission – "Our nucleus of dedicated players will reestablish The 49er Way and lead our organization back to the top of the NFL. These players will represent our core values and beliefs in both their talent and spirt."[104]

Business leaders must constantly ask themselves, what do I value and why? In chapter four we looked at assigning value to your human capital and the Jimmy Johnson value chart. There are numerous versions of the value chart publicly available. Franchises themselves will have their own unique versions, which may be a rule of thumb, or may be updated annually to reflect how highly "best player available" is or is not prioritized over roster "need".

The value chart is a methodology for assessing available talent against each other in a draft process. It is easy to say that the quarterback position is the most valuable over all others. That a wide receiver is more valuable than a tight end. That a left tackle is of greater value than a linebacker. That a pass rusher is more valuable than a running back. It becomes a far more complex evaluation when you start to pit expenditure against specific player traits particularly in a salary cap restricted league. It goes beyond an evaluation of what position do I value more highly than another, to the acquisition costs of a specific talent against the opportunity cost of an alternative selection and investment.

In the 2020 NFL draft, the first three picks were all quarterbacks, with five quarterbacks going all together in the first round (including picks 11 and 15). In terms of draft selections and their impacts on the salary cap, picks one to four were in the $6.0–$6.7m range, picks five to 13 in the $3.0m–$5.6m range, and picks 14 to32 were in the $2.0m–$2.9m range. This can have quite an impact on the salary cap. The fourteenth pick is less than half of the fourth pick.

Now some might ask, what is $3m in a salary cap of $198.2 million for 2020? A measly 1.5 percent; it cannot possibly have any impact on the total output for the coming season. And on face value, that is a reasonable proposition. Just like the economy, however, for a salary-capped roster and the resources acquired within the salary cap, everything is connected. What goes to Peter cannot go to Paul. Three million dollars may be just the amount short whereby you cannot match a competing offer and you lose a valued player in free agency. Conversely, there may be a desired resource in free agency, but your inability to find another $3m prohibits your ability to acquire that resource.

There are many voices in NFL commentary that argue even in a salary cap league, you can find extra money. The most common way is to re-work contracts with current players. Often this involves converting parts of a contract to a signing bonus. Signing bonus are amortized over the life of the contract. Then years may be added to the length of a contract and including 'voidable' years to the back end allowing for pro-rata amounts to be lowered across the life of the contract and extra money found for the current season.

There are four pitfalls here. Firstly, with a win-now mentality, you can assume that those franchises that can deploy this strategy, already have. Any continuing deployment is really only playing at the margins.

Secondly, signing bonuses are paid upfront and may require ownership to redirect cash from other investments. The desirability to fund upfront will vary from franchise ownership to franchise ownership, but again, safe to say, those that can, have. And it can never be a limitless well for continuing to bring payments forward.

Thirdly, under the collective bargaining agreement, contract guarantees need to be remitted into escrow in order that the guarantees are just that[105]. When discussing remuneration for quarterbacks of $30–$50 million per season, it does not sound like much to ensure keeping a player if the guarantee is $100 million or $150 million. In actuality, $50 million is a significant sum in anyone's language when offered the opportunity of investing such a sum over five years or placing it into escrow. Complicated even further if an owner's assets are not particularly liquid requiring divesting in some area or requires borrowing against assets to pay into escrow.

Fourthly, no matter how you cut it, you are mortgaging the future to pay for today. When voidable years are cut, remaining costs are bought to book. Just like any business, there may be some assumptions about likely increases to the salary cap in future years. The NFL collective bargaining agreement contains provisions for how the salary cap is calculated being a percentage of revenue divided by the 32 teams. The ability for individual franchises to influence future salary cap increases is negligible, hence looking to offset voidable years against salary-cap increases is not a science and if executed poorly, will leave franchises exposed.

The trade market is unique as it does not have much of an impact on salary-cap management. The New York Jets knew they had the second pick in the 2020 draft. They formulated their strategy and were going to take a quarterback. As a result, four weeks prior to the draft, the Jets traded their quarterback incumbent Sam Darnold to the Carolina Panthers.

Contract guarantees mean trading a player is much like cutting a player. The franchise still has to account for the salary in their cap management. In 2021, Darnold would count towards $5m of the Jets salary cap. Given trading Darnold did not have any salary-cap savings for Jets, why trade him at all? Is it not better to have a strong backup on the roster in case of injury?

Scheme and philosophy (aka your north star)

Darnold had previously been taken with the third overall pick in the 2018 draft. If Darnold had stayed on and completed the fourth year of his contract, the fifth year was an option at the franchise's discretion. Although it did come with a guaranteed figure, in Darnold's case, the fifth-year option would have been more than $18m. Moving on from Darnold did have a potential impact on the Jets' future salary cap. Alternatively, they could decline the fifth-year option, but at this point Darnold would become a free agent and could go where he pleased without any compensation to the Jets. The Darnold trade secured the Jets a 2021 NFL draft sixth-round pick (no. 226) plus second- and fourth-round selections in the 2022 draft[106].

Using the Jimmy Johnson trade chart, from high to low, depending on where the Panthers finish in future years, the sixth-round points spread are 15–27 points, fourth-round spread 45–116pts, and second-round spread of 270–580 points.

What do you value and why?

Table 9 reflects the actual first-round selection in the 2021 draft. Apart from the quarterbacks, five wide receivers were selected in the first round – those who score most of the touchdowns. There were also five cornerbacks selected in the first round – those who are deployed to stop the wide receivers from scoring. These trends indicate what the front offices value.

Hindsight is a wonderful thing. Looking back now, we can see just one of the five quarterbacks hyped in the 2021 NFL draft would have been available at the San Francisco 49ers original pick number twelve, before they traded with the Miami Dolphins to secure pick number three. General manager John Lynch and head coach Kyle Shanahan valued assurance, giving themselves time to assess their best option, and knowing that they would get to choose from three options at pick number three.

The running-back position is critical to gaining yards, tiring defenses, and maintaining possession. It is an incredibly important position. The downside is that the running back is generally having the ball handed to him by the quarterback and running into tight windows with heavy traffic, lined by the biggest men on the field. It sometimes looks like the first line of an army on the battlefield. There is nowhere to hide, and injuries seem more inevitable than anywhere else.

All teams value the capability and the role of the running-back room. It is just that the position comes with higher risk, and this is reflected in the prioritizing on draft boards. The first running back in the 2019 draft was at pick 24 with the Las Vegas Raiders selecting Josh Jacobs. In 2020, it was pick 32, with the Kansas City Chiefs selecting Clyde Edwards-Helaire. In 2021, there were two running backs selected in the first round: Najee Harris selected by the Pittsburgh Steelers at pick 24 and Travis Etienne selected at pick 25 by the Jacksonville Jaguars. No running backs were selected in the first round of the 2022 draft. In 2023, there were two running backs selected in the first round with Jaymyr Gibbs selected at pick 12 by the Detroit Lions and Bijan Robinson selected at pick eight going to the Atlanta Falcons. The last time a running back went in the top 10 was in 2018 when Saquon Barkley was selected by the New York Giants. What do you value and why?

Finally, not all draft classes are the same. Your current roster has skills and capabilities, and a series of contracts with varying expiring dates. The capability by position in any draft is not going to be the same in each draft. Once you get past the current year, there is a lot of projection involved in determining the talent pool, let alone your roster's ability to secure such talent in a draft order that has yet to be determined. The 2022 draft had only one quarterback selected in the first round and that was Kenny Pickett to the Pittsburgh Steelers at pick 20. Much different to five quarterbacks going in the first fifteen picks twelve months earlier. Leaders are always making decisions on what they value and why.

Table 9. 2020 NFL Draft Round 1

Pick Number	Total Value	Signing Bonus	2021 Salary Cap	Player	Position
No. 1	$36,793,488	$24,118,900	$6,689,725	Trevor Lawrence	Quarterback
No. 2	$35,150,681	$22,924,132	$6,391,033	Zach Wilson	Quarterback
No. 3	$34,105,275	$22,163,836	$6,200,959	Trey Lance	Quarterback
No. 4	$32,910,495	$21,294,904	$5,983,726	Kyle Pitts	Tight end
No. 5	$30,819,641	$19,774,284	$5,603,571	Ja'Marr Chase	Wide receiver
No. 6	$27,085,993	$17,058,904	$4,924,726	Jaylen Waddle	Wide receiver
No. 7	$24,099,069	$14,886,596	$4,381,649	Penei Sewell	Right tackle
No. 8	$21,112,146	$12,714,288	$3,838,572	Jaycee Horn	Cornerback
No. 9	$20,962,628	$12,605,548	$3,811,387	Patrick Surtain II	Cornerback
No. 10	$20,141,390	$12,008,284	$3,662,071	DeVonta Smith	Wide receiver
No. 11	$18,871,957	$11,085,060	$3,431,265	Justin Fields	Quarterback
No. 12	$17,079,793	$9,781,668	$3,105,417	Micah Parsons	Line backer
No. 13	$16,631,757	$9,455,824	$3,023,956	Rashawn Slater	Left tackle
No. 14	$15,885,028	$8,912,748	$2,888,187	Alijah Vera-Tucker	Guard
No. 15	$15,586,352	$8,695,528	$2,833,882	Mac Jones	Quarterback
No. 16	$14,690,255	$8,043,824	$2,670,956	Zaven Collins	Line backer
No. 17	$14,391,564	$7,826,592	$2,616,648	Alex Leatherwood	Right tackle
No. 18	$14,018,202	$7,555,056	$2,548,764	Jaelan Phillips	Defensive end
No. 19	$13,794,176	$7,392,128	$2,508,032	Jamin Davis	Line backer
No. 20	$13,719,508	$7,337,824	$2,494,456	Kadarius Toney	Wide receiver
No. 21	$13,644,833	$7,283,515	$2,480,877	Kwity Paye	Defensive end
No. 22	$13,495,482	$7,174,896	$2,453,724	Caleb Farley	Cornerback
No. 23	$13,346,140	$7,066,284	$2,426,571	Christian Darrisaw	Tackle
No. 24	$13,047,447	$6,849,052	$2,372,263	Najee Harris	Running back

Pick Number	Total Value	Signing Bonus	2021 Salary Cap	Player	Position
No. 25	$12,898,105	$6,740,440	$2,345,110	Travis Etienne	Running back
No. 26	$12,748,736	$6,631,808	$2,317,952	Greg Newsome	Cornerback
No. 27	$12,599,412	$6,523,208	$2,290,802	Rashod Bateman	Wide receiver
No. 28	$12,524,737	$6,468,900	$2,277,225	Payton Turner	Defensive end
No. 29	$11,925,524	$6,033,108	$2,168,277	Eric Stokes	Cornerback
No. 30	$11,608,200	$5,802,328	$2,110,582	Greg Rousseau	Defensive end
No. 31	$11,342,391	$5,609,012	$2,062,253	Odafe Oweh	Outside line backer
No. 32	$11,171,238	$5,484,536	$2,031,134	Joe Tryon	Defensive end

NFL Draft Contracts: Round 2

Pick Range	Total Value	Signing Bonus
Picks 33-41	$9,015,105 to $8,148,893	$3,916,440 to $3,286,468
Picks 42-48	$8,014,479 to $7,073,601	$3,188,712 to $2,504,436
Picks 49-64	$6,924,241 to $5,535,337	$2,395,812 to $1,385,700

NFL Draft Contracts: Round 3

Pick Range	Total Value	Signing Bonus
Picks 65-74	$5,236,500 to $5,100,752	$1,168,364 to $1,069,640
Picks 75-92	$5,086,190 to $4,848,860	$1,059,048 to $886,744
Picks 93-105	$4,834,697 to $4,785,852	$876,144 to $840,620

NFL Draft Contracts: Rounds 4–7

Round	Total Value	Signing Bonus
Round 4	$4,305,688 to $3,979,344	$825,688 to $499,344
Round 5	$3,838,020 to $3,720,148	$358,020 to $240,148
Round 6	$3,694,004 to $3,610,708	$214,004 to $130,708
Round 7	$3,594,832 to $3,556,244	$114,832 to $76,244

Source: Spotrac 2021 NFL Draft Tracker[107]

Jim Collins is a former Stanford Business School professor and globally acclaimed researcher and author on business strategy and what it takes to for companies to endure. He is also the co-author of the Collins Porras Vision Framework along with Jerry Porras. Collins posits that companies and their leaders do not "set" values, but rather they are innately held by their leaders.

Core values and beliefs are instilled throughout the business by concrete actions. That is, what you do and not what you say.

It is not easy from the outside to determine the core beliefs and values of individual franchises within the NFL as intrinsic, beliefs, and values are not always verbalized and harder to observe. The locker room and tape rooms are closed from external eyes, maximizing competitive advantage wherever possible.

Nonetheless, it is fun to look at on-record comments as a means of gaining some insights. While the desired state of being crowned Super-Bowl champions and the mission may be similar across all franchises, the how to varies significantly, with actions underpinned by the intrinsic values and beliefs held by franchise leaders.

Three short examples highlight the intrinsic nature of beliefs and values from the head coaches of the Los Angeles Chargers, the San Francisco 49ers, and the New York Jets.

Brandon Staley was hired as the Los Angeles Chargers head coach for the 2021 season taking the franchise to a winning 9–8 record although missing wild-card qualification for the postseason losing to the Las Vegas Raiders in the penultimate game of the regular season. After the week-two loss to the Dallas Cowboys, and in the lead-up to the week three match-up with the Kansas City Chiefs, Staley shared some insights into his coaching beliefs[108]:

> I think that there are a lot of different ways to play in the NFL. If there was one way to play, we'd all be doing

it. My belief system is to play really thick and physical on blocks, because I know that it has a real impact on what's behind you, so that style of play contributes to how we play behind the D line from a coverage-system standpoint.

Kyle Shanahan, 49ers head coach, has commented on the approach to acquiring talent and the internal conflict of an arms-race mentality when competing within division[109]:

> "I always say let's do it the right way, which there's no right way or wrong way, but like you don't want to have to risk your future to compete in one year, and that's the hardest thing about being in our division".

And here's Robert Saleh, New York Jets head coach, on his coaching philosophy[110]:

> And like I said, it doesn't make it right, everyone's got a different way of doing things, I've just always believed that players have to know that you're in it with them, and it's not a coaches coach, players play, shut the F up do your job; it's we're all in this together. We win together; we lose together; we're locked in arms.

While all three coaches lead with the qualifiers of there is no right or wrong way and that everyone does it differently, the comment is then somewhat contradicted by adding a strong and resolute qualifier – that they do hold their own personal belief and values as to the best way to do deliver the "how to" and they are committed to it despite others doing the "how to" another way.

Scheme and philosophy (aka your north star)

> *"There is a commitment to a philosophy, you know, cause like everybody wants to talk about old Mary, and the run and the pass, but like are you really committed to a system and building some agility within that system week in and week out?"*[111]
>
> –Sean McVay, head coach Los Angeles Rams

Staley's press conference that day later went viral when explaining the importance of the run game[112]:

> ... what I think that the running game does for a quarterback is it gives you some breathers ... You don't need a good running game to be a good play action team, but what you need the running game for is the physical element of the game; there's a physicality to the game that's real ... If you're just a passing team, OK, there's a physical element to the game that the defense doesn't have to respect, OK.
>
> ... That's why I think the run game is important to a quarterback is because it's gonna allow him literally to have more space to operate when you do throw the football ... It's not that you need the run game to throw; it's just what it gives the rest of your skill players ...

To provide contrast, let us look at some philosophies espoused by sportscasters, those from outside the locker room looking in. From Colin Cowherd of Fox Sports and *The Herd* Podcast:

> If they ever write a book on how to win in the NFL, chapter one, get a star quarterback; chapter two protect star quarterback; chapter three develop star quarterback;

chapter four fire coordinator, chapter five get a better offensive coordinator; chapter six get the quarterback weapons; chapter seven make sure you sign him to a long-term deal; the whole league is this now.[113]

John Middlekauff also broadcasts on *The Herd* Podcast with *Three and Out*:

I like the people that have a direct vision of what they want. Now, and once you figure out what works and what doesn't, it becomes pretty unstoppable when you're [a] high-level person, when you're a high-level organization, and that's what the Pittsburgh Steelers are. It's why they've been able to overcome the last couple years of bad quarterback play, now old quarterback play, cause they have so much talent, they draft so well, they have so many impact guys and it's an organizational philosophy.[114]

Dabo Swinney has been the head coach of Clemson University for the last sixteen seasons 2008–2023. His coaching record stands at 213 games for 170 wins at a winning percentage of .798. He has led Clemson to the National Championship beating Alabama twice, 35–31 in 2016 and 44–16 in 2018, and in achieving the feat in 2018 became the first team in the college football playoff era to go 15–0. Clemson was crowned Atlantic Coast Conference Champions six consecutive times between 2015–2020.

Swinney provided some of his insights into philosophy at an awards luncheon in Columbus Valley back in December of 2017:

When I became the head coach in 09 at Clemson, the very first thing I did day one, I set the vision and the

Scheme and philosophy (aka your north star)

philosophy of the program: this is who we are, this is the way we're gonna do things, and here's why …

… The first thing we want for our players is for them to get their education; they're going to get their education; I would rather lose trying to do it right, then to win knowing that we didn't. I played with so many guys that the band cheered for, the people clap for, while they were playing this game, that didn't leave with a degree and then ten years later, it's sad. I've never wanted that for my players.

… So this is how we set the vision the program … we're gonna make sure that our guys get their degree; they get an education; we're gonna make sure that we equip them with tools for life: how to show up on time, how to put in the work, how to win and lose, how to be a good teammate, how to handle adversity, how to handle criticism; tools that you better have when you go out in the real world.

The third thing is I wanted to have a great college experience; let's have some fun; I want them to love their experience, I want to surround him with people that they're gonna love to be around, and the last thing was I want to win a championship, and it's in that order.

In this chapter, we have covered scheme and philosophy by looking at some small insights offered in media conferences from the head coaches of the San Francisco 49ers, the New York Jets, the Los Angeles Chargers, the Los Angeles Rams, as well as sportscasters who watch and report on NFL franchises week in week out. We have looked at one example from the college football system and will finish with one last example that crosses both college and the NFL.

The North Star and North-Star metrics extend beyond

scheme and philosophy. They incorporate your purpose, your core values, and beliefs. They are the "how to". This is not something businesses always do very well. There can be a strong vision, supported by a strong strategy, but the tactics may be prescribed as outcomes and fail to be aligned to any core values and beliefs. Or the core values and beliefs may be just words, and there is misalignment with the concrete actions and processes followed by the business. The "how to" is also critical.

Urban Meyer holds a college coaching record of 219 games across 17 seasons and four different colleges. His wins totaled 187 for a winning percentage of .854 and included three National Championships (Florida Gators 2006 and 2008, and Ohio State Buckeyes in 2014). After performing analyst roles in broadcasting, Myer accepted the head-coach role at the Jacksonville Jaguars for the 2022 season.

During an interview on *Good Morning Football*[115], Meyer shared his strongly held philosophy:

> "I care deeply for players and people and ... I believe that there is greatness in everyone, and it's our job as a leader to find that greatness, and sometimes that's very uncomfortable, sometimes it's not ...
>
> What I always tell people as long as you're keeping score, our job is to win – there's no other job. This is not our job to keep it close; it's our job is to win and in the most difficult environments the great greatness I've been around I would always tell them ... when I needed you the most you gave us your very best, if you're that kind of person ... eventually we'll win. It might take a minute, but we're going to win, so in the hardest most difficult time when I need you the most you gave us your very best."

Scheme and philosophy (aka your north star)

The season prior to Meyer's arrival, the Jacksonville Jaguars finished the season with just the one solo win going 1–15. Thirteen weeks into his first season as head coach and holding a 2–11 win-loss record, Meyer was replaced. The performance on-field was accompanied by a series of missteps both on and off field.

In business, your North Star may be specific metrics to feel confident you are heading in the right direction. What is often unsaid, however, is the metrics are not disassociated from the "how to" – the concrete actions reflecting the business values and beliefs. As in the Meyer example, not being aligned in the "how to" results in separation from ownership, as it does in any business. Whether that is misalignment between board and CEO, board and executive, executive and management, management and business units. While timelines will vary, any such misalignment leads to the same inevitable outcome.

9. All in: culture and legacy

IN THE PREVIOUS CHAPTER WE discussed how values and beliefs may be intrinsic and harder to understand in terms of business drivers. Culture, conversely, is extrinsic: the sum of all moving parts and the series of concrete actions undertaken. Culture is not, however, always easily measurable and has been described as how people behave when no-one is looking. That of course is a narrow interpretation. Culture is both the seen and the unseen.

Examples of performance reflecting culture in the NFL
Joe Judge was the head coach of the New York Giants for two seasons in 2020 and 2021. Judge had a strong coaching pedigree having spent the previous eight seasons assisting Bill Belichick with the New England Patriots. Judge predominately looked after special teams during his tenure, and the Patriots collected three Super-Bowl rings over those years.

Having posted a 4–12 losing record in 2019, under Judge the Giants improved to 6–10 in the 2020 season. The 2021 season wasn't looking better going into week 17, with the team recording only four wins from the first fifteen games. With two games to go, week 17 was against the Chicago Bears who had won only one more game than the Giants at that same juncture. The Giants lost 29–3 to the Bears, and afterwards, Judge faced inevitable questions about his future at the Giant's press conference.

The following is an extract from Judge's comments:

"... Our guys understand how to play together as a team, and understand the process of how they're going through, so I can go through a whole Xs and Os evaluation, go through a roster evaluation, I can go through a lot of things for you right now, OK, I do it every day myself, I go through all that stuff, but in terms of the next step to take, I can tell you right now, OK, I know we are a whole lot closer to where we are going than we are further away ...

...We got more players here who will be we free agents next year, all right, who are in my office every day, begging to come back, I know that ... or players that we coach last year they still called me twice a week talking about you know how much they wish they were still here [even if] they're getting paid more somewhere else, OK, so I know we've got the right foundational pieces in and I know we have some players some key positions that are guys you can build with, and keep carrying on, alright, and we have the right temperament. I know we got the right culture in terms of teaching the players ..."

The Giants play against the Bears generated significant negativity with the Giants passing game finishing at minus ten net yards. At one stage, a Bears kick-off died at the Giants three-yard line. Two plays later, the Giants were downed in their end zone resulting in a safety which saw the Bears get two points and the possession of the football from a free kick.

ESPN football analyst Ryan Clark played 177 games across

thirteen seasons in the NFL. His first two seasons were with the New York Giants, then eight with the Pittsburgh Steelers, and three with Washington in two different stints. He won a ring with the Steelers in Super Bowl XLIII.

The day after the Giant's loss to the Bears, Clarke was scathing on ESPN's *First Take*[116] in his assessment of Judge:

> Now let's point to all the other stuff that Joe Judge was talking about: this team doesn't quit, and you gotta make sure this team is bought in, and we don't have golf clubs in front of our locker, what he's saying is to the Mara family, to the New York Giants fans and to the players is, I don't want you to judge me off of the stuff that you're supposed to judge coaches on, and that's a team progressing, that's a team winning football games, that's a team getting better, because I've done none of those things; the things I want you to judge me on are things that you cannot measure; the fact that people believe in me, you can't know if they believe in me cause you can't measure it. The fact that people are bought in, you can't know that they bought in because you can't measure it, the fact that I received phone calls that I shouldn't be taking ... cause I should be watching film trying to get ready for the next week to win the fifth game that I thought I was gonna win but I promise still only gonna win four. Don't judge me on none of that stuff you can see; judge me on the things that you cannot. I want you to judge me on faith and hope and wishes and dreams, because what you're seeing on film is not enough for me to keep my job.

The key point across both sets of comments is that North-Star metrics cannot be separated from culture. Alternatively, if your culture is not enabling the attainment of your North-Star metrics, the culture needs to change. *Who are you, why do you exist, and why do you do what you do?*

The next week the Giants played divisional rival Washington in the season finale. Scarred from giving up a safety to the Bears having been downed in their own end zone the previous week, the Giants undertook two consecutive quarterback sneaks late in the second quarter from close to their own end zone. The first on second and eleven from inside the two-yard line, and then again on third and nine from the four-yard line. The Giants went on to lose 22–7 to Washington and finish fourth in their division with a season win/loss record of 4–13. Judge's tenure ended that week.

The reality is culture can be measured. The tricky part for growing businesses is to spend time reflecting on how the business evolved from where it has been to where it is now, identifying the key characteristics that helped drive success, as well as those characteristics that inhibited the business from reaching its potential and optimal scale earlier.

Cultural reviews may be initiated as a team-engagement tactic bringing in external expertise so that there is an independent voice receiving feedback from which key themes can be solicited. The science piece of what is needed to make the business successful in the future is not easy and not the result of a survey or focus groups. You cannot lose sight of the "who you are, why you exist, and why you do what you do". If inputs are being derived from sources that are not all in on the "who you are, why you exist, and why you do what you do", the resulting outcomes will be misaligned.

Today the acronym FIFO stands for those workers travelling into remote locations for weeks or months on end, staying onsite or near their working facility, before heading home at the end of a scheduled roster. Fly in-fly out. FIFO is a type of employment seen often in the resources sector such as mining. Prior to this, it was a term sometimes used to reflect the need to achieve cultural alignment. An Englishman would pronounce it – fit in or fook off. Not really an acceptable turn of phrase in the modern workplace but reflects the urgency and need to get culture right in order to achieve results.

'All in' in NFL parlance means leaving nothing on the table, throwing all the chips into the middle to play your next hand in search of the ultimate – a Super-Bowl ring.

There are literally dozens and dozens of inspirational quotes used in football and likewise across all professional sports to help focus attention on the small details, to look to continuously improve, and to keep the eyes on the ultimate prize. Separation comes from the preparation. Champions are made when no-one's looking. The road to greatness is always under construction. It's the biggest game because it's the next game. Every play matters. Small steps in the right direction lead to great results. Bend don't break mentality. Stacking days. Losing is as contagious as winning.

Now there is a degree of indoctrination when you focus on words, and that is needed to develop and embed a specific culture. It is a conscious decision to try to encourage the right mindset, to encourage teamwork and efficiency, and set an expectation of continuously building and improving. When all is said and done, culture is not words; it is action. Being "all in" is not words; it is action.

"Winning is not a sometime thing; it's an all-time thing. You don't win once in a while; you don't do things right once in a while; you do them right all the time. Winning is habit. Unfortunately, so is losing."
– Coach Vincent T. Lombardi

We have looked at Tom Brady's career results and how he has been able to defy ageing to continuously improve. We have looked at the Rams and their pursuit of the 2022 Super-Bowl ring. Both are strong examples of being "all in".

Duckworth describes a culture as the invisible psychological boundaries separating people, and that a distinct culture exists anytime a group of people are in consensus about how things are done around their place and why[117]. Most interestingly, the sharper the contrasts between that culture and how the rest of the world operates, the stronger the bonds among the in-group. Think the Patriot way, the 49er way, differences in scheme and philosophy, differences in player acquisition and development. All the things that make a brand and workplace unique.

Collins is a strong advocate on tactical excellence. Best beats first. Great concept plus poor execution results in business demise. In order to deliver tactical excellence, firms need a culture of discipline, which is about freedom in a framework of values and responsibilities and having the right people who crave wide latitude to do their best work[118].

Growing and evolution pains will always exist for any business as it does with any sporting franchise. Time and again we see examples in professional sport of young people succeeding in their early endeavors, only to experience later that their team is not entitled to a specific result. Regular postseason participation, or even titles, are replaced by long periods of absence.

My favorite examples are in the round-ball game because sadly they offer the greatest heartbreak and greatest reminder of not taking opportunities for granted. Just like the summer and winter Olympics, the staging is only every four years. The road to success is long and littered with obstacles. It is a substantial period of time to be training for something that may or may not happen. To qualify results in great national pride. Failure to qualify impacts the national psyche.

Italy has won the World Cup four times in the years of 1934, 1938, 1982, and 2006. Along with Germany, they hold the second most World Cups behind Brazil with five. Soccer is the most popular sport in the country. The nation has an expectation that they can challenge for the title come World-Cup time.

Italy failed to qualify for the 2018 World Cup. The country was in tears. Brighter times were soon around the corner, with Italy winning the 2020 Euro Cup against quality opposition. Alas, again in 2022, Italy failed at the final hurdle and missed qualification for the World Cup. Previously Italy had qualified for every World Cup between 1962 and 2014.

Italy has not been alone. Despite a strong football pedigree, Sweden failed to qualify for consecutive World Cups in 2014 and 2018. Uruguay has won the World Cup twice, in 1930 and 1950. They failed to qualify consecutively in 1994 and 1998 and also in 2006. There have been additional instances before the 90s for Uruguay. Sport is great reminder that there is no entitlement. Everything must be earned.

When younger players start to age, that realization becomes apparent. You can't be sure how many more opportunities will present themselves. Legacy becomes part of the thinking and wanting to capitalize on what remains of the career. It is only natural that professionals will seek to maximize their earning capacity while they are at the top of their chosen field. In sport, however, once players have achieved a significant nest egg, the next paycheck isn't as important as the legacy of winning one more title. Titles always seem to be the highest vanity metric outstripping individual numbers.

The urgency of achieving another title or maximizing titles in the limited window of remaining years heightens awareness and focus on the "how to" which can't be separated from culture. The head office may have many more years left in the game in comparison to a mature athlete.

Tom Brady is well known for his propensity to encourage a teammate to come back for one more season, put off retirement, or come back out of retirement. Rob Gronkowski is a tight end who played nine seasons with the New England Patriots from 2010 through to 2018 before retiring from the NFL having won three Super-Bowl rings with the Patriots. Gronkowski was retired for just one season before being lured back out by Brady to join him in his debut season with the Tampa Bay Buccaneers.

The Buccaneers won a Super Bowl in that first season with Brady and Gronkowski. The following year the Buccaneers lost to the eventual champions the Los Angeles Rams in the divisional round of the playoffs 30–27. This included coming back from a 20–3 halftime deficit, with the first score after halftime being a touchdown by the Rams moving them to a 27–3 lead. Brady led a comeback to tie the game 27–all with less than a minute left, however, it was sufficient time for the Rams to gain from a couple of long passing completions and kick a field goal as time was expiring.

Tom Brady announced his own retirement from the NFL on February 1, 2022. The retirement was short-lived with a further Brady announcement on March 13, 2022, advising he was coming back to the Buccaneers for his twenty-third season of football. With that commitment, Brady started hitting the phones during free agency. Firstly, encouraging Russell Gage wide receiver from the Atlanta Falcons to join the Buccaneers, which Gage duly did before the end of the first week of free agency. Brady was also on the phone to the Buccaneers running back Leonard Fournette who had just come off contract and was a free agent. As Fournette tells the story, he was visiting the New England Patriots during the second week of free agency when he received a call from Brady opening with "Man, what your ass doing up there?" Fournette re-signed with the Buccaneers shortly thereafter.

It is not usual for businesses to create incentives for team members to attract talent to their operations. It can be a little tricky to understand the depth of personal relationships, and the vouching going on during the hiring process given attached incentives, but in talent-short markets, all initiatives are on the table for consideration.

It is a strong indication of a player being all in if they are attempting to convince other talent to join their team.

Culture is tricky. If a player's unrest becomes public, it does not necessarily mean that they are not all in. Nor that the front office, coaching, or ownership are not all in. What it does mean is that all stakeholders have skin in the game, and a view on the "how to" – whether that "how to" is considered part of their responsibilities or not.

The big NFL story heading into the 2021 season was news breaking on draft day that Aaron Rodgers, quarterback for the Green Bay Packers, was disgruntled and did not want to return to the franchise. The Packers had recorded a 13–3 winning record for the season and had just missed out on qualifying for the Super Bowl losing to the Tampa Bay Buccaneers 31–26 in the NFC Conference Championship game. Rodgers had passed for 4,299 yards achieving a 70.7 percent passing completion rate. Later Rodgers would be named the Most Valuable Player (MVP) for the season. Apart from winning a Super-Bowl ring, there was not much to be disappointed with for the season, so the news came as a shock.

After 16 seasons in the NFL and one Super-Bowl ring, Rodgers is expected by many pundits to achieve Hall of Fame status as soon as he becomes eligible (minimum five years retired from the league).

While there was much media speculation about the reasons for Rodgers' being disgruntled, we can only ever go by the words of the person himself. Appearing on ESPN's *SportsCenter* for anchor Kenny Mayne's final show[119], Mayne asks Rodgers for his response to the view that people have been conditioned to believe management is always right because their loyalty to the team is paramount, and that players are bad actors when they stand up for themselves. Rodgers responded with:

> ... I think sometimes people forget what really makes an organization, and you know history is important, you know legacy of so many people who come before you, but the people, that's the most important thing, that people make an organization. People make a business, and sometimes that gets forgotten. You know, culture is built brick by brick, the foundation of it by the people ... not by the organization, not by the building, not by the corporation, it's built by the people, and I've been fortunate enough to play with a number of amazing, amazing people, and got to work for some amazing people as well, and it's those people that build the foundation of those entities, and I think sometimes we forget that ... With my situation, look it's never been about, you know, never been about the draft pick, picking Jordan, I love Jordan, he's a great kid, a lot of fun to work together, love coaching staff, love my teammates, and I love the fan base, and Green Bay; [it's been an] incredible, incredible 16 years. It's just kind of about a philosophy, maybe forgetting that it is about the people that make the thing go. It's about, it's about character; it's about culture; it's about doing things the right way ..."

Culture is very much about the how to, and all stakeholders have a vested interest. From winning next season, to the capacity to win in future seasons – the approach to taking care of business has a direct impact upon individual's and their own legacies.

"My dad told me growing up, like why the Niners are like the Niners, why the Yankees are like the Yankees, what a difference between a first-class organization is and everyone else, how there is only about five teams in the league, and this changes year to year, but this is what he told me growing up, that are actually really trying to win and that's all that matters is winning; other people are just trying to survive."[120]
– Kyle Shanahan, San Francisco 49ers head coach

Examples of performance reflecting culture in the cricket

In section 4.3 Chip on your Shoulder, we covered the rise of the West Indies in the 1960s and 1970s to become the best team in world cricket achieving a run of fifteen years where they did not lose an international test series between 1980 and 1995.

Australia had an extraordinarily strong cricket team in the 1970s. From 1972 through to 1977, the Australians went undefeated in eleven consecutive test match series winning eight and drawing three. As one team ascends, in this case the West Indies, another declines. From 1977 through to 1984, Australia played in 21 test match series, winning just seven, losing nine and drawing five.

The West Indies were visiting Australia for a five-test series in November of 1984. The first test in Perth was a comfortable win by an innings and 112 runs for the West Indies. The Australians did not fare much better in the second test held in Brisbane, batting first and being dismissed for 175. The West Indies scored 424 in reply, and Australia was again dismissed relatively cheaply for 271. The West Indies scored the necessary 26 runs for the loss of two wickets to win the game by eight wickets.

Following the second test, Australian captain Kim Hughes resigned. Having led the nation in 28 test matches, Australia had recorded only four wins, losing 13 and drawing 11. Allan Border was named as Hughes' successor as captain heading into the third test. The West Indies won the third test by 191 runs to claim the series. The fourth test was drawn, with Australian winning the last test for a series loss of 3–1.

Following this series loss to the West Indies, Australia would win just two of their next 11 test match series, losing six and drawing three.

Bob Simpson was a former Australian test cricket captain, who played 62 test matches between 1957–1978. Simpson scored 4,869 test runs at an average of 46.81, his highest score being 311. Along with Border, Simpson became pivotal in turning around Australia's fortunes when in 1986 he was named the first ever coach of the test team. Simpson brought with him a new approach to professionalism and hard work, particularly in the field and batting and would stay in the role for a decade.

Australia's 1989 Ashes series against England in England heralded the establishment of a new Australian cricket team culture. Within Australian media circles, Border had been criticized as being too friendly with the English players. The team itself were criticized as being too accepting of losing. The Australians under Border had won the 1987 World Cup

50-over tournament but had yet to capture that same form in the test match cauldron.

The 1989 Ashes series would change this and along the way earned Border the nickname of "Captain Grumpy". When it came to play, everything the team did became hard-nosed and determined. Most of all, it was about standards and the Australian players expecting more from themselves.

In the first test, Australia batted first and amassed a mammoth 601 runs for the loss of just seven wickets. Opener Mark Taylor, playing in just his second test series, scored 136 in the first innings. In his previous four innings against the West Indies, he had registered scores of 25, three, three and 36. Steve Waugh top-scored with 177 and remained not out when the declaration was made. This was Waugh's first test hundred in his forty-second test innings. England were dismissed in their first innings for 430. Australia batted again declaring at three wickets for 230, leaving England to chase 402 for victory. Terry Alderman took five second-inning wickets ending with 10 wickets for the match, and spearheading England's dismissal for 191.

Australia won the second test comfortably by six wickets. The third test was drawn, before Australia won the fourth test by nine wickets and fifth test by an innings and 180 runs. The final test was drawn but the damage had been done with Australia winning the series 4–0.

Border would go on to captain Australia in another 14 test match series, winning seven, drawing four, and losing only three.

Border's final test match as captain was against South Africa in Durban, South Africa, March 25-29, 1994. By that time, Border held the record as test cricket's highest ever run scorer with 11,174 at an average of 50.56 (now held by Sachin Tendulkar from India with 15,921 runs at an average of 53.78). Border also held the record for most test matches as captain finishing with 93 matches as captain[121] (later passed by Graeme Smith from South Africa in 2012) winning 32, losing 22, one tied test, and 38 draws for a winning percentage of 34.4.

A hard-nosed, gritty, winning culture had been established and embedded.

Border was succeeded as captain by Mark Taylor. Taylor built on Border's legacy going on to captain Australia in 50 test matches between 1994–1999 – winning 26 tests, losing 13, and drawing 11 for a winning percentage of 52. While Border had achieved a win/loss ratio of 1.45, Taylor had raised this to new heights achieving a ratio of 2.0. Where Border had to scrap and come from behind, Taylor had inherited a team where the youngsters had become hardened professionals and generational talents in leg-spin king Shane Warne and fast-bowler Glenn McGrath had warmed up and were working into their strides before becoming legends of the game.

With such weapons at Taylor's disposal, he was able to maintain the culture of determination and grit, building upon it with a heightened attacking mindset. The formula was codified. Bat first. Score more than 400 in the first innings. Set attacking fields. Bowl the opposition out twice. Let Warne weave his magic on day five with well-worn pitches affording the greatest spin.

Taylor was succeeded as Australian cricket captain by Steve Waugh. It is always a matter of conjecture looking in from the outside. My personal view is that Waugh was more aggressive than Taylor, but probably not quite as attacking. The distinction here is that aggression reflects going for the win, while attacking reflects the nature of field placements, the why and how bowlers were used, and times of declarations giving the opposition an opportunity to win thereby incentivizing them not to play for a draw.

Waugh captained Australia 57 times between 1999–2004. With the evolution of the side, grit combined with attacking prowess, now combined with heightened aggression, Waugh achieved more than double Taylor's win/loss ratio coming in at 4.55 securing 41 wins, nine losses and only seven draws.

For the sake of completeness, much has been written about Waugh's tenure. Waugh coined the term "mental disintegration" which meant a ruthlessness from the Australians to ensure resounding wins and psychological destruction of the opposition. It has been said the level of sledging was over the top and demonstrated poor sportsmanship, and while the Aussies won well, their behavior was not a shining-star example in losing. Putting the diversity of views on the sledging aside – the results were superior to any seen before or since.

The world record for most consecutive cricket test match wins is 16 tests. This has been achieved by Australia twice. The first was from October 14, 1999 to February 27, 2001 under Waugh's tenure (although Waugh did miss one of these matches through injury).

The second time was after Waugh retired and when Ricky Ponting had taken over the reins from Waugh as test captain. It was achieved during the period of December 26, 2005 to January 2, 2008.

Ponting's last test as captain was the Boxing Day fourth Ashes test against England in Melbourne in December 2010. A finger injury would keep him out of the fifth test in Sydney. He would resign as captain after the Cricket World Cup in March 2011 and continue playing tests until December 2012. Ponting captained Australia for 77 tests and continued the attacking and aggressive identity of the team. He would become the most winning Australian captain, winning

48 times, losing just 16 tests, and drawing 13. The win/loss percentage dropped only slightly to 3.0.

The team culture and identity of attack and aggression would begin to wane after Ponting's tenure. There have still been periods of success, but the domination and sustained excellence had gone. All future Australian test captains were world-leading players in their own right. The results, however, dropped.

Michael Clarke captained Australia 47 times from 2011–2015, winning 24 test matches, losing 16, and drawing seven for a win/loss ratio of 1.5. Steve Smith followed captaining Australian in 35 tests across 2014–2021, winning 19 times, losing 10, and drawing six for a win/loss ratio of 1.9.

Table 10. Most Matches as Australian Cricket Captain (Minimum 25 test matches) as of January 2024

Player	Span	Mat	Won	Lost	Tied	Draw	W/L	%W	%L
WM Woodfull	1930–1934	25	14	7	0	4	2.00	56.00	28.00
R Benaud	1958–1963	28	12	4	1	11	3.00	42.85	14.28
RB Simpson	1964–1978	39	12	12	0	15	1.00	30.76	30.76
WM Lawry	1968–1971	25	9	8	0	8	1.12	36.00	32.00
IM Chappell	1971–1975	30	15	5	0	10	3.00	50.00	16.66
GS Chappell	1975–1983	48	21	13	0	14	1.61	43.75	27.08
KJ Hughes	1979–1984	28	4	13	0	11	0.30	14.28	46.42
AR Border	1984–1994	93	32	22	1	38	1.45	34.40	23.65
MA Taylor	1994–1999	50	26	13	0	11	2.00	52.00	26.00
SR Waugh	1999–2004	57	41	9	0	7	4.55	71.92	15.78
RT Ponting	2004–2010	77	48	16	0	13	3.00	62.33	20.77
MJ Clarke	2011–2015	47	24	16	0	7	1.50	51.06	34.04
SPD Smith	2014–2021	38	21	10	0	7	2.10	55.26	26.31
PJ Cummins	2021–2024	28	17	6	0	5	2.83	60.71	21.43

Source: ESPN cricinfo

Now the words may have publicly remained voiced from Australian test players after Ricky Ponting left the game, the steely resolve, the determination, the attacking approach, the aggression were all still mantras, but the results did not align.

And there were other major indicators to come to signify that the culture had changed.

First was the scandal known as Sandpapergate. Australia was visiting South Africa for a four-test series in 2018 for what was expected to be a close affair. Australia won the first test in Durban by 118 runs. South Africa won the second text in Gqeberha by six wickets. The third test was in Cape Town.

South Africa won the toss and elected to bat and were dismissed for 311 early on the second morning. Australia's first innings totaled 255 ending early on the third morning. With South Africa batting a second time, it was during day three that Sandpapergate occurred.

Television cameras zoomed in on Australian opener Cameron Bancroft who looked like he was using a foreign object on the ball to alter its surface, which is against the rules in cricket.

There are two common types of swing a bowler can achieve in cricket. Conventional swing is achieved with the new ball. With the bowling hand gripping the ball down the middle of the stitched seam with the index and middle fingers, the seam is slightly tilted in the direction the bowler wishes the ball to swing and keeps the shiniest side of the leather ball on the opposite side of where the bowler wants the ball to swing. When the game begins, the ball is in the same condition on either side. A key ingredient is for the bowler to release the ball keeping the stitched seam asymmetric throughout the ball's flight. Speed of flight and wind hitting the ball cause the swing.

Reverse swing happens when the smoothest side of the ball is on the opposite side. The ball degrades naturally, and teams focus only on protecting, cleaning, and shining one side of the ball. Allowing degradation on the other side to amplify and speed of flight are also critical factors.

In the modern game, given protected wickets and cricket pitches prepared to ensure batsman have a good opportunity to entertain, teams have rushed to move as quickly as possible to an environment that is conducive to reverse swing. It is not permissible to artificially speed up that process.

The television footage of Bancroft was conclusive in that he was in possession of a yellow foreign object, as best he did to disguise it. The umpires quizzed Bancroft during the game, and by the end of the days play, word had spread throughout the world. Sheepish interviews were given.

South Africa were dismissed on day four for 373 leaving Australia 430 runs required to win. Despite reaching 57 runs without loss, the Australians collapsed losing all 10 wickets for 50 runs, dismissed for 107 resulting in a 327-run loss for the Australians.

The Australian captain Steve Smith, vice-captain David Warner, and Cameron Bancroft were all stood down by Cricket Australia (the board of Australian cricket) for the fourth test, and an investigation was immediately launched. While having no knowledge of the ball tampering that was to occur, coach of the side Darren Lehmann announces that he was resigning his position effective immediately after the completion of the fourth test. Australia went on to lose the fourth test by 492 runs and the series 3–1.

Smith and Warner receive twelve month bans from Cricket Australia and Bancroft nine months. Then there was a series of internal reviews as to how this incident could have occurred on the watch of the current governance model.

Smith was replaced as captain by Tim Payne, and Warner replaced as vice-captain by Pat Cummins.

Renewal always occurs after a crisis. A little over two months after the scandal broke, the Cricket Australia chief executive resigned giving twelve months' notice. The chair of the board resigned before the end of 2018 as did other directors.

Tim Payne's reign as Australian captain lasted 23 tests matches, winning 11, losing eight, and drawing four. Payne resigned in November 2021 after reports began to emerge of a sexting scandal that was investigated back in 2017. The nature and outcomes of the investigation didn't stop Cricket Australia from appointing Payne captain in 2018.

The final major incident that reflects a growing cultural divide between the past and the present was the appointments of cricket coach for the Australian cricket team. Darren Lehmann's resignation as coach following Sandpapergate led to the appointment of Justin Langer. Both men were grounded in the Australian cricket team culture developed during the nineties and early 2000s.

Lehmann played 27 test matches for Australia between 1998–2004 scoring 2,909 runs at an average of 45.0. He holds the record for the most first-class runs domestically in Australia in the four-day Sheffield Shield/Pura Cup competitions, playing 147 matches and scoring 13,635 runs at an average of 54.97. His first-class runs total almost doubles when you included seasons played in England for Yorkshire (25,795). An attacking batsman, Lehmann was very unlucky not to play more test matches.

Justin Langer started his test career as a stoic, mentally tough player, who played 105 test matches between 1993 and 2007. As his career progressed, and he became a formidable opening pair with Matthew Hayden, his game became more expansive and attacking. He ended his career with 7,696 runs at an average of 45.27. Throughout his career, Langer demonstrated a steely resolve, a strong love for the baggy green cap, and was the ultimate loyal teammate.

When Lehmann abruptly resigned, Langer was considered

the safe pair of hands to restore pride into the baggy green and a culture of being part of something bigger than oneself – the "how to".

One of Langer's trademarks is his intensity, the type of character trait which was going to be needed for the long road back. After the South Africa scandal, there were series losses to Pakistan 1–0 and India 2–1, before winning three of the next four test series, with the fourth drawn. There were murmurings of player unrest with Langer's intensity.

Australia then lost a tough series to India 2–1 in Australia ending in January 2021, before going on to claim their first World Cup T20 title in November 2021.

The T20 World Cup was quickly followed by Australia retaining the Ashes against England in Australia with a 4–0 drubbing in the five-match series. Langer was offered just a six-month contract extension by Cricket Australia despite the recent success, which he declined.

The player murmurings displayed the cultural divide between the past and the present. Unlike many other sports, the coach in test cricket is the support, the captain is the decision-maker. It is why the test cricket captain is referred to as the second most important job in Australia just behind the prime minister. There are ebbs and flows on whether the captain and/or coach participates on the team-selection panel. But once the selections process is done, the coach builds the player and team capabilities, and the captain decides strategy and deploys the tactics on game day. There is always collaboration, but historically the lines have been clear on roles and responsibilities.

In taking over from Tim Payne as Australia's cricket test captain, Pat Cummins was always going to make changes and determine his own scheme and philosophy that would best achieve success.

The treatment of Justin Langer by Cricket Australia did not go down well with Langer's peers, those who played with him, and were part of establishing the previous culture. An important driver at that time was that entitlement did not exist anywhere. It was very difficult to make it into the Australian cricket team, and if players were ever dropped, it was incredibly difficult to get back in.

Steve Waugh was dropped due to poor form and spent eighteen months on the sidelines across 1990/91 missing two test series. Matthew Hayden debuted in 1994 playing just one test match against South Africa registering scores of 15 and five, before being dropped and not getting a second chance for two and a half years. Hayden went on to play a total of 103 test matches scoring 8,625 runs at an average of 50.73.

Justin Langer had played the first of his six test matches by November 1994, before he too was dropped, and then had to wait over two years for his next opportunity. Adam Gilchrist was Australia's best wicketkeeper/batsman and played ten years of test cricket between 1999–2008. Gilchrist's career ended with 96 test matches, scoring 5,570 runs at 47.60, taking 379 catches, and making 37 stumpings. Gilchrist debuted just shy of his twenty-eighth birthday, kept at bay for so long because of the wicket-keeping prowess and useful batting contributions of Ian Healey. Healey played 119 test matches, scoring 4,356 runs at an average of 27.39, taking 366 catches, and making 29 stumpings.

The point here is that Langer's generation came through at a time of unparalleled success. Nothing was gifted; everything had to be worked for. Grit demonstrated by both individuals and team were at levels that were through the roof. The culture that embodied this time was specific, and for those graduating from that time, the culture was a critical part of the success.

It is accurate that Australia lost a lot of experience between 2007 and 2009. Warne (145 test matches), McGrath (124 test matches), and Langer (105 test matches) all played the last of their test cricket in 2007. In 2008, Gilchrist (96 test matches) and Brett Lee (76 test matches) played their last tests. In 2009, Hayden played his last test (103 test matches).

It cannot be dismissed, however, that the drop in win/loss ratios over the last decade simply represents a generational drop in talent level. The talent levels in the current team are obvious, and they are clearly capable of competing with anyone.

That is also not to say that today's current group demonstrate entitlement.

What I am suggesting is that sustained excellence is underpinned by culture, and the moving away from Justin Langer as coach of the Australian cricket team represents a shift away from the historically successful Australian cricket team culture. Only time will tell whether the new culture, or as they inanely say in politics the "reset", has been successful. One thing that cannot be hidden from is that the benchmark has previously been set and will always be the yardstick used to measure future success.

We covered context and the Cricket Australia financial position after the first 15 months of COVID-19 in section 2.2, and that revenue generated from test series hosted in Australia involving England and India subsidize the costs of hosting touring teams from other nations.

Twelve months later, and the sport had generated a profit of $4.9m for the year ending June 30, 2021.

Table 11. Cricket Australia Financial Position 2018–2021 (Year Ending June 30)

Profit & Loss ($'000)						
Year	2016	2017	2018	2019	2020	2021
Total Revenue	339,787	303,490	399,265	485,901	390,098	414,705
Total income/(loss) for the year	35,727	(51,295)	(10,759)	9,902	(43,155)	4,862

Balance Sheet ($'000)						
Year	2016	2017	2018	2019	2020	2021
Total Assets	371,412	317,717	276,128	240,785	195,178	265,201
Total Liabilities	221,517	219,117	188,287	143,042	140,590	205,751
NET ASSETS	149,895	98,600	87,841	97,743	54,588	59,450

These financial figures include having hosted India in a four-test match series.

For the next financial year, and the year ending June 30, 2022, the future Cricket Australia financials will include having hosted a five-match Ashes series against England. The risk for the sport is that the two main drivers of revenue have already visited Australia shores on the four-year rotation.

Financial head winds heading into the financial year commencing July 1, 2022, include inflationary pressures across the world; challenges with global supply chains and inhibited by extending COVID-19 shutdowns in Shanghai, China for months on end; the war in the Ukraine interrupting energy markets with sanctions placed on Russia; and wheat market interruptions with Ukraine supply inhibited due to the conflict.

All these costs pressures will have an impact on the sport competing in a tighter fiscal environment for the discretionary entertainment spend by fans attending sporting contests.

A big question remains for Cricket Australia and the future health of the sport in the country. It is not yet clear the impact on brand reputation and consumer sentiment from the Sandpapergate scandal, resignation of captain Tim Payne, and the replacement of national treasure Justin Langer as coach all in relatively quick succession.

When the 2017–2022 Memorandum of Understanding (MOU) between Cricket Australia and the Cricketers Players Association expired, it was replaced by an updated MOU for just 12 months[122]. The bulk of the summer cricket season will be completed by February 2023, thus giving the governing body ample insight into likely financial position by June 30, 2023.

"There is nothing more hollow than words, particularly in this day of social media; people can only be judged by their actions."
— John Middlekauf, *Three and Out* Podcast

---

10. Coaching mindset

DUCKWORTH'S RESEARCH ON GRIT CONCLUDES that a fixed mindset about ability leads to negative explanations on adversity with the result being that people give up on challenges and, as a pattern, avoid them in the first place. Conversely, those with a growth mindset adopt optimistic ways of explaining adversity that results in perseverance and seeking out new challenges that ultimately make an individual stronger[123].

A coaching mindset in professional sports is the equivalent of a growth mindset in business. It is a focus on how to realize the full potential of individual members of the team, as well as lifting standards of the team as a collective over time. It works, brick by brick, as the coach sets the foundation; improves the capability of individuals and the team day by day during the pre-season, day by day during the regular season, season by season; inducts new players into the standards; and decides when current players are unable to meet the evolving and heightened standards. It is a two-way street. Coaches coach, but players need the discipline of meeting this grind of continuous improvement as an expectation.

The NFL provides a strong indoctrination into the coaching mindset, principally because coaching is a profession. The pathway to an NFL career starts in high school.

High school head coaches can expect to be remunerated and better than other sports. Interest in football increases market opportunities. As such, coaches work the requisite number of hours developing schemes, playing philosophies, and player improvement plans to maximize performance. Coaches may earn better future opportunities in their profession based on the performance and achievement of their teams. Moving into the college system, the top echelon of coaches earn high seven-figure salaries. In the NFL, the top coaches are also on high seven figures with a select handful going into eight-figure territories.

For athletes seeking to find their way into the NFL, coaches and programs are key factors in deciding which school to attend; athletes know that the right system and right coaching will amplify their development and maximize opportunities down the road.

Franchise owners in the NFL also know that coaches and quality of program are their keys to success or otherwise at the elite level.

The 2021 NFL season was the first as a head coach for Robert Saleh joining the New York Jets. His professional coaching career to this point started with five years in the college system from 2002–2005 with Michigan State, Central Michigan, and Georgia. This was followed by 16 years in the NFL with the Houston Texan (2005–10), the Seattle Seahawks (2011–13), Jacksonville Jaguars (2014–16), and the San Francisco 49ers (2017–2020). He held the position of defensive coordinator for the full four years at the 49ers before gaining the Jets head coach position.

A mantra that Saleh regularly espouses is that of "all gas, no brake". Explaining how this mantra embeds with playing groups a "getting better mindset", Saleh has said[124]:

The one thing that they can't lose touch with is the fact that they need to find a way, every single day, to go to bed better than when they woke up, and that mindset and how you do that, from when you wake up, to how you eat, how you dress in the morning, shower, prepare, rehab, regen, practice, study, all of it ... it's all geared towards that mindset and that's what that all gas no brake mantra kind of means to us in terms of you are going to bed better than when you woke up, not only through our help but through the investment being put back into yourselves.

Prior to Saleh's arrival, Adam Gase was head coach at the Jets for two seasons registering win-loss records of 2–14 in 2020 and 7–9 in 2019. Prior to Gase, the head coach was Todd Bowles who was in charge for four seasons registering win-loss records of 4–12 in 2018, 5–11 in 2017, 5–11 in 2016 and 10–6 in 2015. The Jets last postseason appearance was in 2010.

Saleh's first year in charge doubled the number of wins in Gase's last season, albeit with an extra game, registering a 4–13 win-loss record.

Heading into the 2022 draft, the Jets had a total of nine picks, with pick numbers four and 10 in the first round, pick number 35 and 38 in the second round, pick number 69 in round three, pick numbers 111 and 117 in round four, and pick numbers 146 and 163 in round five.

During the draft and after the Jets first two selections, it became apparent which players were likely to still be available later in the first round. The Jets secured a trade with the Tennessee Titans sending pick numbers 35, 69, and 163 to the Titans in exchange for pick numbers 26 and 111. That gave the Jets a third selection in the first round, and four players inside the top 38 which resulted in the Jets selecting cornerback Ahmad Gardner at no. four, wide receiver Garrett Wilson at no.10, defensive end Jermaine Johnson II at no.26, and running back Breece Hall at no. 38.

After the completion of the 2022 off-season mandatory mini-camp, Saleh was interviewed on *The Rich Eisen Show*[125] providing some insights into his coaching mindset heading into his second season in charge:

> "The objective of this whole youth movement is to get these guys as much playing time as possible, so they get scarred like a veteran, while they have youthful legs, and if you could get them thinking and playing like a veteran while they're still running what they did at the Combine, then you have chance to be a very explosive roster. So does it hurt to watch? Is it painful? Is it a rollercoaster ride? Is it stressful? Absolutely, but in our opinion, and if you're able to ride it out, and you can develop these guys the right way, and you've got guys who are made of the right stuff, like we feel like we have, where they're gonna grind and they're gonna find ways to get things done. We really do think the potential of this team is pretty cool and it's gonna be fun to watch these guys grow."

Professional disciplines can start as early as high school in football and becomes entrenched at the highest college level. Offensive and defensive Rookies of the Year in the NFL are not only standouts on their teams, but standouts across the league making major contributors in their first year out of college.

If we look at the opportunities to coach playing talent as a life cycle, it starts in high school. Then there is a funneling and concentration as the best talent is recruited by the best programs in college. In nominating for the NFL draft, the best talent is invited to participate in the NFL Combine. As a key component of the draft process, franchises are permitted to undertake 30 meetings, bringing desired draft nominees into their facilities for interviews, meetings, and physicals. There are years of college tape available for franchises to review along with their own franchises scouting reports to determine a list of 30.

After the draft, franchises can sign Unrestricted Draft Free Agents (UDFAs), who are those who were unsigned through the draft process. They can also sign any other active players who remain free agents, or those returning from long-term injuries who are without a contract.

Franchises are limited to 90 players during the offseason on their rosters. As the offseason workouts commence, players may be waived and new players signed based on the assessment of players on the 90-man roster. Throughout these offseason workouts and mandatory minicamps, players are being coached and strengths and weakness identified.

Throughout August the 90-man roster is first cut to 85, then to 80, and then to the final squad size of 53. A practice squad of 16 is in addition to the 53-man squad.

Coaching occurs prior to entering the NFL at high school and college. Then with squads of 90 and throughout the process of cutting to 53, and then throughout the season to improve the performance of individuals and the team itself.

Let's look at the coaching mindset through this progression, firstly with college.

The coaching mindset was apparent early on with Dabo Swinney as head coach at Clemson. Swinney relays his own experiences of pursuing football in college at Alabama[126]:

"There is no elevator to success; there is no app; you gotta to put the work in, and the thing I love about the game of football, as much as the game has changed and different things, [is] its hard work ... and the other thing I learned through the game of football, is you can outwork people ...

... What I learned is that you can outwork people, you can outthink people, you can out want people, you can out effort people, you can out tough people, [and] that's what the game taught me [that] you can out believe people."

The San Francisco 49ers selected quarterback Trey Lance with the third pick of the 2021 draft. Lance's rookie season was playing as back-up quarterback to Jimmy Garoppolo. Lance played in six games during the 2021 season, including two as starter when Garoppolo was injured. Lance made 71 pass attempts for 41 completions at 57.7 percent, passing for 603 yards in total at an average of 8.5 yards per completion, and having five touchdowns and two interceptions. He also rushed for 168 yards at an average of 4.4 yards per rush scoring one more touchdown.

Heading into the 2022 draft, the 49ers made it known they were open to a trade for Jimmy Garoppolo clearing the way for Lance to become the starter. Niners head coach Kyle Shanahan shares some insights[127] into his coaching mindset moving from a veteran in Garoppolo to a second-year player in Lance and how to create an offense for a starter who has a limited sample size in the NFL:

"... There's certain principles to what you think a quarterback has to do, you know, and for everybody. I mean you'd love him to be able to do the drop-back game, the play-action game, you'd love to move him out on bootlegs, you'd love to have big throws, short throws, screens, everything, and there's a time in every game that you usually need one of those, so you try them at everything, and almost every quarterback at this level is capable of doing everything, but you find how consistent they are, and there's gonna be certain areas that are his strengths, and certain areas that are weaknesses, just like every other quarterback I've coached and you put them through all that and you don't try to hide it; you try to understand it; there's usually nothing that you can't do, but you find out what's hard on a person, so you do it that if you absolutely have to, and you always try to find avenues to where you put them in an advantageous situation where they're confident, cause they know this is automatic, you know they can do that, and eventually people take that away and you gotta go to the next thing, and you gotta get good at that so you can bring the other thing back, and I think that's kind of the story in every position.

The Lance example gives an insight into the coaching mindset entering a pre-season with a specific individual and specific position in mind. In this case, the most important position in football: the quarterback.

Mike McDaniel was the offensive coordinator for the 49ers for the 2021 season, having spent the previous four years at the 49ers as the run-game coordinator. He had previous NFL coaching experience with the Houston Texans, Washington, Cleveland, and Atlanta.

The 49ers hold weekly media sessions throughout the season. After winning their season openers against the Detroit Lions and the Philadelphia Eagles, McDaniel gave some insight in the coaching mindset during the season[128], where weekly games and recovery windows provide narrower opportunities for skills development:

… That's the whole deal week in week out, you're building towards the end, so you don't really ever be like alright finished product because, right there, you just lost your edge, and whether you're getting exposed now or in a couple of weeks, the end is coming, so there's where you know Kyle does a good job of trying to build that culture. I think everyone buys into it, where it had, you're always building to be your best self and our best team and that's progressing through the year. We may have a great game, we might have a terrible game, that means nothing to the next week. So I think it's awesome to get a win, when you have a lot of yards and plays left on the field, so that's the silver lining to it but, whether you win or lose you're trying to look at it that same way so that you can try to be your best football team in the homestretch, when you're trying to get a playoff berth, or you're trying to win home field or whatever your team and your performance has allowed you to do in the whole season at the end.

Following the 2021 season, McDaniel successfully landed the head coach job with the Miami Dolphins.

These four examples of Swinney's coaching mindset in college with Clemson, Saleh's investment in youth with the Jets, Shanahan preparing a new young quarterback with the 49ers, and McDaniel's coaching mindset philosophy in season, all demonstrate that the coaching mindset is a process. There is no finish line. Once you have settled on a team list, it is all about focusing on realizing the potential of your human capital and lifting standards over time.

10.1 Iron sharpens iron

You will sometimes hear the phrase "iron sharpens iron" dropped in an NFL press conference by coach or player. The origins of the phrase are from the bible "As iron sharpens iron, so one person sharpens another" (Proverbs 27:17).

The meaning is literal. In isolation, iron is dulled through usage overtime. Two or more pieces of iron working together, however, can be maintained and enhanced, that is, sharpened. In professional sports, the phrase goes deeper to mean earning opportunity and taking accountability. Accountability by not just looking in the mirror, but rather by allowing others to uncover and identify weaknesses to be worked on and accepting the challenge of working with others to improve skills in those weaknesses over time.

"The one thing we talk about at Clemson all the time, there is no entitlement, you know, you come to Clemson you're going to be empowered, not entitled. There's no entitlement."

– Dabo Swinney, head coach, Clemson Tigers

Whether in business or professional sport, confronting the facts and accepting accountability are some of the most difficult aspects to navigate for any operation.

Bill Walsh was the mastermind coach who started the 49ers glory run in the 1980s. He had spent the bulk of his coaching assistant career with the Cincinnati Bengals (1968–1975), followed by a year with the San Diego Chargers in 1976, before becoming the head coach of Stanford in the college system. Two years at Stanford preceded his appointment as the head coach of the 49ers in 1979, a position he then held for a decade. Walsh was the coach who secured the 49ers first ever Super-Bowl win. He went on to secure three visits to the Super Bowl, winning all three (the seasons of 1981, 1984, and 1988). During this time, Joe Montana quarterback and Jerry Rice wide receiver became household names.

Walsh's leadership philosophy was based on establishing a *standard of performance*. Critical to future success was the character of coaches, players, and personnel. In his book, *The Score Takes Care of Itself*, Walsh makes two comments that are more forthright that you would typically find in any strategy book about business:

> More people are familiar with losing than winning. Consequently, losing is not that difficult to deal with, in the sense that we've all faced it, lived it, and are familiar with the fallout it can produce. We have seen people lose heart, self-destruct, turn on one another, and become disloyal."[129]
>
> It is also my opinion that the lack of the "stick-with-it" attitude is accompanied by a certain lack of intelligence; not always ... The thick-witted person can't deal with the hard knocks after a while, and that's when the complaining begins.
>
> Some define character as simply aspiring to high ideals and standards. I disagree. Many people have lofty aspirations. Unfortunately, aspiring isn't enough. You must also have the strength of commitment and sacrifice to adhere of those standards and ideals in both good times and bad.[130]

Just to get to the starting line of *iron sharpens iron*, it all starts with character.

> *"We have a pyramid of success over there in the football building, and it starts with 'be a champion'. And I always tell the players, you gotta be a champion before you ever gonna win a championship."*
> – Nick Saban, head coach, Alabama Crimson Tide

In a professional sports context, players drive each other to reach new heights. They are battle hardened through competition. In the NFL, it starts with the off-season 90-player roster. The roster participates in organized team activities (OTAs). In OTAs there is an absence of genuine contact, however, the simulations are game intended, players are competing, honing their skills, and getting ready for a season which may or may not eventuate for some. The roster is slowly culled down over the next three months to 53 with a practice squad of 16. Franchises can play at the margins with individuals recovering from longer-term injuries being on the injured reserves list. Ultimately, the competition is fierce, and it is a fine line between being a team player and sharpening the iron of a teammate and being individually accountable, to being cut and looking for another opportunity.

Comments[131] from 49ers head coach Kyle Shanahan give some insight into the complexities and balancing act involved with sharpening iron and accountability:

> "I would never come in and say I want to see guys getting on each other more and stuff but, I do truly believe that, you know, the good teams, players hold each other accountable. We always got to do it as a coaching staff and things like that ... and you do do that, but when it gets real is when players do it to each other and, there's

ways to go about it, you don't have to get in people's face and yell; you gotta do it whatever way that gets the right result, and the more ... guys you have do that to each other, I think the stronger you can get, but you don't just do that to do that, some guys do that and it looks the wrong way cause they're doing it for the wrong reasons, but no matter how you are, when you do and your intentions [are] right, guys usually respond."

Heading into the 2021 NFL season, the NFC West Division was broadly seen as the most competitive. The Los Angeles Rams, the Arizona Cardinals, the San Francisco 49ers, and the Seattle Seahawks all had rosters capable of qualifying for the postseason. More than 35 percent of a team's 17 games are played in division. It is simply not possible for all four teams within a division to qualify for the postseason.

Not only do your coaches and teammates prepare the battle hardened during the preseason and throughout training during the season, but your competition also does during regular season games. We covered the 49ers postseason charge in the chapter on grit. By the end of the regular season, the Rams had qualified top of the division with a win-loss record of 12–5, just beating out the Arizona Cardinals 11–6 for the divisional title, and closely followed by the 49ers with 10–7, with Seattle registering a 7–10 win-loss record.

The 40 wins across all four teams in the NFC West was the most of any division, and ended up seeing the Rams, Cardinals, and 49ers qualify for the postseason. The NFC West was the only division with three teams to qualify for the postseason, while there were three divisions with only one team qualifying for the postseason. Iron sharpens iron. It should have been no surprise then (noting it was for many), that the 49ers beat the Dallas Cowboys and Green Bay Packers on their way to a Conference Championship match-up with NFC West divisional title winner the LA Rams for a place in the Super Bowl. History shows that the Rams went on to take all comers and win.

Heading into the 2022 season, the NFC West division was no longer looking the strongest of all with that title passing to the AFC West. The AFC West division is home to the Kansas City Chiefs who at that stage had qualified for two of the three previous Super Bowls, winning one. While the Chiefs lost star wide receiver Tyrek Hill in a trade to the Miami Dolphins, they were led by the mercurial star quarterback Patrick Mahomes II. The Denver Broncos were also in the AFC West and secured via off-season trade, the Seattle Seahawks superstar quarterback and previous Super-Bowl champion Russell Wilson, while also picking up 49er free agents defensive tackle DJ Jones, offensive tackle Tom Compton and cornerback K'waun Williams.

The remaining two franchises in the AFC West were also active in free agency and trades, with the Las Vegas Raiders picking up Green Bay Packers star wide receiver Davante Adams and Cardinals edge rusher Chandler Jones. While the final team in the division, the Los Angeles Chargers picked up star cornerback JC Jackson from the New England Patriots, and a trade with the Chicago Bears secured edge rusher Khalil Mack.

On paper the AFC West had become the strongest division in football. Injuries aside, not all four teams can make the postseason, but those that do qualify will be battle hardened having faced the stiffest of competition to get there and ready to take on all comers. Iron sharpens iron.

Coaching mindset

"One of the things that is understood [is that] great players wanna be coached hard. I've never met a great player [who didn't] wanna be pushed. I talked to Tony Dungy recently about Peyton Manning, Payton wanted to be coached hard, Brady wanted to be coached hard, Kobe Bryant wanted to be coached hard, all great players do; the rest of the guys are insecure. If you're really great, you want people to get the most out of you ...

... "Sean McVay got very frustrated with Jarred Goff, started holding him accountable for all the turnovers, not knowing the playbook, not having the ability to go deeper into the playbook; he had to call Jarred Goff's audibles for him, he held him accountable, Sean McVay should, and the Rams today are better for it.

"The reason the NFL ratings this year, have you seen them? They're going through the roof, any show including ours that is connected to the NFL, up, up, up. Why? Because it's like a real workplace, you can hold people accountable. The NBA in my opinion panders too often to stars; the great players want to be coached hard."

– Colin Cowherd, The Herd[132]

It can be a really fine line between knowing how hard to push to sharpen the skills of individual team members and the skills of your team more broadly. The best performers want to be coached hard. The up-and-commers need to be coached hard so that they can realize their ceilings.

Within such a need, there is a real risk of running two-speed operations, where the best performers and up-and-commers are treated differently to others in the team. Holding people accountable to different standards lowers the benchmark rather than fulfils the potential.

Walsh's leadership philosophy was to be aggressive in pushing the envelope:

> Aggressive leaders – effective ones – push individuals hard, and then we push harder, knowing that one of our responsibilities is to get that extra effort necessary for an organization to achieve top results. A good leader believes that he or she knows the secret (or secrets) for bringing a group of people up to a maximum productivity, and in fact, if you don't know how to do it, you'll soon be gone.[133]

10.2 Becoming elite and the Tiger Woods model

Imagine a packed stadium of 80,000 fans. How many of those fans could walk down to ground level and onto the field converting a place kick 20 yards out from right in front of the goal posts?

There is no science or dataset to support my question. I would imagine the age ranges of people attending any sporting contest would start at newborn through to octogenarians. I suspect you could count the number of attendees in their nineties or past one hundred on one hand.

Twenty yards out does not sound very far. It does not look very far either. My best guess for a diverse group of people attending would be that anyone who has played any level or type of football aged from 14–40 years old, 80 percent could make that kick eight out of 10 times. That is, they would be more than competent. For someone in that age range who has not played any level of round ball sports, maybe the percentage drops by more than half with 80 percent able to successfully convert zero to three out of 10 attempts. For attendees outside of those age ranges, it would be a steep drop away on the bell curve slope the older one gets.

What if this scenario was halftime entertainment, and the home team had put up $20,000 as a prize? How would the pressure of a potential $20,000 windfall, just one kick attempt and 80,000 fans cheering affect the outcome?

Sports professionals are faced with a similar situation week in, week out. Only the location of the kick is twenty or more yards further back, while half the crowd is booing and the other half cheering to encourage successful execution. The crowd noise is at first deafening, and followed by silence after the kick, while fans await to assess the direction and flight of the ball. Then back to deafening as the crowd start to understand the trajectory of the ball and can anticipate the result. And rather than a cash prize, there is less than two minutes on the clock, and a successful kick means the difference between winning and losing.

How do they do it under such pressure?

There has been much written about the 10,000 hour or ten-year rule for achieving mastery. Intended to refer to complex cognitive fields, the 10,000 hours is symbolic rather than a prescriptive number and intended to indicate that the volume of work required to achieve mastery is significant. Within this context, it is a good symbol across all professions. The principles apply across both professional sport and business. That is, it is the doing aspect, and that it is a significant body of work and experience to achieve mastery in anything.

Let's go back to the opening scenario of a sports fan picked randomly out of a packed stadium of 80,000 fans and invited down to ground level to convert a place kick from right in front 20 yards out and in front of the goal posts. If that fan had a sample size or data set of 10,000 previous kicks similar in nature, how confident would they be feeling about knocking the ball over in between the goal posts. No matter the crowd noise or the pressure of a potential $20,000 windfall, they would be feeling pretty confident they could block out the noise and successfully convert.

It is a universal truth in sport that the athletes with the most blessed physical attributes do not necessarily end up with the best of all-time records. Athletes with less natural talent still succeed, some of whom reach the pinnacle of their chosen sport.

At the invite-only NFL Combine, approximately 300 athletes undergo a series of physical tests. While there are specific tests for specific positions, there are five drills that generally all athletes participate in: the 40-yard dash, the vertical jump, the shuttle run, the bench press, and the broad jump.

The 40-yard dash is a straight-line sprint intended to test explosiveness off the line. Times will vary. The speediest have run in the 4.2s, but generally 4.3–4.4s are exceptionally quick, going upwards to mid to late fives for the bigger-bodied athletes.

Leg power and explosiveness is tested in the vertical jump and broad jump, both from a standing start with both feet planted. The bench-press tests arm strength via the number of repetitions of a 225lb weight. Agility and lateral speed are tested in the shuttle run which is a three-cone drill over 20-yard runs. The player lines up on the gridiron perpendicular to the end-zone lines. Starting with one hand grounded along with both feet, they first run as fast as they can for five yards to the right, bending down to touch the line, then going back to the left for ten yards bending down and touching the line again, before coming back past the starting place five yards to the right.

The results of these tests give insight into the explosiveness of the athlete. But do the fastest runners always turn into the best players? Have the greatest players always been the highest and longest jumpers? Or the athletes who can make the most repetitions on the bench press? No, it doesn't work that way.

It does not mean that athletes strong in these areas can't turn into the best players. Similarly, it does not mean that they will turn into the best players. The exhibited strength does not even guarantee that an individual athlete will be less likely to experience significant injuries.

Speed is of course a great asset. The intangibles, however, include technique and anticipation. Being able to read what the opposition will do before they do it. Then there is a saying in the NFL that separation comes from preparation. The offensive team in the NFL can have no more than six eligible receivers on the field for any play called. Preparation refers to scheming and execution. Having a quarterback fake a handoff to a running back, having receivers block or run variations of routes, are all intended to create misdirection affording separation for the receiver/s that the play is designed for. Then, of course, is the catching. One cannot have a case of the dropsies when the pressure is on. Once the separation has been achieved, execution requires the appropriate finish.

Tiger Woods has been a global icon since he was an infant. Woods has 15 career golf majors second only to Jack Nicklaus (18 majors). Woods first appeared on television at age two on *The Mike Douglas Show.* His interest in golf started from six months of age fueled by watching his father Earle Woods hit practice balls in a makeshift driving net in the garage. Tiger started using the practice net from 11 months of age. At age just two, he walked out onto his first regulation golf course playing a par 36 for nine holes and scoring 48. At age just three, he entered his first aged tournament for those ten years of age and under and won it[134].

Becoming elite is a process. It starts with an innate desire that fuels passion, that then motivates hard work. In Tiger's case, the 10,000 hours started exceedingly early. It is easy to dismiss the 10,000-hour rule. It is not a science. It is not linear. If it were a prescriptive rule, everyone would be doing it. Tiger was a natural; it was always going to happen.

Taking that line of thought too easily dismisses the hard work involved. Too often in this day and age, we hear people say, "work smarter, not harder". It is akin to suffering from the grandfather clock disease. It takes the pendulum from one extreme end to the other. Grit and hard work cannot be substituted. To borrow another NFL saying, champions are made when no-one is looking.

A better lens to view the 10,000-hour rule is to ask oneself the question "if I am forging a career in a profession where others have undertaken 10,000 hours and I haven't, can I expect to outperform my competition?" And the answer to that is clearly no.

To revisit one of Dabo Swinney's quotes in the previous chapter: "What I learned is that you can outwork people, you can outthink people, you can out want people, you can out effort people, you can out tough people; that's what the game taught me, you can out believe people." If you haven't put in the requisite hours, you are only cheating yourself.

What I mean by the Tiger Woods model is simply a child starting out at a noticeably young age. The 10,000-hour rule does not shorten the labor but mastery is achieved earlier than others who start out in the sport later. If the child happens to stumble across an immediate aptitude and passion for a specific sporting endeavor, they are on the road to success. Nothing guaranteed of course. Hard work and quality hours honing their skills must follow.

Venus and Serena Williams picked up tennis rackets at the age of four and three, respectively. Venus went on to record seven grand slam titles, while Serena went on to record 23 grand slam titles. They paired together to win three gold medals in the women's doubles competition at the Olympics, with each picking up an individual gold medal in the women's singles. Venus also collected a silver medal in the mixed doubles[135].

Starting out early, combined with grit and determination provides a head start. It is not particularly unique. It happens in swimming all the time. Your children go along to the local pool to learn how to swim. Once they can swim 25 meters proficiently, there is not much else to do other than graduate to squads or finish up. If they progress to squads, they start pounding laps under tutelage.

Other sports such as soccer have organized aged competitions across the world commencing at under sixes.

When discussing the USA's qualification for the 2022 Qatar World Cup in soccer, sportscaster Colin Cowherd was optimistic of the USA getting some wins, but not of being one of the teams that could take out the tournament[136]:

> And here's my concern, in a lot of the other places in the world that have great soccer teams – Argentina, Brazil and a lot of these other places, their kids aren't prep-school kids and they're not you know Academy kids; they're like a lot of our great athletes in America in the NBA and NFL and baseball. They didn't grow up with much, and they got a chip on their shoulder, and they'll kick your arse.
>
> ... If you look at the history of the world and sports

and who wins, it is, it's not the wealthy kids, it's not the BMWs in the backseat going to school kids. It's kids that have been doubted and they've had to fight for everything in their life, and they get out in the field or a court, and you do not wanna compete with them.

The point on hunger and desire is well made. And the earlier it is, the quicker an athlete moves through the 10,000-hours rule for mastery and can focus on becoming great.

Often overlooked with the 10,000-hour rule is that the time served is about quality. Duckworth refers to this as deliberate practice. Of the many facets to an athlete's game in any sport, there is going to be a series of strengths and weaknesses. Once an athlete has developed and holds clearly established strengths, how much time is put into raising the bar in these strength areas? How much time is invested in improving weaknesses? There are only so many hours in the week, month, and year. Achieving the best balance and optimizing improvement is where the science truly comes in.

Golf looks like a simple game. For anyone new to the sport, it looks as simple as the selection of a club that is comfortable and suitable for your height, swinging as hard as you can in the direction of the hole, finding the green, and putting the ball into a sizeable hole. Nothing too complicated there.

In reality golf is a highly technical game, from bend of the knees, straightness of the back, placement of the ball within your stance, bottom-hand placement, top-hand placement, thumb location, back swing, weight transfer from back leg to front leg, achieving a square club face at contact, and follow through. You must have all mechanics aligned to achieve consistency.

If you practice bad habits or poor technique, it does not matter how many hours are put it, improvement will be minimal if any. What it will do is embed your bad habits, so that the ceiling for improvement is minimized rather than maximized. The 10,000 hours must be about quality.

Bill Belichick was the head coach who masterminded the New England Patriots rise to the top securing the Patriots first ever Super-Bowl win against the St Louis Rams in the 2001 season. The Patriots had been to the Super Bowl twice previously losing in the 1985 season 46–10 to the Chicago Bears, and again in the 1996 season losing to the Green Bay Packers 35–21.

By taking the Patriots to the Super Bowl nine times between the 2001 and 2018 season, collecting six Super-Bowl titles, Belichick would oversee the achievement of the Patriots mission of "We are building a big, strong, fast, smart, tough, and disciplined football team that consistently competes for championships".

Belichick is famed for not offering up much in media conferences and keeping his cards close to his chest. Sometimes you can get a snippet of insight into his philosophy one of which is a direct reference from Sun Tzu's *Art of War*, being "Play to your strengths and attack your opponent's weaknesses".

The implication for elite athletes is that the opposition will plan to create situations where you do not get to showcase your strengths on game day, but rather scheme to amplify your weaknesses.

To become an elite athlete, it is a delicate balancing act. You cannot ignore working on your strengths, but you also need to invest in eliminating your weaknesses.

Here is a quote from Bill Walsh on how the elite dedicate themselves to always honing the fundamentals.

> "You never stop learning, perfecting, refining – molding your skills. You never stop depending on the fundamentals –

sustaining, maintaining, and improving. Jerry [Rice] and Joe [Montana], maybe the best ever at their positions, at the last stages of their careers were still working very hard on the fundamental things that high-school kids won't do because it's too damn dull."

If we accept that the 10,000-hour rule is about quality and deliberate practice, then there must be an appreciation of the coaching that goes into designing the quality of the practice and generating the maximum return for the effort an athlete is putting in. Otherwise, the playbook would be stock standard, and everyone would be following the same formula. That is, coaching is a separator on the quality aspects of the 10,000-hour rule.

We have used examples of coaching anecdotes throughout this book. There is just one more area to cover, and that is in relation to mentoring and coaching that may assist shorten the 10,000-hour rule.

Tiger Woods and Williams sisters' careers both demonstrated examples of great athletes starting out in their sporting professions before the age of five supported through the commitment of dedicated parents. Nonetheless, part of the support framework provided by the parents in both instances was introducing their children early to professional coaching[137].

A more rigorous coaching framework happens in swimming and soccer earlier in life than other sports. It is also available in tennis. As a means of getting children exercising, parents can engage professional coaches in group or individual bookings. Age is no barrier, just the investment capacity of parents. The more practice earlier in life helps to avoid bad habits and techniques and shortens the time to achieve proficiency. Imagine a six-year-old having a weekly tennis lesson through to ten years of age, and their capability of performing competitively against another ten-year-old who has just taken up the sport. It is quite an early advantage that may never be overcome by the child starting later.

History is littered with successful father/son playing duos in professional sports. Particularly in the sports played with a ball. It does not require the father to have been an all-time great. Having played in the professional system means a game of catch or shooting baskets immediately includes mentoring on proper technique. Again, shortening the 10,000-hour rule.

The PNC Championship is an annual golf tournament where winners of golf majors team up with a family member and play against other major winners and a family member. In 2021, Tiger Woods teamed with his twelve-year-old son Charlie. The Woodses finished second in the event behind John Daley and his son John Daley II.

Charlie Woods has an incredibly smooth golf swing, and he shone during the PNC Championship smoking balls off the tee and dropping long putts[138].

At the end of the tournament, Tiger gave an interview which should give a glimpse of having one of the worlds all-time greats as a golfing mentor. As Tiger shared:

> "As I have explained to him, as my dad explained to me, no matter how many people are around you, whether its zero or millions; it doesn't matter; it's the same shot. It doesn't change. It's exactly the same shot. The ball's not moving; it's just sitting there. Now you've got to hit the shot. And so whether he's playing at home with his buddies, or he's playing with me, or he's playing in tournament golf, or he's playing in front of tv crews, it doesn't matter; it's the same exact shot. And just having that mindset and he's starting to understand that and learn that, and he showed that today."

Imagine having the world's best golfer taking an active interest and guiding your development in golf from a young age. That is quite an advantage. Let us look at some other sports.

In the NFL, the most famous of these family combinations started with Archie Manning who was a quarterback across 13 seasons 1971–1984, ten of which were with the New Orleans Saints, one with the Minnesota Vikings, and two with the Houston Oilers[139]. The Oilers would later move to Tennessee for the 1997 season eventually becoming the Tennessee Titans from the 1999 season onwards. Archie Manning was selected to play in two Pro Bowls and across his career threw for 23,911 yards and 125 touchdowns.

Archie had two sons, Peyton and Eli. Peyton was enshrined into the NFL Hall of Fame in 2021 having played 13 seasons with the Indianapolis Colts (1998–2010) followed by four seasons with the Denver Broncos (2012–1015). He missed the entire 2011 season due to a neck injury. Peyton collected two Super-Bowl rings, one with each franchise, in the 2006 season with the Colts and the 2015 season with the Broncos. Across his career, he passed for 71,940 yards completing at 65.3 percent with 539 touchdowns.

Eli Manning's career spanned 16 seasons all with the New York Giants from 2004–2019. Like Peyton, Eli, too, collected two Super-Bowl rings interrupting the Patriots juggernaut on both occasions being the 2007 and 2011 seasons. In total, Eli passed for 57,023 yards completing at 60.3 percent with 366 touchdowns.

Imagine passing the football in that backyard as a kid after school. It would be quite the initiation.

Mike Shanahan has 308 games of head coaching experience in the NFL spanning 1988–2013. Prior to the NFL, he spent seven years in the college system followed by four years with the Denver Broncos in the offensive coordinator and wide receiver coaching positions before securing his first head coach opportunity with the Los Angeles Raiders. He spent two years with the Raiders before returning to the Broncos for two seasons – firstly as a quarterbacks coach, and then as offensive coordinator. This was followed by three years as offensive coordinator/quarterbacks coach with the San Francisco 49ers before returning to the Broncos and performing the head-coach role for fourteen seasons collecting back-to-back Super Bowl wins in 1997 and 1998 seasons. His head-coaching career finished with four seasons in Washington.

Shanahan's son, Kyle, is today the San Francisco 49ers head coach. The Shanahan's have a connection to the 49ers last Super-Bowl win back in the 1994 season which was Mike's last as offensive coordinator/quarterbacks coach before securing the head-coach job with the Broncos. The 49ers beat the San Diego Chargers 49–26 in Super Bowl XXIX, with Kyle being a ball boy that day for the 49ers. As Kyle forged his own coaching career, he led the 49ers to Super Bowl LIV for the 2019 season. Despite losing that day to the Kansas City Chiefs 31–20, the Shanahan's became the first father/son duo to reach the Super Bowl as head coaches.

John Bosa was a tight end playing 31 games across three seasons with the Miami Dolphins 1987 through 1989. Bosa has had two sons enter the NFL. Joey was selected with the third overall pick in the 2016 draft and has since played eight seasons with the Chargers for a total of 93 games making 321 tackles and 67 sacks as a defensive end. Younger brother Nick went one better as was drafted second overall in the 2019 NFL draft. He has played 68 games across five seasons making 209 tackles and has 53.5 sacks credited.

Quality of coaching and mentoring from an early age gives anyone a head start towards achieving mastery. Whether it is hand-eye coordination, technique or understanding schemes, it all goes to racking up the 10,000-hour rule faster.

It is not just the NFL. In the Australian Football League, there is a father/son draft concession rule to enable a family's name to continue with their franchise team where there has been a past major contribution. As a general guide, this major contribution has been an entry point of 100 senior games by the father for the nominating team.

The most famous example is Gary Ablett Senior and his two sons Gary Ablett Junior and Nathan Ablett. Father Gary Senior is one of only six players to have kicked more than 1,000 goals in the Australian Football League as a full forward/half forward. He played in four grand finals, however, his team the Geelong Cats were unsuccessful on each occasion. Gary Junior played midfield in a career across the Geelong Cats and Gold Coast Suns scoring 445 goals and sits inside the top 100 all-time goal scorers in the AFL. He collected two Brownlow Medals over his career, the equivalent of a league Most Valuable Player (MVP), and two premierships. Other notable father/son combinations predominately with the one franchise were Tim and Jobe Watson at the Essendon Bombers, Sergio and Stephen Silvagni at the Carlton Blues, and Jack and Tom Hawkins at the Geelong Cats.

In the National Rugby League, there are many examples too. Some of the best included Steve Rodgers and son Matt Rodgers (both played predominately for the Cronulla Sharks, represented their state and Australia, with Matt being a dual representative also playing Rugby Union for Australia), Ivan Cleary and his son Nathan (current coach and halfback for the reigning premiers the Penrith Panthers, Ivan played first grade for four clubs), Wayne Pearce (Balmain Tigers, NSW State of Origin representative and Australian test match representative) and his son Mitchell Pearce (Sydney Rooster,

Newcastle Knights, NSW State of Origin representative), Eric Grothe Senior and Eric Grothe Junior (both played predominately for the Parramatta Eels and represented NSW and Australia). There are many, many more examples like John and Scott Sattler, John Morris and his twin boys Josh and Brett, Mark and Justin Horo, Rod and Joel Reddy, Craig and Dean Young, John and Aaron Raper, and Bill and Brett Mullins.

In Major League Baseball some of the more famous examples have been Ken Griffey Senior and Junior and Bobby Bonds and Barry Bonds. In the NBA, the 2022 NBA Champions the Golden State Warriors, had three examples alone with Steph Curry (father Dell Curry), Klay Thompson (father Mychal Thompson) and Garry Payton II (father Garry Payton I).

One final point to make about becoming elite. At the individual athlete level, to be recognized as elite, performance needs to be at the highest level, and consistently so over a long period of time. The ability for a wide receiver to catch a contested ball one-handed is a great capability, but it is not a technique schemed for, and it is not a high-percentage play that can be delivered consistently over time.

There is a grind involved to become elite. Firstly, the grind to become proficient, and then the grind to be able to deliver performance higher than most over a sustained period.

Duckworth uses the formula of talent equaling how quickly skills improve when an individual invests effort, while achievement is what happens when the athlete takes their skills and applies effort to them[140]. Effort is represented twice in this equation:

$$\text{Talent} \times \text{Effort} = \text{Skill}$$
$$\text{Skill} \times \text{Effort} = \text{Achievement}$$

Elite is not just capability and capacity. It must result in achievement.

When the pressure is on, can the athlete stand up and make a play with a better than 50:50 chance of success. Elite is having completed the grind and knowing that you can deliver despite any pressure that is on.

In the NFL, the Kansas City Chiefs became the first franchise in more than 20 years to win back-to-back Super Bowls on February 12, 2024 when they defeated the San Franscisco 49ers 25-22. The last franchise to achieve this feat was the New England Patriots in the 2003 and 2004 seasons. Prior to this, there have been seven other occasions. The first two Super Bowls were won back-to-back by the Green Bay Packers for the 1966 and 1967 seasons. The Pittsburgh Steelers have achieved the feat twice for the 1974 and 75 seasons and the 1978 and 79 seasons. The Miami Dolphins went back-to-back in the 1972 and 73 seasons, the San Francisco 49ers in the 1988 and 89 seasons, the Dallas Cowboys in the 1992 and 93 seasons, and the Denver Broncos in the 1997 and 98 seasons. All up, it occurred three times in the 1970s, once in the 1980s, and twice in the 1990s. And now only twice since the turn of the century.

It has become harder to win a Super Bowl in the NFL. The draft and salary cap to a degree keep the process tighter and closer. There is much investment in the coaching, training facilities, and science to maximize the chance of success. Sometimes luck can play a part. A bounce of the ball. A refereeing decision. A draft pick becomes an all-time great.

Mostly, however, it is about the grind. Having the motivation and desire to consistently put in the hard work, improve individually, and as a team, and ultimately win. Winning itself can impact motivation and desire.

Bill Walsh talked about this as the success disease[141]:

"When you reach a large goal or finally get to the top, the distractions and new assumptions can be dizzying. First comes heightened confidence, followed quickly by over confidence, arrogance, and a sense that "we've mastered it; we've figured it out; we're golden". But the gold can tarnish quickly. Mastery requires endless remastery. In fact, I don't believe there is ever true mastery. It is a process, not a destination. That's what few winners realize and explains to some degree why repeating is so difficult. Having triumphed, winners come to believe that the process of mastery is concluded, and they are its proud new owners.

Success disease makes people begin to forgo, to different degrees the effort, focus, discipline, teaching, teamwork, learning, and attention to detail that brought "mastery" and its progeny, success. The hunger is diminished, even removed in some people."

These lessons are somewhat more difficult to assess in business. In professional sport, you literally have hundreds of hours of tape available. Young talent in college play anywhere between one and four years, and then enter the NFL. After completion of the four- or five-year rookie contract, there comes the responsibilities of securing a new contract. Being able to see with your own eyes the strengths and weaknesses of individual athletes and how they have been enhanced or not over the years. The ability to assess their level of production year in year out.

Being elite is a process. Some of your competition, whether internally or externally, have started clocking up their 10,000 hours before turning six years of age. It is too easy to dismiss the Tiger Woods model as a sporting phenomenon only. Children who have found interests that they become passionate about have their mastery clock ticking earlier. It would be arrogant to believe that one can get ahead with less work than others. Interests could be completing puzzles, solving problems, and have a natural affinity with numbers and mathematics. If you can write code before your teenage years, are you better placed than someone who cannot code to test, trial, and invest sweat equity in building a product that you believe addresses a gap in the market? Of course, you are.

It does not need to be limited to mathematics. It could be that a child who loves reading and knocks over hundreds of books more than their peers by their teenage years. Are they better placed to understand communication techniques and be able to apply language to solve business problems? As a general rule of thumb, yes.

Starting early does not guarantee that an individual will become elite, but for those coming into a new sector or profession, the question becomes whether you are willing to outwork people? What is the level of your intrinsic motivation?

For the business more broadly, it is to understand that the 10,000 hours is also about quality. Conscious practice. If the playbook were stock standard, everyone would be doing it. Quality is also about coaching, getting the maximum return for the effort being put in. Do the same thing, get the same result. People need to be provided with tools that help them succeed. Competitive advantage can be gained by shortening the 10,000 hours, not through fewer hours, but through better hours. The elite benchmark is what it is.

"Pro sports – baseball, basketball, football, tennis, golf, whatever, F1, NASCAR – the highest level of anything is difficult and it's so much easier to hunt than be the hunted because the wind blows the fastest at the top of

the mountain, everyone is gunning for you, its human nature right. Everyone's gunning for Bezos. Everyone's gunning for Elon. Everyone's gunning for Mahomes and Brady and Rodgers. You know it's easy to be the up-and-comer; it's kinda easy to be Josh Allen, like he's got nothing to lose, like even last year and obviously this year, you know a little more pressure; it's hard when there's tangible pressure."
– John Middlekauff *Three and Out – Herd* Podcast 9 November 2021

10.3 Team first and the locker room

Leadership guru and author Simon Sinek tells a profound, yet humorous story about his time working with the US Navy Seals. Sinek asked members of the Seals which of their team were selected to progress through to Seal Team 6 – Seal Team 6 being the elite of the elite. Their response was a graph where the y axis vertical line represented performance and the x axis horizontal line represented trust. No-one wanted a team member in the left corner of the graph representing low in performance and low in trust. Naturally the high in performance and high in trust quadrant was the most desirable.

The balance between performance and trust, however, was a preferred trade-off in performance rather than trust. Where high in performance and low in trust represented a toxic leader, and team members preferred a middling performer with higher trust. The throw-away line being, "I may trust you with my life, but do I trust you with my money and my wife?"[142].

Developing trust in the workplace takes time. True leaders

are predictable in action and their situational responses. They consistently represent values, show appreciation and care, take personal responsibility reviewing how things can be improved, and admit mistakes. They are open and honest, solicit feedback, and act on feedback. They self-sacrifice for the greater good.

In team sports, the winners have players who stand up in the biggest moments on the biggest stages. I remain in awe of the final quarter in Super Bowl LVI where Rams quarterback Matthew Stafford constantly targeted eventual MVP and wide receiver Copper Kupp. Having lost wide receiver Odell Beckham Junior before halftime, the Bengals knew what was likely coming in the form of targeting passes towards Kupp, and the open windows were ever so slight. But cometh the hour, cometh the man. It was the elite of the elite icing the game. Kupp would make eight catches for 92 yards in the Super Bowl, collecting two touchdowns in the process.

Successfully climbing the mountain makes it easy to forget the factors that got you there. What secures the opportunity to perform on the biggest stage is the grind. Week in, week out, preseason, and regular season. And it is not just the grind of the individual, rather the grind as a collective – as a team. Everyone has a role to play, sacrificing personal interest for what is in the team's best interest.

Kupp was consistently a high performer throughout the 2021 season. All the time, he was banking trust credits with head coach Sean McVay and quarterback Matthew Stafford. The trust credits came not just from game performances but from putting in the hours of grind with the quarterback in preparation for games. The result of this trust is that when the game was on the line and the Super Bowl ring up for grabs, McVay and Stafford were going to do everything they could to get the ball into a catch window for Kupp.

The Stafford–Kupp relationship expedited trust building in just their first season together. The two ballers who shared a similar passion for football would often have breakfast together throughout the year just chewing each other's ear talking ball and watching tape. With no other coaches or teammates involved, Kupp equated the time spent together as being an additional 500 hours of extra time on the season[143].

Relationship-building takes time. Developing trust takes time.

To engender trust requires open and honest communication. It also means establishing standards and creating an environment where every team member is accountable to those standards.

Mike White was an assistant coach of the San Francisco 49ers during the Bill Walsh years. Reflecting on Walsh's coaching abilities, White refers to Walsh as a problem solver. Walsh could identify the problems, and plan and successfully execute the fixing of those problems. In one such example of the execution, White said of Walsh:

> "For example, he knew that organizations have leaders within, not just one leader, the CEO or head coach, but interior leaders who make possible or prevent what the guy in charge is trying to accomplish. In football, they're called locker-room leaders, and ultimately they play a major role in creating the culture of team – instilling either a positive or negative mindset. Every organization has them: influential people who've got your back – or [are] putting a knife in it.
>
> Bill understood that at one end of the scale there were locker-room leaders who were positive and supportive and at the other end influential players who were very negative. Most important, he understood that all the

guys in the middle could go one way or the other; they were up for grabs."

One of Jim Collins most influential business books is *Good to Great* first published in 2001. The same sentiment White refers to in the example above, Collins uses in his metaphor of driving a bus, meaning a chief executive steering a business in a certain direction. Collins' metaphor references first who, then what, meaning that you get the right people on the bus, the wrong people off the bus, and determining who to put into each seat prior to deciding which direction to take the bus in. This is a pre-requisite for moving companies from good to great, just as the process Bill Walsh used when first becoming the head coach of the 49ers. Sometimes it even means moving on highly skilled team members, if they are not demonstrating a team-first mentality nor buying into the vision the direction the bus is headed.

Nick Saban has been the most successful head coach in college-football history, winning six national championships with the Alabama Crimson Tide (2009, 2011, 2012, 2015, 2017, 2020) and one with the Louisiana State University (LSU) Tigers back in 2003.

Saban's college head coaching career started with the University of Toledo staying just one season before joining Bill Belichick's Cleveland Browns in the NFL as defensive coordinator for four seasons 1991–1994. He then returned to the college system as head coach of Michigan State University for five seasons (1995–1999), followed by a five-season stint with LSU (2000–2004). He was later offered the head coach role at Alabama in 2007 where he has remained ever since.

In a keynote provided to the Coaching Character Initiative in 2012, Saban connects the bus metaphor with creating a team[144]:

Coaching mindset

"... The big part of being on the team is you have to be able to communicate with other people, and you have to work with other people, and you can never have any team chemistry for this reason: mediocre people don't like high achievers, and high achievers don't like mediocre people, so if everybody doesn't buy into the same principles and values of the organization, at the same high standard, you're never going to be successful. Just like our spring practice right now, you know what my goal of spring practice is? Get the right guys on the bus, get them in the right seats, and get the wrong guys off the bus.

So one of these days you're gonna be working in an organization and somebody's gonna try to do that to you, so which one of those people do you wanna be? Do you wanna be somebody they're trying to get off the bus because you're satisfied with mediocre performance? Because you can never have any team chemistry in your organization if everybody is not committed to the same standard and the same things. You know when I worked for Bill Belichick, we had one sign in the building. It was "do your job".

Once you have embedded your standards, and team members are holding themselves and each other accountable to those standards, a key indicator of whether there is broader trust in the operating environment are examples of team members willing to self-sacrifice for the greater good.

Deebo Samuel is a wide receiver for the San Francisco 49ers. Samuel was selected by the 49ers with pick 36 in the 2019 NFL draft. Being a second-round pick, Samuel's rookie contract was for four years (first-round picks have a fifth-year option at the discretion of their franchise). The 2021 season was Samuel's third season in the NFL.

We covered the journey of the 49ers 2021 season in the chapter on grit. The 49ers started the season with a 3–5 win-loss record. Going into week 10 they were up against the 7–2 Los Angeles Rams in a game where a loss could end the 49ers playoff aspirations.

It was this game against the Rams that Samuel was asked to take on more responsibility for the greater good, and in doing so, created a hybrid role later termed by Samuel himself as a "wide-back" – a combination of wide receiver and running back.

In the eight games before the Rams, Samuel had 49 receptions from 81 targets for a total of 882 yards at an average of 18 yards per reception. He also made six rushes for a total of 22 yards at an average of 3.7 yards per rush. In the three games prior to the Rams, Samuel was not called to rush at all in any of those games, which is fair enough as rushing is the dominion of the running back.

All that changed in the must-win clash with the Rams.

In the Rams game, Samuel made five receptions for 97 yards at an average of 19.4. He was down on targets, but the reception and yards were very similar to his production across the first eight games. What changed was that in addition to these receptions, Samuel was called upon to rush five times, almost doubling his rushes in total from the first eight games. He totaled 36 yards at an average of 7.1 yards per rush.

After beating the Rams 31–10, the 49ers continued with this hybrid use of Samuel for the remainder of the season going on to a 5–2 win-loss run, and eventually qualifying for the postseason.

In those last eight games of the regular season, Samuel had 28 receptions for 523 yards at an average of 18.7 yards per reception. And he had 53 rushing attempts for 343 yards at an average of 6.5 yards per rush.

In the first eight games of the season, Samuel had four receiving touchdowns and one rushing touchdown. In the second half of the season, Samuel had two receiving touchdowns and seven rushing touchdowns. (NB. Samuel missed week 13 against the Seattle Seahawks, playing 16 regular season games in total).

The rushing production increased even more in the post-season, where Samuel had 10 rushes against the Dallas Cowboys in the wild-card round, another ten rushes in the snow against the Green Bay Packers in the NFC division playoff, and seven rushes against the Rams in the NFC Championship game.

Samuel was all in. He was happy to modify his role to do whatever it took to maximize his team's chances. No example epitomized his commitment more so than the wild-card round matchup with the Dallas Cowboys. After the Niners secured a turnover, Samuel re-entered the field shouting out to head coach Kyle Shanahan "Hey Kyle, Kyle, let's go" intimating to get Samuel the ball. Samuel continued his encouragement in the preceding huddle telling his teammates, "Let's go put the ball in the box; let's go". Shanahan called the play for Samuel, with Samuel taking the quarterback hand-off thirty yards out from the Cowboys' end zone, running to the right, before cutting back in heavy traffic, and going on to score a touchdown.

Running over to coach Shanahan after the touchdown, Samuel was picked up on field microphones saying, "See I told you. I told you. Let's go."

The rookie-contract system in the NFL has a lot of strengths in providing certainty for franchises investing in talent development. It does have weaknesses though. One of those being the sliding scale of salaries from pick number one through to pick 262. Franchises tend to select based on need to address a gap in their capability, more so than taking the best player available. Teams trade future draft picks without really knowing the value of those picks because finishing position on the ladder determines how high in the selection order a team picks, and that finishing position is unknown when the trade is made. There are differences in talent between draft classes from year to year. A deeply talented draft class puts downward pressure on salaries throughout the draft class, whereby a shallower draft class may mean teams "reach" on talent projections. Either way, the marketplace does not determine pricing over the four-year period of rookie contracts, which can lead to market distortions.

The other weakness is when a player on a rookie contract, in this case Deebo Samuel, turns in an all-star season directly optimizing the output and results of the team, yet attracting a salary at the lower end of those on the 53-man roster. By not tying production and performance to salary across the roster, inequity is created and is a variable that can impact the locker room.

Whether on the playing field or as part of a team in business, it takes a lot of trust to ask a team member to step out of their comfort zone and look after a new responsibility, one which they may not necessarily desire, for the greater good.

To maintain trust, it is important for business leaders to not misuse that commitment by becoming complacent. When things are going well, other issues and the squeaky wheels can distract from looking after those that have demonstrated the team-first mindset.

In Samuel's case, despite the success of carrying the 49ers offense in the second half of the season, contract discussions did not proceed as desired entering into the final season of his contract. This led to Samuel requesting a trade in the lead-up to the 2022 NFL draft.

To the credit of 49ers management, Samuel, and his

representatives, what caused the disenchantment to lead to a request for trade has not been aired publicly.

In this vacuum, it left media and social media to speculate. Just like a business can war game scenarios and strategy development, the same can be done for careers and contract negotiations.

Heading into the final contract year for a second-round rookie, you could understand the personal need to achieve financial security during contract negotiations. Maslow's hierarchy of needs does not change.

Some of the speculation in Samuel's case included whether a dual-use role will result in a shorter shelf-life? The shelf-life for running backs is generally shorter than wide receivers due to the heavy hits taken over time; will dual use result in a shorter shelf life? Or reduce length of the next contract? Or given that wide receivers are generally paid more than running backs in the NFL, will the dual use reduce Samuel's yearly earning capacity? Will the amount of guaranteed money included in the contract enable the player to put financial concerns aside and just focus on being all they can be?

I highlight this scenario only to reinforce the need to take care of key personnel, particularly those that have self-sacrificed for the greater good. When a team member has gone above and beyond and filled a void for the greater good during the previous season, goodwill needs to be reciprocated. Trust and team first need to be mutual.

Eventually, Samuel re-signed with the 49ers on August 1, 2022, which is the first day pads come on at training camp. The contract extension was for three years with a total value of $71.55m including a guaranteed $58.1m and a signing bonus of $24.035m[145]. At a 49ers media conference after training that day, Samuel was asked if his type of usage had been a sticking point leading to his request for trade.

Samuel emphatically responded[146] that this proposition was false saying:

> "... You can turn on the tape, go back to the Cowboys game, it kinda shows what kind of player I am, and also, you can go turn on the pro-bowl tape, and like what I said about being a wide back, I don't mind, you know what I am saying, doing whatever it takes for this team to win."

Adding further evidence to the proposition being inaccurate was Samuel's contract including added incentives for rushing; $650,000 for 380 or more rushing yards per year and $150,000 per year for three or more rushing touchdowns, with incentives capped at a maximum $650,000 per year.

During the second half of the season and through the postseason, Samuel inspired his teammates and elevated the team's performance.

In business, if you need to move a person into a different role to address fallibility elsewhere in the operations, their goodwill cannot be misused by keeping them there longer than negotiated. They will be putting to the side their own career aspirations and potential remuneration and professional standing. Team-first mentality needs to be all-round.

Let us look at two more recent examples of having a team-first mentality particularly as it relates to remuneration in a salary-cap restricted world.

Los Angeles Rams wide receiver Cooper Kupp had an extraordinary 2021 season. Prior to being awarded the MVP in the Rams Super-Bowl victory, Kupp had 145 receptions in the regular season for 1,947 yards at an average of 12.7 yards per reception along with 16 touchdowns becoming the first player since 2005 to take out the receiving triple crown of most receptions, receiving yards, and receiving touchdowns in the season.

Kupp had a further 33 receptions for 478 yards in the postseason averaging 14.5 yards per reception and scoring another six touchdowns.

Since the 2021 season represented the first year of a three-year contract extension for Kupp and he had just led his team to Super-Bowl glory and achieved the best stats for any wide receiver during the year, one might have anticipated that a pay rise was the order of the day. Despite his stellar season, Kupp was not going to hold out to force the issue heading into the new season (to "hold out" means a player refuses to turn up to pre-season training until a new contract is signed).

Andrew Siciliano of NFL Network reported at the time that Kupp had said,

> "I don't think that's the approach that I take. There's a place you want to be. There's a place that I think is fair. I'm not trying to beat anybody. I'm not trying to compare myself to anyone else."

By early June 2022, Kupp had signed an extension for an additional three years taking him through the 2026 season with the Rams. The contract was valued up to $80 million which placed him fourth on the league wide receivers list for average salary per year.

After playing just one game in his rookie season, Patrick Mahomes II became the starting quarterback for the Kansas City Chiefs in the 2018 season. In his first full season, Mahomes led the Chiefs to the AFC Conference Championship where they were beaten by the New England Patriots 31–37.

The following year, in just his third season, Mahomes went

one better, reaching not only Super Bowl LIV, but leading the Chiefs to claim the title defeating the San Francisco 49ers 31–20.

Following Super-Bowl success, and despite still having two years remaining on his rookie contract, the Chiefs and Mahomes signed a ten-year $503m contract extension that included $25m in incentives. The Chiefs returned to the Super Bowl the following season, albeit with a different result, this time going down to the Tampa Bay Buccaneers 31–9.

You will recall that the salary cap dropped to $182.5m for the 2021 NFL season, down from $198.2m the previous year and reflecting the challenging COVID-19 conditions. The salary cap bounced back for the 2022 season placing a limit of $208.2m on team salaries and reflecting better economic conditions as society learned to live with COVID-19. With the lifting of the salary cap, contract benchmarks for NFL's elite players also began to rise.

Heading into the 2022 training camp for the Kansas City Chiefs, star quarterback Patrick Mahomes II was asked about spiraling salaries:

> "It's awesome for, not only the quarterback market, but for just the market of players in general. You want the salary cap to keep going up; you want players keep getting more and more money … When I signed my deal, I knew I was gonna be pretty set for life regardless of what the market kind of happens … Money is one thing, but when you get the Super-Bowl rings at end of your career, I think that's going to be the thing that that you look back upon …"

When asked whether it was important to him to be the top-paid quarterback, Mahomes was firm that it wasn't a priority, explaining: "You always want to get paid, like I said, take care of your family, but I wanna have a great team around me as well and so whatever way that is, I'm gonna make sure I have a great team for me around me the rest of my career."

This mindset is evidence of the team-first mentality and the ability to win over the locker room. Salaries are a balancing act and one player, not even the quarterback, can solely carry a team.

To support this assertion, let us look at the last four years heading into the 2022 season and the top 20 highest earning contracts across each of those seasons.

Quarterbacks represented 18 of the top 20 highest earning contracts in 2018, 16 of the top 20 highest earning contracts in 2019, 17 of the top 20 highest earning contracts in 2020, and 15 of the top 20 highest earning contracts in 2021.

Across those four seasons, Tom Brady was twice the successful quarterback winning Super Bowl LIII with the New England Patriots beating the Los Angeles Rams 13–3 and as the winning quarterback in Super Bowl LV with Tampa Bay Buccaneers beating the Kansas City Chiefs 31–9. The other two were Patrick Mahomes as the Kansas City Chiefs quarterback beating the San Francisco 49ers in Super Bowl LIV 31–20, and Matthew Stafford as quarterback of the Los Angeles Rams beating the Cincinnati Bengals 23–20 in Super Bowl LVI.

In the year the Chiefs won, Kansas City did not have anyone in the top 20 highest contracts (as Mahomes was in the third year of his rookie deal). Despite winning twice across those four seasons, Tom Brady's contract placed eighteenth highest in 2018, fourteenth highest in 2019, sixteenth highest in 2020 and nineteenth highest in 2021.

Across those four seasons, no-one in the top 14 of highest

average annual value contracts ended up with a Super-Bowl ring in that same season. Across those same seasons and contracts list, 12 of those players missed the playoffs altogether in 2018, 13 missed the playoffs in 2019, seven missed the playoffs in 2020, and nine missed the playoffs in 2021.

It is not the purpose of this exercise to get into spit balling which franchises may have overpaid for an asset or to identify production that was short of contract remuneration. Certainly, injuries impeded achievement in several instances.

What the analysis does suggest is that by paying certain players the highest contract values annually, investment capability in other areas is inhibited. The best players like Brady and Mahomes understand this, and once they reach a standard of living that they are comfortable with, it is no longer about vanity metrics of being the highest paid, but rather that the outcome of their services and those of their teams optimizes the number of Super-Bowl rings.

The locker room understands this too. Any relative sacrifice by the best players affords the opportunity to invest in other areas and maximize the production of the collective. And then it becomes a team game. Building upon strengths and addressing weaknesses. As Bill Belichick has often been quoted "It's not about collecting talent; you are building a team."

Of course, the converse is also true. If a franchise invests heavily in star talent and that star talent is either unable to achieve a level of production commensurate with that investment, or unable to lift the production of teammates around them, then the lack of value is magnified, and management will be quick to move away from any ongoing investment.

Highest-paid NFL players ranked by the average annual value of their contracts according to Over the Cap.

2018[147]	2019[148]
1. Aaron Rodgers (QB) Green Bay Packers $33.5m (Missed playoffs)	1. Russell Wilson (QB) Seattle Seahawks $35m (Lost Divisional Round)
2. Matt Ryan (QB) Atlanta Falcons $30m (Missed playoffs)	2. Ben Roethlisberger (QB) Pittsburgh Steelers $34m (Missed playoffs)
3. Kirk Cousins (QB) Minnesota Vikings $28m (Missed playoffs)	3. Aaron Rodgers (QB) Green Bay Packers $33.5m (Lost NFC Conference Championship)
4. Jimmy Garoppolo (QB) San Francisco 49ers $27.5m (Missed playoffs)	4. Jared Goff (QB) Los Angeles Rams $33.5m (Missed playoffs)
5. Matthew Stafford (QB) Detroit Lions $27m (Missed playoffs)	5. Carson Wentz (QB), Philadelphia Eagles $32m (Lost Wild Card Rounds)
6. Derek Carr (QB) Oakland Raiders $25.005m Missed playoffs	6. Matt Ryan (QB) Atlanta Falcons $30m (Missed playoffs)
7. Drew Brees (QB) New Orleans Saints $25m (Lost NFC Conference Championship)	7. Kirk Cousins (QB) Minnesota Vikings $28m (Lost Divisional Round)
8. Andrew Luck (QB) Indianapolis Colts $24.594m (Lost Divisional Round)	8. Jimmy Garoppolo (QB) San Francisco 49ers $27.5m (Lost Super Bowl)
9. Alex Smith (QB) Washington $23.5m (Missed playoffs)	9. Matthew Stafford (QB) Detroit Lions $27m (Missed playoffs)
10. Khalil Mack (OLB) Chicago Bears $23.5m (Lost Wild Card Round)	10. Derek Carr (QB) Oakland Raiders $25m (Missed playoffs)
11. Aaron Donald (DE) Los Angeles Rams $22.5m (Lost Super Bowl)	11. Drew Brees (QB) New Orleans Saints $25m (Lost Wild Card Rounds)
12. Joe Flacco (QB) Baltimore Ravens $22.13m (Lost Wild Card Round)	12. Khalil Mack (OLB) Chicago Bears $23.5m (Missed playoffs)
13. Russell Wilson (QB) Seattle Seahawks $21.9m (Lost Wild Card Round)	13. Alex Smith (QB) Washington $23.5m (Missed playoffs)
14. Ben Roethlisberger (QB) Pittsburgh Steelers $21.85m (Missed playoffs)	14. Tom Brady (QB) New England Patriots $23m (Lost Wild Card Round)
15. Eli Manning (QB) New York Giants $21m (Missed playoffs)	15. Aaron Donald (DE) Los Angeles Rams $22.5m (Missed playoffs)
16. Philip Rivers (QB) Los Angeles Chargers $20,812,500 (Lost Divisional Round)	16. Joe Flacco (QB) Denver Broncos $22,133,333 (Missed playoffs)
17. Cam Newton (QB) Carolina Panthers $20.76m (Missed playoffs)	17. Julio Jones (WR) Atlanta Falcons $22m (Missed playoffs)
18. Tom Brady (QB) New England Patriots $20.5m (Super Bowl Champions)	18. Nick Foles (QB) Jacksonville Jaguars $22m (Missed playoffs)
19. Sam Bradford (QB) Arizona Cardinals $20m (Missed playoffs)	19. Demarcus Lawrence (DE) Dallas Cowboys $21m (Missed playoffs)
20. Ryan Tannehill (QB) Miami Dolphins $19.25m (Missed playoffs)	20. Eli Manning (QB) New York Giants $21m (Missed playoffs)

2020[149]	2021[150]
1. Patrick Mahomes (QB) Kansas City Chiefs $45m (Lost Super Bowl) 2. Russell Wilson (QB) Seattle Seahawks $35m (Lost Wild Card Round) 3. Ben Roethlisberger (QB) Pittsburgh Steelers $34m (Lost Wild Card Round) 4. Aaron Rodgers (QB) Green Bay Packers $33.5m (Lost NFC Conference Championship) 5. Jared Goff (QB) Los Angeles Rams $33.5 (Lost NFC Divisional Round) 6. Kirk Cousins (QB) Minnesota Vikings $33m (Missed playoffs) 7. Carson Wentz (QB) Philadelphia Eagles $32m (Missed playoffs) 8. Dak Prescott (QB) Dallas Cowboys $31.5m (Missed playoffs) 9. Matt Ryan (QB) Atlanta Falcons $30m (Missed playoffs) 10. Ryan Tannehill (QB) Tennessee Titans $29.5m (Lost Wild Card Round) 11. Jacoby Brissett (QB) Indianapolis Colts $27.9m (Lost Wild Card Round) 12. Jimmy Garoppolo (QB) San Francisco 49ers $27.5m (Missed playoffs) 13. Matthew Stafford (QB) Detroit Lions $27m (Missed playoffs) 14. Derek Carr (QB) Oakland Raiders $25m (Missed playoffs) 15. Drew Brees (QB) New Orleans Saints $25m (Lost NFC Divisional Round) 16. Tom Brady (QB) Tampa Bay Buccaneers $25m (Super Bowl Champions) 17. Philip Rivers (QB) Indianapolis Colts $25m (Lost Wild Card Round) 18. Alex Smith (QB) Washington $23.5m (Lost Wild Card Round) 19. Khalil Mack (OLB) Chicago Bears $23.5 (Lost Wild Card Round) 20. Aaron Donald (DE) Los Angeles Rams $22.5 (Lost NFC Divisional Round)	1. Patrick Mahomes (QB) Kansas City Chiefs $45m (Lost AFC Conference Championship) 2. Josh Allen (QB) Buffalo Bills $43m (Lost AFC Divisional Round) 3. Dak Prescott (QB) Dallas Cowboys $40m (Eliminated Lost NFC Wild Card Round) 4. Deshaun Watson (QB) Houston Texans $39m (Missed playoffs) 5. Russell Wilson (QB) Seattle Seahawks $35m (Missed playoffs) 6. Aaron Rodgers (QB) Green Bay Packers $33.5m (Lost NFC Divisional Round) 7. Jared Goff (QB) Detroit Lions $33.5m (Missed playoffs) 8. Kirk Cousins (QB) Minnesota Vikings $33m (Missed playoffs) 9. Carson Wentz (QB) Indianapolis Colts $32m (Missed playoffs) 10. Matt Ryan (QB) Atlanta Falcons $30m (Missed playoffs) 11. Ryan Tannehill (QB) Tennessee Titans $29.5m (Lost NFC Divisional Round) 12. TJ Watt (OLB) Pittsburgh Steelers $28.003m (Lost AFC Wild-card Round) 13. Jimmy Garoppolo (QB) San Francisco 49ers $27.5m (Lost NFC Conference Championship) 14. DeAndre Hopkins (WR) Arizona Cardinals $27.25m (Lost NFC Wild-card Round) 15. Matthew Stafford (QB) Los Angeles Rams $27m (Super Bowl Champions) 16. Joey Bosa (DE) Los Angeles Chargers $27m (Missed playoffs) 17. Derek Carr (QB) Las Vegas Raiders $25.005m (Lost AFC Wild Card Round) 18. Myles Garrett (DE) Cleveland Browns $25m (Missed playoffs) 19. Tom Brady (QB) Tampa Bay Buccaneers $25m (Lost NFC Divisional Round) 20. Khalil Mack (OLB) Chicago Bears $23.5 (Missed playoffs)

Source: Over the Cap

I do not wish to overplay the need for key-position holders to sacrifice remuneration for the benefit of the team in order to have success. The truism is that businesses need to balance capacity to pay in any hiring or retention decisions. In salary-cap leagues, this investment capacity is noticeably clear cut, even allowing for the capability to borrow from the future to pay for today. For businesses, capacity is somewhat blurrier as capability to invest can be found through other mechanisms, such as budgeted for increased revenues to pay for any increased investment, capital raising, or debt borrowings to free up liquidity to invest in additional salaries.

For players, winning supports both the team brand and the brand of individuals which then presents other opportunities. So, while a lower salary may be accepted, additional income may be found elsewhere. Taking a higher salary accompanied by poor team outcomes such as regularly failing to qualify for the postseason will inhibit the ability to attract endorsements and additional income from off-field business opportunities.

Forbes publishes an annual list of highest-paid athletes incorporating off field earnings in addition to on-field earnings. For 2022, the highest-earning NFL player was Tom Brady with his off-field earnings of $52m dwarfing his on-field earnings of $31.9m for a total of $83.9m.

Winning in business also opens up other opportunities. It may be new customers or investors are attracted to your brand and market position. For individual team members, it may be new opportunities within the business or outside the business. Whichever is the case, the pre-requisite is a team-first mentality.

One final comment on team first and the locker room. Inclusivity is a pre-requisite to team first and ultimately success. It means to be accepting of differences and coming together united in the same cause. It does not mean decision-making by committee or consensus. It does mean everyone has a role to play for the team to achieve its full potential.

Professional sport, arguably more than any other business, requires unity and inclusivity. Not even in basketball, where there are only five players on court at any one time, can one single player carry the entire team to victory. There may be pockets of six minutes where an individual player dominates, but whether it is in offense or defense, everyone needs to contribute consistently within the role that has been designed for them to complement the rest of the team. The NBA has super teams where two or three elite players come together to maximize the chance of winning the season, but even then, the supporting cast is important to achieve that objective.

John Lynch is the current general manager for the San Francisco 49ers joining the franchise in 2017. Lynch had a 15-year NFL playing career from 1993–2007. His first eleven seasons were spent with the Tampa Bay Buccaneers collecting a Super-Bowl ring in Super Bowl XXXVII, followed by four years with the Denver Broncos. Over those years Lynch made nine Pro-Bowl appearances and was selected first-team All Pro for three consecutive years 1999 to 2001.

In 2021, Lynch was enshrined into the NFL Hall of Fame. The concluding remarks[151] of his enshrinement speech encapsulates the importance of inclusivity in team sports as a pre-requisite for success:

> "Before concluding, I want to state the National Football League is the greatest metaphor for life that I've ever known. It challenges each and every one of us who plays this great game in every way possible. Everything about the game is hard and tests your will. It compels every man who puts on a uniform to not only do their best but to be their best.

In football, we quickly discover that we're only as strong as our weakest link, and if we're to achieve the goals that we set for ourselves, we must all learn to play together and pull together.

Each of us comes from a different walk of life, but when we huddle up, we huddle up as a team. It doesn't matter where we come from or your background. All that matters is the fulfillment of one goal: victory.

Tonight, I advocate that we take the lead of football and huddle up as a people, as a great nation. Let's find the common ground through our shared values. Let's celebrate and learn from our differences. Derrick Brooks from Pensacola, Florida; Warren Sapp from Apopka, Florida; and John Lynch from Solana Beach, California, have. So, too, can all of you."

11. Customer experience, go-to-market and your distribution platform

The rise of the platform business

BACK IN 2014, I HAD the opportunity to host an event in Australia where Randi Zuckerberg presented on the top ten technological trends that were empowering entrepreneurs. Zuckerberg espoused a future where every person is a media company.

Instinctively, this position was consistent with what one might anticipate, after all Zuckerberg had been one of the first employees at Facebook before going on to establish her own media company. At the time of 2014, Facebook was into its tenth year and had zoomed past one billion active monthly users.

Reflecting on the years that have passed since 2014, however, Zuckerberg's proposition happened far more rapidly than I anticipated, was more encompassing, and to such as degree that the lines between professional and social networks converged. Personal brands moved out of the shadows of corporate brands with the prevalence of platforms such YouTube, Twitter, LinkedIn, TikTok and Instagram providing individuals with instant access to new audiences across the world.

Platform technologies have been the go-to model for investors: build once and sell multiple, maximizing return on investment. There were three main commercialization models: shopping cart with mark-up on sales; subscription-based cloud services; or if a platform was freely available to consumers, then the users were the product, and rapid scaling for the business meant demonstrating exponential growth in active users on the platform in order to be more and more attractive to investors and to advertisers.

In 2015, Tom Goodwin who was senior vice president of strategy and innovation at Havas at the time, coined a catchphrase that went viral on social media and captured the essence of the power of platform technologies:

> "Uber, the world's largest taxi company, owns no vehicles. Facebook, the world's most popular media owner, creates no content. Alibaba, the most valuable retailer, has no inventory. And Airbnb, the world's largest accommodation provider, owns no real estate.[152]

There have been many variants since Goodwin's catchphrase; the essence, however, is the same: low overheads, low infrastructure costs, cross border software solutions, friction removed from supply chains, underutilized assets monetized and democratized, global markets, enhanced transparency around pricing, and digital ranking systems of participants.

Goodwin was making the case that the largest profitability up for grabs was found at the customer interface: the layer between those with the supply and who were holding the bulk of costs and the market being where the money was.

In my mind, Amazon and Google were the first of these platform businesses. Amazon founded by Jeff Bezos in 1994 and operationalized as an online bookstore from

1995. Google founded September 4, 1998, in Menlo Park California by Larry Page and Sergey Brin. That is not to say there were not others, rather that Amazon and Google clearly won their markets, securing early adopters, building out their core product from which other innovations were organically developed or acquired in.

Successful platforms that followed Amazon and Google are Facebook founded in 2004, YouTube founded in 2005, Twitter founded in 2006, Airbnb founded in 2008, Uber founded in 2009, Instagram founded in 2010, Snapchat in 2011 (upon the relaunch of Picaboo as Snapchat), and TikTok in 2016. All these platform technologies were enabling the future where every person was a media company.

Rockstar platform businesses were also being established outside of the United States such as Spotify out of Sweden in 2006 for audio streaming and Shopify out of Canada also in 2006 for e-commerce and enabling online retailing.

The 2000s were the diffusion and inflection point on the market S curve for platform technologies. As the market matured with more and more entrants, further competition was created by traditional businesses digitally transforming in order to compete at the customer interface layer whether that was business to consumer or business to business.

Microsoft was founded in 1976 as an enterprise software business and started shifting to cloud and mobile first during the 2000s. Apple has become synonymous with innovative and market leading new hardware. Apple started the transformation to a platform business with the introduction of the iTunes store in 2003 and the App Store in 2008.

An influential example of a traditional business making the digital shift is Netflix. Founded in 1997 by Reed Hastings and Marc Randolph in Scotts Valley California, Netflix opened as a DVD rental business minus the traditional shop fronts. Supply of customer orders was via mail with DVDs arriving and being returned via post. Twelve months later and Netflix.com was established as an online presence for the renting of these DVD movies. Rapidly evolving, the next 12 months saw a membership-subscription service launched, followed by a recommendation system based on member ratings 12 months after that.

Streaming becomes the gamechanger

The game changer for Netflix was the move to streaming in 2007, followed by streaming onto mobile devices from 2010. Netflix expanded into Australia in 2015, with 12.2 million people in Australia having access to a Netflix subscription as of 2020. I remember the early days of Netflix in Australia not being seamless, with buffering not just occurring at the beginning of the program, but also would interrupt the program during the stream. It was not a lot, but it did occur regularly and affected the customer experience. Today buffering interruptions have been eliminated.

As one would expect, as platform technologies matured and optimized market share in their relevant areas, new opportunities needed to be found for business growth. For some businesses, this meant extending past just the customer interface layer and into content production.

Netflix start original programming in 2013[153] with programs such as *Hemlock Grove, Arrested Development, Orange is the New Black* and *House of Cards*, which becomes the first internet-streamed service program to win three Primetime Emmy Awards.

In 2016, YouTube trekked a similar path creating a new division called YouTube Originals. *Cobra Kai* was one of YouTube's first successes, a spin-off series from the Karate Kid movies. Two seasons of *Cobra Kai* were streamed on YouTube

Originals before exclusive rights were transferred to Netflix. Original content production lasted six years as a product at YouTube, before YouTube Originals was discontinued at the beginning of 2022 to focus on enabling content creators.

With streaming technologies maturing and greater customer acceptance of streaming as a method of content delivery, traditional businesses started to pivot to ensure their own reinvigoration. The big one was Disney.

Disney has been active in the acquisitions market over the last thirty years. Some of the more notable content-producing assets included acquiring Pixar from Steve Jobs in 2006, Marvel in 2009, Lucas Films and the Star Wars assets in 2012, and 21st Century Fox in 2019. Initially it looked like Disney had reached mass of such scale that continued business growth had required its broadening out to become an ecosystem play – one where multiple brands and audiences would co-exist rather than Disney continuing to organically grow new stories of its current stable of characters and introducing new characters overtime.

In 2012, Disney and Netflix entered into a licensing agreement which started with a collection of Disney classics, and from 2016 broadening into access for new movies from Disney, Pixar, and Marvel, at the same time as they were made available to other pay television networks. The Netflix streaming rights were all encompassing across online, mobile, tablet, internet-connected televisions, gaming consoles, and other streaming boxes.

By the time this licensing agreement was due to expire at the end of 2018, Disney had announced its own plans to establish a streaming service.

This really would not have come as a surprise to anyone. As platform businesses moved into content production, traditional content producers would need to constantly review

Customer experience, go-to-market and your distribution platform

their broadcast and distribution channels to ensure optimal business outcomes.

Bob Iger succeeded Michael Eisner as chief executive officer of the Walt Disney Company in 2005. In assuming the CEO role, Iger went about executing on three strategic priorities: firstly, investing available capital into high-quality branded content; secondly, embracing technology as an opportunity for its own potential; and thirdly, going global in a much more focused way[154].

Disney went about doubling down on technology as an enabler for more than a decade. Their technology acquisitions were not just limited to studios for animations and computer-generated imagery (CGI) in support of the high-quality branded content priority.

It also included acquiring video game developer Avalanche Software in 2006, securing a 30 percent stake in Hulu TV in 2009, the acquisition of online social network game developer Playdom in 2010, the acquisition of UTV Software Communications in 2011 (that had both broadcasting as a core capability along with content production), and in 2016 buying a 33 percent stake in BamTech with an option to buy a controlling stake in 2020.

BamTech grew out of Major League Baseball Advanced Media, spinning out as its own streaming division in 2015[155].

Determining go-to-market strategy

As a business strategy, taking minority stakes in technology partners gives a corporate investor a unique look under the hood to best understand enabling potential. Coupled with Disney experimenting on building its own streaming platform, they were well placed to make an informed decision on go-to-market strategy.

In 2017, Disney acquired a further 42 percent stake of

BamTech becoming the majority owner. By 2019, Disney had taken a majority stake of Hulu.

Disney+ was launched in 2019 built on the BamTech technology and announcing Disney as a platform business, while also promoting Disney's ecosystem. Open the Disney+ app on your smart tv and your header menu options include Disney, Pixar, Marvel, and Star Wars. Each of these header menu options takes you into the specific Disney, Pixar, Marvel, or Star Wars universe.

From a standing start in November 2019, Disney+ subscriptions have soared. True to the Iger strategic priority, it is a case of quality over quantity. While Disney+ has a much smaller library than Netflix or Amazon, Disney Plus subscriptions increased by 36.1m to a total of 151.2m as of July 2, 2022, up from 116m twelve months earlier[156].

Netflix, on the other hand, experienced its first decline in membership subscriptions during the first quarter of the 2022 financial year. The total number lost was just over 200,000 globally from a base of 221.85m. It was, however, the first quarterly decline in Netflix's ten-year history and was accompanied by an immediate 35 percent fall in the share price that day and losing over $50b in market capitalization.

Rather than being a one-off, the very next quarter also saw an additional reduction of almost one million memberships. Competition, household sharing, and uncertainty of how COVID-19 restrictions previously expedited streaming uptake were identified as the key contributing factors[157]. The household sharing factor is a critical one. The model originally implemented minimized any friction for new-user adoption – exactly what all businesses should be aiming to do with any new product or service. Once a market becomes saturated however, evolving the monetization of household sharing can ignite new revenues for Netflix. Conversely, if the price elasticity of demand is misunderstood, tinkering with the monetization model may challenge customer loyalty.

Technology, platforms, and ecosystem lessons from pro sports

What business lessons can be learned from professional sport when it comes to technology, platforms, and ecosystems?

Technology has been embraced at all levels within professional sport. Firstly, for developing team tactics by analyzing data trends. That is, analyzing data to identify an individuals' strengths and weakness, and designing plays and match-day tactics that amplify opportunities to take advantage of a team member's strengths, while minimizing opportunities to have their weaknesses exposed. The same analysis occurs at a team level whereby the management may seek to understand the percentages for success of a specific play under a specific set of circumstances. Strength and conditioning analysis seek to understand when a player requires rest to perform at their optimum. Advances in safety equipment can be optimized to best protect against injury.

The area where technology has had the biggest impact, however, has been in broadcasting. For better or for worse, microphones on the field, microphones on the referees, and cameras and microphones in the change rooms bring the viewing audience as close as possible to the action as and when it happens.

For this question, however, I want to dive into professional sport as a business taking a helicopter view of the customer experience, go-to-market strategies, and technologies used as distribution channels.

It is no coincidence that the sport at the top of the tree, namely the NFL, does these three areas the best. How is it possible that the sport with the fewest weeks in the regular season competition (32 teams, playing 17 games each over 18 weeks) creates the most value?

The first ingredient is clarity on who the primary customer is. For the NFL, it would be easy to say the primary customer is the fan. However, it is not. The primary customer for the NFL is the broadcast partners.

It would be easy to say that the primary customer for broadcast partners is the fan. However, it is not. The primary customer for the broadcast partners is advertisers. This is akin to the business model for some technology-platform businesses where consumers get free access to the platform, and advertisers pay to be able to access targeted markets at scale via the platform.

The principal attraction of sport as entertainment is the ability for a viewing audience to watch the play unfold live. When that capability is optimized, the league gains the multiplier effect of engagement with the sports-gambling market. The sports-gambling market is only attractive to a viewing audience of live sport. No-one is going to watch a game on reply or a game on delay if they have wagered on the outcome. Results and contest outcomes must be available instantaneously.

Attendance at stadiums on game day and wagering aspects aside, live sports provide an opportunity for satellite events to run concurrently, whether that is a social in-home function with family and friends or public social settings such as bars and clubs.

Discrete productization enables the NFL's success

The NFL media rights are very lucrative and characterized by the absence of exclusivity, not something that is easily achievable. In a similar manner to the topic of being 'all in' for franchises in chapter eight, exclusivity in business arrangements commonly assures both the product/service owner and their contracted service provider have a shared interest in maximizing success.

The NFL have been able to thread the needle on exclusivity through the segregation of games to create distinct separate products based on geography and game-day allocations. The regular season has historically been separated into four products[158]:

- AFC games on a Sunday afternoon – a media partnership with CBS dating back to 1998.
- NFC games on a Sunday afternoon – a media partnership with FOX that dates back to 1994.
- Sunday Night Football – a media partnership with NBC that dates to 2006[159].
- Monday Night Football – a media partnership with ESPN.

Each of these traditional media businesses responded to the threat of streaming companies by broadening into this new technology market themselves: CBS has streaming capability through Paramount+ owned by its parent company, ESPN has streaming capability through ESPN+, NBC has its own has streaming capability through Peacock TV owned by its parent company, and Fox has its own has streaming capability through Tubi. Tubi was acquired by Fox in 2020, funded by divesting its five percent stake in another streaming service Roku[160].

Threading the needle on exclusivity has not always been the case for the NFL and indeed became trickier with the establishment of NFL Network in 2003. Owned entirely by the National Football League, NFL Network was a 24-hour seven day a week media company dedicated to covering news and analysis, celebrating all things NFL. It launched with an agreement in place with DirecTV providing access to 11.4m homes in the US and intended to branch into agreements with cable operators going forward[161]. In 2006, this extended to broadcasting games with the advent of another discrete NFL product – Thursday Night Football.

Thursday Night Football initially launched as an eight-game stretch of regular season games in 2006 and was broadcast exclusively on NFL Network. It grew to thirteen games and remained exclusively on NFL Network through to the 2013 season.

For the 2014 and 2015 seasons, Thursday Night Football was expanded to the full 16 regular game season and broadcast on CBS along with NFL Network. Then, for the 2016 and 2017 seasons, a streaming component was introduced. CBS and NBC split the rights to Thursday Night Football for these two seasons while also remaining on NFL Network. Games were streamed on Twitter in 2016 and Amazon in 2017.

Fox secured a five-year agreement from 2018–2023 for Thursday Night Football superseding the CBS/NBC deal, however, the requirement for games to also be available on NFL Network remained, as well as streaming on Amazon.

When the new media agreement was up for negotiation, Amazon was awarded exclusive access to Thursday Night Football although those games would still be broadcast on free over the air television in participating teams broadcast markets. Fox relinquished the final year of their five-year agreement with Thursday Night Football transitioning to Amazon one year early.

Maximizing coverage and revenues, the NFL has adopted what they term a "tri-cast" model on media rights, treating free-over air television, cable and digital/streaming as separate distribution channels. Digital and streaming is often referred to as Over-The-Top (OTT) media services which means direct

Customer experience, go-to-market and your distribution platform

to consumer via the internet and bypassing cable, broadcast, and satellite television channels.

The NFL has used multiple partners and strategies to develop international audiences for games over the years. An agreement with Sky Sports in the UK has been in place since 1995[162]. In 2017, the NFL partnered with Over Tier to stream games into 61 countries across Europe. This was expanded to 181 countries in 2019 to include Australia, Brazil, Japan, Mexico, and India[163].

The NFL's platform play came in 2022 with the launch NFL+[164] – the NFL's own exclusive subscription-based streaming service. In the US, NFL+ replaced NFL Game Pass. NFL+ subscribers have access to local and primetime games on mobile and tablet devices. For those outside the US, subscribers have access to all games live. The NFL+ app sits on your phone or tablet right next to the Disney+, Netflix, Amazon, and Apple apps. Outside the US, it also enables games to be viewed on smart televisions for home-theatre viewing. In the US, it is mobile and tablet devices only.

Now many would dispute that NFL+ is a platform technology. The common understanding of a platform being the foundational technology upon which other businesses are built or enabled – either through access to data via APIs (Application Programming Interface) that integrate with third-party products and services, or access to the foundation technology code base so that others can add value by building on top of the foundations. In the NFL+ case Apple's iOS operating system and the Android operating systems would be considered the platform technologies that have enable the build of NFL+ so that it can be housed across a variety of different hardware and streamed to mobile users anywhere.

The NFL does have a developer portal, however, access is limited only to NFL partners and clients.

Why do I contend NFL+ is a platform technology? Because it is a product that enables an ecosystem of other businesses that deliver digital products and services. Namely, that future where every person is a media company. Data exchange may not be integrated and automated, however, in a digital world, the data exchange occurs 24 hours a day, seven days a week, 365 days of the year. We will look at how after considering the macro context.

In March 2021, the NFL concluded its new media distribution rights agreement. The agreement was for an 11-year period 2023 through 2033[165]. While the total value was not officially announced by the NFL, it was widely reported across the *New York Times*, *Forbes* and CBS that the total value exceeded $100b and represented a significant increase on the previous agreements.

The tri-cast model of free-to-air television, cable, and streaming continues with Amazon locked in for Thursday Night Football and streaming over the agreement duration. Super Bowls are shared across CBS (2023, 2027, 2031), FOX (2024, 2028, 2032), NBC (2025, 2029, 2033), and ESPN/ABC (2026, 2030). The new agreement also locked in utilizing the streaming capabilities of all their partners via Amazon, Paramount+, Fox digital platforms, Peacock, and ESPN+.

In a challenging economic climate, the NFL had a strong negotiating position being able to point to NFL games being 24 of the top 25 and 77 of the top 100 most watched television programs in the past five years.

The US broadcast television ratings season are conducted over September through May period each year. For the 2020–2021 ratings season[166], NFL games registered as the top eight most watched individual shows, headed by Super Bowl LV between the Tampa Bay Buccaneers and the Kansas City Chiefs. Almost 93 million viewers tuned in to CBS to witness the Buccaneers winning 31–9. The second largest audience was also on CBS with an audience of 42.5m tuning into the AFC Championship game between Kansas City and the Buffalo Bills.

In the following ratings season 2021–2022, the NFL continued to dominate, taking out three of the top four viewing audiences of original television programs with three or more episodes. The highest rating program was NFL Sunday Night Football on NBC, followed by NFL Thursday Night Football on Fox and NFL Network. Third place was *Yellowstone* on Paramount Network, followed by NFL Monday Night Football on ESPN.

Of the twenty most watched networks in 2021–22, the top six were CBS (owned by National Amusements Inc.), NBC (owned by Comcast Corporation), Fox Broadcasting (owned by Fox Corporation), ABC (owned by Walt Disney), Fox News Channel (owned by Fox Corporation), and ESPN (owned by Walt Disney Company). All six have an interest in seeing the NFL succeed.

In threading the needle on exclusivity, the NFL has been able to achieve the involvement of the all the major media brands in the United States.

There are two key words for any business leader to remember, and they are capacity and capability. They apply at a micro-level for an individual business, and at the macro level for an economy-wide view. Capacity is holding, or having the ability to acquire, the necessary size, infrastructure, and resources to deliver any new product or service. Capability means the competence to deliver that product and service at the scale and quality expected.

The NFL's media partners are the best of the best, all holding the capacity and capability to ensure that the NFL product pushed out into the marketplace is the best of the best.

The size of the investments in NFL product by media partners is of such quantum, they too need to be fully committed to ensure the product is of the highest quality in order to capture a suitable return on their investment.

The quid pro quo for the NFL is that they have a mutual obligation to best support their media partners. One way they achieve this is through the segmentation of the product into Thursday Night Football, Sunday Night Football, and AFC and NFC on Sundays meaning that their media partners do not directly compete against each other in a specific product category.

The main way, however, is that the NFL has packaged the delivery of any game in a manner designed to maximize opportunities for media partners. There is one hour of game time in football scheduled over four quarters of 15 minutes each. The game clock stops when each play ends, except for the last two minutes of each half where the game clock will continue if the ball is downed in the field of play (although it stops if the offensive player takes the ball out of the field of play).

Despite just one hour of play, a broadcast generally extends over three and a quarter hours per game not including any pre or post games shows also scheduled by the broadcasting network.

In the first quarter, a viewer will see on average six breaks of two minutes each allowing a broadcaster to play four 30-second advertisements. The breaks will occur when there is a changeover between the offensive and defensive after a touchdown, a field goal, or the offensive team punts. Hence it is possible to get two quick commercial breaks together even if there has only been two minutes of playing time.

Another two-minute changeover at the completion of the first quarter. Rinse and repeat. A 13-minute halftime break allows for broadcaster analysis and additional series of commercial breaks[167]. Again, rinse and repeat for the second half. The broadcast time is extended if a game is tied at the end of regulation time.

This pattern is just for regular season games. The Super Bowl grand finale extends much longer.

The NFL's commitment to broadcast partners is entrenched into the rule book

The television broadcast partnerships are so important to the NFL that broadcast requirements are documented in the NFL Rulebook. For example, Section 5 on Timeouts:

> Item 2. Length of Timeouts. Charged team timeouts shall be two minutes in length, unless the timeout is not used by television for a commercial break. Timeouts shall be 30 seconds in length when the designated number of television commercials have been exhausted in a quarter, if it is a second charged team timeout in the same dead-ball period, or when the Referee so indicates game stoppages.

An example to optimize the viewing experience and maintain brand standards is contained in Section 4 on Equipment, Uniforms, and Player Appearance:

> ARTICLE 1. GENERAL POLICY. Throughout the game-day period while in view of the stadium and television audience, including during team pregame warm-ups, all players must dress in a professional manner under the uniform standards.

An example to protect NFL partners from competing interests is also contained in Section 4:

ARTICLE 7. LOGOS AND COMMERCIAL IDENTIFICATION. Throughout the period on game-day that a player is visible to the stadium and television audience (including in pregame warm-ups, in the bench area, and during postgame interviews in the locker room or on the field), players are prohibited from wearing, displaying, or orally promoting equipment, apparel, or other items that carry commercial names or logos/identifications of companies, unless such commercial identification has been approved in advance by the League office. The size of any approved logo or other commercial identification involved in an agreement between a manufacturer and the League will be modest and unobtrusive, and there is no assurance that it will be visible to the television audience.

You can start to see the lengths the NFL has gone to in order that maximum value is generated for the game and its media partners. NFL football is a product made for broadcast television and streaming.

At a fundamental level CBS, NBC, Fox, ESPN, and Amazon are not competitors in the NFL marketplace. Each has a separate NFL product to nurture. That said, when advertising revenue is the focus for each, they do compete in a more important market which is access and long-term relationships with businesses needing to promote their products and services to relevant demographics. Investment by a business with one network may or may not be replicated with other networks.

Partner ecosystems afford the NFL a multiplier effect

Each of the NFL's media partners build their own ecosystems around the NFL product to gain more eyeballs and enhanced customer loyalty, which in turn allows maximum value in securing their own commercial partnerships and advertisers.

Let us look at some examples of the ecosystems being fostered by some of these networks.

As the broadcaster of Monday Night Football, ESPN programs more than eight hours of football content each Monday during the season including *NFL Rewind*, *NFL Live*, and *Monday Night Countdown* before the scheduled game of Monday Night Football. Following the game, *SportsCenter* recaps the action from the game.

SportsCenter holds down multiple places in daily programming utilizing a variety of regular anchors as hosts and covers all the major sports, latest games, and results. *NFL Live* is programmed five days a week.

For the past two seasons, ESPN2 have hosted a second broadcast of Monday Night Football for 10 weeks of the season featuring Peyton and Eli Manning as hosts. The format replicates any mancave or sports bar informal chat environment between friends while watching a broadcast – only the analysis is led by Hall of Famer Peyton, and his future Hall of Famer brother Eli who collectively hold four Super-Bowl rings with guests dialing in to contribute.

Outside of Mondays, ESPN also has substantial football coverage on Sundays with *Sunday NFL Countdown* programed for three hours in the lead-up to Sunday games. Simultaneously on ESPN2 is *Fantasy Football Now* also airing for three hours. On Sunday evenings is *NFL Primetime* broadcast on ESPN+ recapping highlights from the day's games and providing analysis.

In the lead-up to Sunday games is *NFL Matchup* on Saturday mornings previewing upcoming games. There is a staple of daily (Monday to Friday) sport shows such as *Get Up, First Take* and *Around the Horn* which cover all the major sports. During the football season, there is strong coverage of the NFL.

There is also a plentitude of daily talk shows dedicated to football and hosted by former NFL players on the ESPN Radio Network.

ESPN Fantasy is a platform across the web and mobile app conducting fantasy leagues for multiple sports; the largest, however, is the NFL with 11 million participants[168] and over 17 million teams for the 2022 NFL season.

Fantasy sports leagues as a marketplace is not insignificant. The NFL provides a platform itself via NFL.com. Others competing with ESPN include CBS Sports, DraftKings, FanDuel, Sleeper, and Underdog Fantasy.

Fantasy leagues place participants at the heart of being a general manager in their preferred league. Selecting players before the season, making roster moves for upcoming games due to injuries or specific players being on a bye week, and making in-season trades. Fantasy players need to be passionate and committed. It is very frustrating to post a low weekly total because you were not paying attention and had two players on the active fantasy roster who were on bye weeks. It is a great audience engagement tool, bringing players back to the platform each week.

The ESPN.com website is a treasure trove of sports data. For the NFL, it includes historical statistics for the performance of every franchise by season, and similarly for every player. ESPN.com has been used as the source for much NFL-player data referenced in this book. It also has an excellent draft cast that provides live updates of the annual NFL draft. As the draft progresses and players are selected, the filter capability allows users to identify which players remain available and engage in conversations on social media and chat groups about which players they hope their team selects with their next pick.

Customer experience, go-to-market and your distribution platform

Conglomerates such as Disney hold powerful abilities to amplify messages across their stable of companies. Disney's first amusement park, Walt Disneyland, was opened in Anaheim California in 1955. Today, there are 27 such amusement parks across the globe.

In the week leading up to Super Bowl LVI (2022) being hosted at Sofi Stadium in Inglewood California, ESPN's NFL Live was moved from the regular studio and broadcast from Disney California Adventure Park at the Disneyland Resort in Anaheim, California. NFL content brought the eyeballs, and the California Adventure Park was quite the backdrop with brilliant sunshine. You could not imagine better advertising for Disney or the theme and amusement park stable.

It does not end there when watching ESPN. I have often witnessed others in the Disney stable advertising during commercial breaks such as the Disney cruise ship experience.

Naturally while these are separate companies in the Disney stable and need to be independently financially profitable, it is quite the way to amplify brand and product to targeted demographics.

Hence CBS, NBC, Fox, ESPN, and Amazon have all built and maintain their own ecosystems to nurture the NFL product.

Multi-channel distribution strategies to amplify reach and satisfy customers by their preferred means

I will refrain from providing an equivalent high-level overview of each in comparison to the ESPN ecosystem, but I do want to share an example from Fox before highlighting the broader ecosystem. I have been a regular listener to Colin Cowherd's *The Herd* even though I am based in Sydney Australia. *The Herd* with Colin Cowherd is a three-hour program broadcast live in studio each weekday on cable television via FS1 (Fox

Sports 1) and simultaneously via Fox Sports Radio and the iHeartRadio station.

I cannot access the cable television station FS1 from Australia, and the 2am start time during the Australian winter months (or 5am during the summer months) is not really an attractive proposition for tuning in live on Fox Sports Radio or the iHeartRadio app. The show, however, is edited efficiently and drops on Apple Podcasts around 6am each morning during winter months which is perfect for the morning commute. It's a little less attractive dropping at 9am in the Australian summer months, but nonetheless, very timely to stay abreast of current news and not feeling that you are catching up on information that is stale in today's 24-hour news cycle. *The Herd* covers NFL, NBA, and MLB as well as college football and a little dropped in on international topics of interest such as the Summer Olympics and the Soccer World Cup.

Television viewership for *The Herd* has reached an episode high of 290,000 viewers[169], while each show is radio simulcast across more than 250 stations. Highlights are posted to the Fox Sports website, a dedicated *The Herd* YouTube channel, Facebook page and to Twitter, amplifying key pieces of content. Colin Cowherd has 1.6 million followers on Twitter, *The Herd*'s Twitter account has 433,000 followers, Cowherd's Facebook page has 466,000 followers, *The Herd*'s Facebook page has 1.6m followers, while the YouTube channel has 1.1m subscribers. In 2019, *The Herd* attracted in excess of 70 million total listens across all platforms[170].

To borrow from Cowherd's introduction each morning welcoming his listeners, "wherever you may be, however you may be listening". This is one of the lessons from professional sports applicable to any business, and that is deploying relevant content via a multi-channel strategy so that your core demographics can consume via their preferred means, when and how they desire.

One of Cowherds stablemates at Fox Sports Radio is Dan Patrick with *The Dan Patrick Show*. Patrick is the three-hour radio show directly preceding *The Herd*, also simulcast on the iheart radio. Back in 2020 each show was live streamed on YouTube, however, has since moved over to Peacock TV with popular interviews and segments posted to the dedicated YouTube channel. *The Dan Patrick Show* has over 450,000 followers on Twitter and 211,000 on Facebook.

Rich Eisen started as a 26-year-old television sportscaster with ESPN, spending seven years there (1996–2003) before being the first on-air talent signed to join the NFL Network in 2003. Eisen hosts *NFL GameDay Morning* during the football season, and anchors NFL specials such as the *NFL Draft* and *NFL Scouting Combine*.

Over the last decade, there has been a trend towards consolidation across global media organizations integrating television, streaming, and other digital offerings with traditional print (now paywall protected newspapers). Talent is shared across platforms. There is also scope for talent to maintain their own brands delivering their own products.

Eisen, for example, hosts and broadcasts the three-hour *Rich Eisen Show* every weekday. It has previously been live-streamed on YouTube, however, currently streams on the Roku Channel. The Roku channel is free on all Roku devices (Samsung Smart TVs, Amazon Fire TV and the Roku app), while *The Rich Eisen Show* is simulcast on SiriusXM which is to radio broadcasting what Spotify is to music streaming. It is also syndicated on 50 stations on the terrestrial radio network and later posted on the cumulus podcast network. *The Rich Eisen Show* has 525,000 subscribers on YouTube, 117,000 followers on Facebook, and 120,000 followers on

Twitter, while Eisen himself has 1.3m followers on Twitter.

The motivation of contrasting Cowherd, Patrick, and Eisen is to reiterate the need for a multi-channel approach towards servicing target markets, while highlighting the diversity of their distribution platforms to achieve their multi-channel strategy. Their distributions channels overlap in some areas and are totally different in others. The content is pushed out both in video format and also solely in audio format. Their shows are broadcast live each week and made available as play on demand shortly thereafter. Interesting interviews and segments are cut and recut, pushed out on social-media channels such as YouTube and Twitter, all for the purpose of drawing interest into the full show. All three are making their content available to their target markets to consume how and when they wish to consume.

Live-streaming capability is available across all social media such as Instagram, Facebook, and LinkedIn. Twitter Spaces and Clubhouse provide audio-based chat rooms. YouTube, however, was first to market and has set the pace for monetization that others aspire to. There are a range of monetization strategies that YouTube makes available to content creators through their Partner Program. Monetizing a channel through ads doesn't require being a participant in the YouTube Partner Program, however, content does need to meet advertiser-friendly guidelines.

There are minimum thresholds to participate in the YouTube Partner Program. Upon acceptance, additional ways to generate revenue include channel memberships, YouTube Premium revenue, attached shopping carts, and super chat participation in live streams.

When Google advised that it was discontinuing YouTube Originals at the beginning of 2022, it did so with reference to two million creators being supported in the YouTube Partner

Program and having paid more than $30 billion to content creators, artists, and media companies in the previous three years[171].

Through YouTube, current and retired professional sports people have been able to build and maintain their brands both during and post their professional sporting careers. In this respect, Pat McAfee has been a standout.

McAfee played eight seasons and 127 NFL games as a punter for the Indianapolis Colts from 2009–2016. He punted 575 times for 26,669 yards at an average of 46.4 yards and played twice in the Pro-Bowl.

In 2019, McAfee launched a three-hour daily sports program in his own name broadcasted live weekdays on YouTube.

Play-on-demand access to *The Pat McAfee Show* is available direct from YouTube and also available in audio-only form as a podcast from Apple and Spotify. Today, *The Pat McAfee Show* has 2.14m subscribers on YouTube, 2.8m followers on Twitter, 1.3 million followers on Instagram, and 615,000 followers on Facebook. The success of the show led to a deal with ESPN announced in May of 2023, whereby the *The Pat McAfee Show* would air live weekdays simultaneously on ESPN, ESPN+, and ESPN's YouTube channel[172].

Just like all industries, the internet has democratized sportscasting and commentating. It is not just traditional media, current and past professional sportspeople providing content creation; there are any number of content creators that focus on a sport or a brand providing commentary on topical issues.

As mentioned in the opening chapter, one of my favorite podcasts is *Haberman & Middlekauff*. High-school buddies who have taken various routes in sports commentating and NFL scouting amongst other things, they have developed a YouTube show that provides a lot of San Francisco 49ers content and boasts 18,500 subscribers, and push play-on-demand audio via podcasts published to Apple and Spotify.

Apart from YouTube's monetization strategies, larger productions often secure sponsors and advertising for their programs which are references in word and image during the live stream in addition to any YouTube advertising.

Content creation has become a burgeoning industry as demonstrated by the more two million content creators supported through the YouTube Partner Program. It takes time to build an audience, irrespective of your adopted platforms. Like all new business opportunities, however, the best time to start is now.

Platform selection is not without risk. Competitive offerings to YouTube do exist. For example, Vimeo in video hosting, and Twitch and Rumble in live streaming. It sometimes feels that there is not a lot of transparency around suspensions of accounts due to breaching community guidelines, nor certainty around timelines for having suspensions revoked. Then there are new technology entrants arriving all the time to challenge the status quo.

New companies entering the media landscape may choose to stream direct from their own website, or launch with a purpose-built app, separating the challenges of platform distribution and audience acquisition. Understanding your audience, or target market if the audience is not yet validated, is critical.

A non-sports example of customer experience, go-to-market and distribution platform

Let us look at one non-sporting example of customer experience, go-to-market and your distribution platform.

Top Gun: Maverick was the long-awaited sequel to the

1986 *Top Gun* film starring Tom Cruise and Val Kilmer. Produced by Paramount Pictures, it was originally slated for a July 12, 2019 release date, however, was pushed back to June 24, 2020 to accommodate flight sequences using new technology and planes.

In the lead-up to the AFC Championship game between the Kansas City Chiefs and the Cincinnati Bengals, Tom Cruise appeared in a hype video for CBS Sports. While it was a promotional video for the AFC Championship game which was also being broadcast by CBS, it did include clips from the upcoming film release, as well as being narrated by Cruise to the *Top Gun* anthem. CBS is owned by Paramount Global, which also owns Paramount Pictures. Another example of strategically leveraging value across assets.

Fox was the NFL's broadcast partner for Super Bowl LIV held on February 2, 2020 at the Hard Rock Stadium in Miami, in a game won by the Kansas City Chiefs 31–20 over the San Francisco 49ers. The Super Bowl constantly attracts the largest television audience in the United States each year and attracts the most expensive advertising. Upcoming cinema attractions are a staple, and in 2020, a new trailer for *Top Gun: Maverick* was dropped ahead of its June 24, 2020 release date. Other movies advertised during the Super Bowl included *No Time to Die* (James Bond), and four from the Disney stable: *Black Widow, Loki, The Falcon and the Winter Soldier*, and a final trailer for *Mulan*.

Super Bowl advertising provides the biggest audience of the year and the best opportunity to create awareness, even if it comes with a correspondingly large price tag.

By March 2020, cinemas in the United States were being closed due to COVID-19. The March release of *Mulan* was postponed. The May 2020 release date of *Black Widow* was postponed. *Top Gun: Maverick* pushed back to July, and then further postponed being pushed back to December 2020.

By September 2020, cinemas were open at more than half pre-pandemic levels[173], although it fluctuated and went back down during the winter months. Even as more cinemas re-opened, movie-goers remained cautious.

It was a real balancing act, choosing when and how to launch. Disney eventually released *Black Widow* to the smaller number of cinemas on July 9, 2021, however, electing to do so while simultaneously releasing on Disney+. Paramount Pictures continued to wait almost another year until cinema opening and attendances returned to some level of normalcy, eventually releasing *Top Gun: Maverick* on May 27, 2022.

These were massive decisions for both Disney and Paramount Pictures of which customer experience, go-to-market, and distribution platforms were central. There were undoubtedly other factors such as the compacting of schedules impacting other movie assets in production, finding time in calendars to maximize awareness and promote their movies, and risk assessing any release delays and how that may date a script and the effect on the audience.

What history does tell us is that the hybrid release of *Black Widow* at the cinema simultaneously with release on Disney+ resulted in the movie's star Scarlett Johansson taking Disney to court for contract breach, arguing the dual release cannibalized the theatrical gross and thereby causing loss of box office bonuses. A confidential settlement was reached.

Top Gun: Maverick would go on to record Cruise's highest-ever opening weekend at the box office. At the time of writing, the movie had entered the top 12 highest-grossing movies of all time.

The key point here is that, despite the unknown variable of cinema openings and attendances given concerns over COVID-19 contagion, Paramount Pictures continued to show patience pushing back the release of *Top Gun: Maverick* until such times as a cinema audience could be maximized. They were clear on who their target market was, and that target market's preferred distribution platform. Disney did not show the same patience. The eventual distribution platform for both movies had a material impact on gross revenues.

12. Politics and sport: there is no escaping the macroeconomic environment

THERE IS A COLLOQUIAL SAYING that politics and sport should never be mixed. The global pandemic, however, demonstrated that the world of professional sports is no different to any other industry and is joined at the hip with the political landscape.

This is not a case of party specific political persuasion influencing sporting leagues or vice versa. It is simply the effect of government policy settings on all citizens irrespective of the party in power at the time.

You do not need to be an economist to understand that economics is about scarcity. Highly desired goods and services in short supply attract larger prices. Less desired goods and services in abundance attract lower prices.

At any given point in time, the economy is in a state of equilibrium. When government policy settings change, signals are sent to the marketplace incentivizing private sector investment or divestment.

For example, for seven straight years between 2013 and 2019, government spending in the United States was consistently in the range of 35 percent of Gross Domestic Product

(GDP)[174]. Over that same period, Australia had greater variance in the range of 36 percent – 39 percent of GDP. Both significantly jumped in 2020 responding to the initial onset of the global pandemic with government spending rising to 45.3 percent of GDP in the United States and 44.73 percent of GDP in Australia.

GOVERNMENT EXPENDITURE AS A PERCENTAGE OF GROSS DOMESTIC PRODUCT (GDP)

	2012	2013	2014	2015	2016	2017	2018	2019	2020	2021
Australia	36.58	36.48	36.86	37.39	37.36	36.86	37.00	39.01	44.73	42.32
United States	37.21	35.84	35.43	35.19	35.55	35.41	35.47	35.73	45.30	42.36

The term "investment" really needs to be stricken from the political class's lexicon. It has been misused to divert attention away from any reasonable assessment, simply substituting for the word "expenditure". If an elected official cannot articulate a projected return over a specified timeframe, it is not an investment.

At a high level, when an elected official prosecutes the case for an investment, it does not necessarily require the stipulation of a financial return; it can be a social return. The social return, however, must be measurable both quantitatively and qualitatively. If such measures are absent, it is an ideological argument.

In actuality, all investments, even social ones, can be articulated as financial outcomes. For example, an investment in a new jobs creation plan should result in savings to public expenditures in welfare or increases in tax receipts. A new policy investment in expanded childcare should result in improved workforce participation rates.

GDP measures the value of goods and services produced by a nation over a specified timeframe. The previous GDP chart is an annual increment. GDP is commonly used as the default indicator for the government of the day to imply that a growing economy means growing living standards. Not even GDP per capita is a quality measure of rising living standards – if those living standards are not being broadly experienced across all citizens.

Nonetheless, when public spending significantly jumps, it means inevitable disruption to market equilibrium with capacity and capability being drawn away from current pursuits to address government priorities and government identified need. When these needs cannot be satisfied by the capacity and capability of the domestic industry, and at a price point the purchasing government is willing to pay, the products and services are imported.

Once public administration has experienced increased resourcing, it becomes exceedingly difficult for public bureaucracies to be weaned off. It is like the shared services of a large conglomerate expanding substantially (a metaphor for public services administration), done at the expense of reducing customer-facing roles (a metaphor for income generating goods and services of private sector businesses). You are increasing the cost base of the business yet reducing the income production capacity. Scalability and efficiency possibilities aside, all other things being equal, it is not sustainable. The only way to pay for an increasingly inefficient model of delivery is to raise the prices for your customers (increasing taxation of your citizens).

Public sector employment in Australia pre and post pandemic provides a strong example. Over the four financial years ending June 30, 2019 – June 30, 2022, Australian full-time jobs rose 7.7 percent while part-time jobs rose 1.1 percent for an aggregate of 5.6 percent increase in all jobs. Over that same period, public sector employment rose 18.3 percent while the accompanying wages bill rose 25.6 percent increasing from $166.9b to $209.6b, a rise of $42.66b.

EMPLOYMENT IN THE AUSTRALIAN ECONOMY

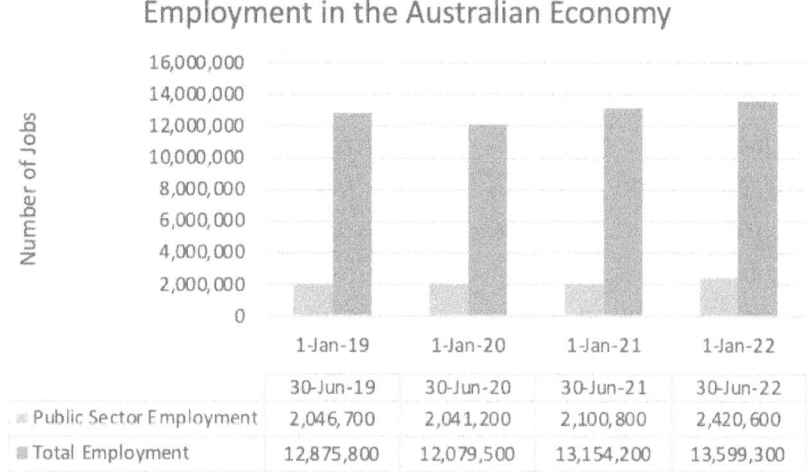

	30-Jun-19	30-Jun-20	30-Jun-21	30-Jun-22
Public Sector Employment	2,046,700	2,041,200	2,100,800	2,420,600
Total Employment	12,875,800	12,079,500	13,154,200	13,599,300

The significant bump in public sector employment occurred 15–27 months after the onset of the global pandemic indicating a new normal, and little appetite to wean off during the economic uptick.

Now in the private sector, there are competitive forces keeping those companies focused on ways to meet customer need, constantly looking for means to reduce overhead and opportunities to improve product-market fit and customer satisfaction – otherwise inefficiencies will see them bow out to the competition. Government monopolies, however, have no such competitive pressures.

Venture capital sometimes receives a bad rap for distorting the market. At one level, there are thousands of start-ups seeking investors to bring their product to market, or to scale their business. When large venture capital invests, it does so by selecting one team over another, bringing their business expertise, their networks, and customer introductions to that team which offers the ability to ignite the growth of that product over its competitors.

In the fintech world, venture capital observes big incumbents that are slow to move and highly regulated, seeing an opportunity to disrupt and erode market share. The sheer quantum of transactions and credit means many start-ups are attracted to enter the market. The markets themselves, however, have not really grown, so the pie has not changed; it is simply a high-volume market that affords the potential to be lucrative if new entrants can demonstrate an ability to create new forms of value or displace incumbent market share. The potential market distortion only comes when one product and company are substantially better funded than its competitors to exploit market opportunities. Why? Because the pure laws of supply and demand do not drive pricing and neither does the true cost of production. The startup subsidizes the costs of production to attract and quickly scale its user base.

In 2020, we observed an immediate and steep loss of jobs. There was a resulting dampening of consumer sentiment and demand as uncertainty spread like wildfire, resulting in plummeting economies. Governments in developed economies responded by injecting unprecedented stimulus into their economies hoping for a J-curve bounce back and avoiding a deep and long recession.

Economic growth came roaring back due to the stimulus as lockdowns began to subside, and we were left with hyperinflation compounded by challenges remaining in global supply chains, and a new energy and food crisis as the Russia–Ukraine war bunkered down.

Forget venture capital. The biggest distortion of markets comes from public policy and accompanying government spending. In the short term, injecting additional funds into the economy stimulates demand, leading to higher consumption and investment which can positively impact GDP. This is a temporary sugar hit, however, and can have negative long-term consequences. Increasing levels of public debt need to be serviced, with higher interest payments both due to the volume of debt and a higher interest rate environment, leading to the need to broaden or raise the tax base.

Inflationary pressures continue to rise as demand outstrips supply. Much of government stimulus spending in the year 2020 was quite rightly focused on supporting people and businesses affected by lockdowns rather than investments in productive assets meaning resulting economic growth was not for the long-term nor sustainable. Compounded by significant inflation across 2022 and 2023 meaning rising debt servicing costs.

In today's world, what should be productive assets are highly politicized. Developed economies do not seem to exit cyclical economic cycles. Keynesian economic principles of increasing government investments to cover a lull in private-sector spending, and then pulling back when private investment picks up, just does not happen in practice. The modus operandi seems more to be that any road, railway, tunnel, airport, renewable energy, or other infrastructure project is a worthwhile investment because it will automatically become a productive asset while amplifying the opportunity for re-election in a marginal seat. Productivity gains are loosely calculated and a secondary consideration if a consideration at all.

The size of government purchasing power and their political imperative means resource allocation is distorted. An investment in a road must see the road in use by a specific date so it can be demonstrated an elected leader has delivered for their constituents. And if investments need to be increased during the project to ensure milestones are met, the public bureaucracy is more than happy to pay overs. Cost does not meaningfully come into this equation. What these political imperatives do is price signal to the market drawing resources away from other private-sector pursuits to satisfy a ribbon cutting ceremony opportunity.

There is one example of this political imperative having a long-term effect on the Australian economy, and another that could have amplified the situation if the incumbent party had been re-elected. The first was the JobKeeper subsidy enacted in the final quarter of the 2020 financial year.

The program was later reviewed by the federal Parliamentary Budget Office finding that at least $38b went to companies where turnover did not fall below the program thresholds during the period they claimed support[175]. At one level, when faced with an economic cliff, responsiveness is critical. Bureaucracy cannot get in the way of the objective, and any slowness to issue financial support would have resulted in job losses. On another level, execution is everything. And that is now $38b that needs to be funded by the tax system going forward having supported businesses that were not the demographic intended, the real target being those in the most need. Worse still, in a prolonged period of deficit budgets, interest is being paid on the aggregated public "investment".

The second example was funding commitments that were made by both major parties in the lead-up to the 2022 federal election. Independent bodies sometimes exist to bring together expertise and provide impartial advice to government on achieving policy objectives. Infrastructure Australia is one such example established to provide expert advice on delivering better infrastructure for all Australians.

In the lead-up to the 2022 Australian Federal Government elections, the incumbent governing party committed to a new $16.5b infrastructure spend of which just 15 percent of projects had been endorsed as priorities by Infrastructure Australia as priorities. Not surprisingly, many of these projects were to be found in marginal seats[176]. All investments are an opportunity cost. Capital invested in one place cannot be invested in another. Of new project infrastructure spend, 85 percent was going to go to areas not identified as priorities by the independent body – so why have an independent body? Presumably not being identified as a priority by the independent body meant they were not going to be an asset that was more productive than those they did identify as a priority.

To consider the impact of government spending, both the wise and unwise, it can be commonly presented in graph form as government spending as a percentage of GDP. This is fine to clearly show any deviations from historical norms. It does not, however, give a sense of the enormity of the task at hand.

Given the size of the US economy compared to Australia's, it also not valuable plotting the burgeoning levels of government debt of both on the same chart. The US debt levels[177] dwarfing Australia's lend rise to thinking that there is not a problem in Australia. It is of course all relative.

U.S. NATIONAL DEBT OVER THE LAST 100 YEARS

Inflation Adjusted - 2022 Dollars

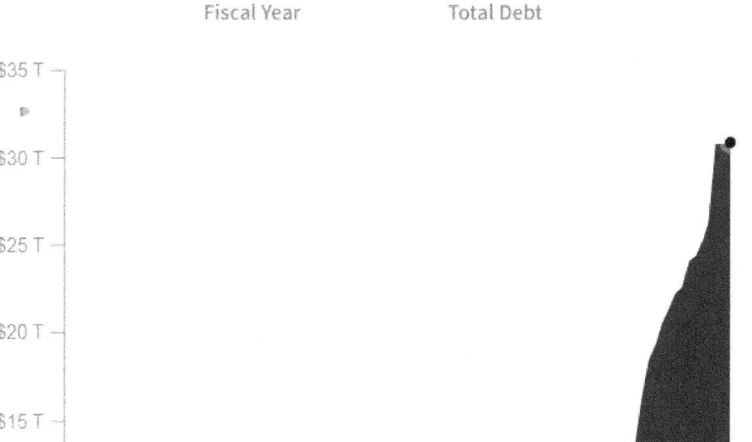

Visit the Historical Debt Outstanding dataset to explore and download this data. The inflation data is sourced from the Bureau of Labor Statistics.

Last Updated: September 30, 2022

AUSTRALIAN GOVERNMENT NET DEBT

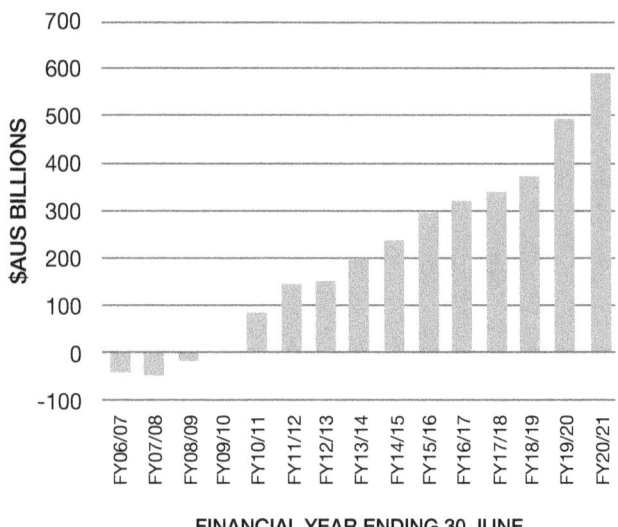

FINANCIAL YEAR ENDING 30 JUNE

The debt curves for both countries start slowly, and then grow exponentially. Neither government has been able to extricate itself from increased spending since the Global Financial Crisis (GFC) in 2007–2009. A decade later, and the next financial shock being the global pandemic was much more impactful than the GFC, yet in the current environment debt servicing requirements require increased resourcing.

Now many economists posit that the debt levels are fine and can be comfortably serviced as a percentage of the broader economy. The politics is that governments are always reluctant to increase taxation, perceived to penalize their citizens for an inability to fund their expenditure commitments. This is compounded by a reluctance to increase corporate tax rates for fear of putting the brakes on private investment and new jobs creation.

The key difference between a government managing a national economy and an individual citizen managing their household budget is that the citizen has a finite productive working life of approximately 45 years. Citizens are hopeful that they have built a sufficient pool of productive assets and working capital after those 45 years to fund their lifestyle through the retirement years. The alternative being to rely on government funded pensions and/or the continuation of work into the golden years.

Governments, however, have no such time imperative. Conceptually, there is no finite timeline for the economy or a nation. Hence the temptation to continually kick the can down the road.

When it comes to the economy, everything is connected. If migration inflows significantly outnumber outflows, there are implications on the costs of housing whether that be through purchase prices or rental agreements. Increasing supply takes time, yet there is an increased pool of consumers competing for the same limited number of resources as soon as migration inflows are larger than the outflows. As a result, there is upward pressure on prices.

It is not entirely true that a growing population guarantees a growing economy, however, in Australia with 85 percent of employment in services, it is a good way to keep GDP ticking over. Of course, neither Rome, nor schools, nor hospitals, nor roads along with housing can be built in a day. So there is a trade-off where GDP growth papers over policy failures elsewhere.

The key point of these macroeconomic examples is that if government public policy does not balance investments in productive assets and essential services, we see a distortion of resource allocation. And what is worse is that there is no intention of paying down the outstanding debt levels, only increasing them, further distorting resource allocation. Not too dissimilar to a pyramid scheme really.

A point in case was the suggestion in 2023 of the US mint pressing a $1 trillion dollar coin. The US has a legal limit placed on the amount of money the government can borrow. In January 2023, the US government reached the debt ceiling of $31 trillion. Lifting the debt ceiling is not uncommon, but when nearing the limit, it is used as a political lever to achieve deals for support to pass a rise. The conceptual strategy of minting a trillion-dollar coin is that it is then deposited with the US Federal Reserve as a way of not needing to borrow more money and a way of bypassing lifting the debt ceiling.

The only real commitment governments demonstrate is a focus on growing the economy as a way of increasing receipts of taxation and hoping that inflation eats away at the value the gross numbers mean in terms of purchasing power. In 2022 and 2023, inflation played its part, but was still only at the margins of raising extra revenue for governments.

What does public policy have to do with sport? As much as they might try otherwise, elected leaders make all decisions through a political lens. The decision-making process is a funnel of trade-offs, and the overriding influencers of decisions are not productivity and efficiency.

The reality is that elected leaders can, and do, intended, or otherwise, directly impact the hosting of sporting competitions by creating policy settings that are either conducive to league success or hinder it. At this level, sporting leagues and franchises are just like any other advocacy group, needing to ensure they secure their share of the public purse, demonstrating how such an investment generates a return for their local community (which starts with the same constituents represented by the elected leader), and providing their tribe with a better experience.

The reason why the NFL, NBA, AFL, and NRL successfully navigated the onset of the global pandemic is related to the size of their fan bases. Not the size of the participation rate. The size of the paying customer base. The bigger your tribe, the quicker you gain the attention of publicly elected officials. Access is shaped by the degree of potential for negative voter sentiment.

The fan bases of the NFL, NBA, AFL, and NRL represented uniquely large cohorts of voters, giving them each the direct ear and timely access to elected officials where they could share their concerns and whiteboard solutions. Then the access to capital gave each of these sporting codes unhindered access to the top virologists, epidemiologists, and biosecurity experts in their fields.

Once risk-management plans were put in front of health officials, with elected officials in the background concerned with upsetting voters, it left little wiggle room. If not a return to playing now, why not? If not now, then when? If not a return of crowds and full capacity now, why not? If not now, then when? All difficult questions for health bureaucrats and elected officials to answer in the face of the unknown. These sporting codes were able to use their voter clout to return to the sporting field most expeditiously, leaving others in their wake.

Netball Australia and the professionalization journey

As one example for contrast, I will use netball in Australia. In terms of Australians participating in sport, athletics including running and jogging has the highest amount of participation with 3.48m participants, followed by swimming with 3.23m and cycling with 2.56m. Netball has the highest number of females 15 years of age and over participating with 525,000[178].

There is no commonly accepted definition of what a professional sport is, varying from the elite players receiving some form of payment to elite players earning more than

50 percent of their annual income from playing. For me, a professional sport is one that organizes itself without most of its funding coming from the public purse.

In Netball Australia's case, it is not a good sign that the lead write-up for their annual report comes from a representative of the Australian Sports Commission followed by the chair of the board of directors and chief executive officer. For the financial year ending December 31, 2021, government grants were $10.4m while sponsorship was $12.5m.

The asset base peaked in 2015 with $10,598,412 being held in net assets. This dropped by 28.8 percent the following year in 2016, and while holding flat for the next three years, the value of the asset base was eroded by inflation.

Table 12. Netball Australia Financial Position by Financial Year Ending December 31[179]

Year	Revenue	Expenses	Surplus/ (Deficit)	Net Assets
2022	$38,733,839	$38,433,938	$299,901	**$458,619**
2021	$30,004,232	$34,373,068	($4,368,836)	**$158,718**
2020	$28,741,639	$31,549,842	($2,808,203)	**$4,527,554**
2019	$29,835,698	$29,788,538	$47,160	**$7,332,216**
2018	$29,308,680	$29,242,770	$65,910	**$7,269,311**
2017	$26,830,272	$27,222,383	($392,111)	**$7,182,553**
2016	$15,853,286	$18,974,228	($3,120,942)	**$7,546,484**
2015	$27,563,112	$27,185,587	$377,525	**$10,598,412**

Fighting to survive the onset of the global pandemic in 2020, the asset base dropped 38.2 percent and was all but wiped out the following year. Netball Australia had no access to capital and no momentum, and now having lost $7.2m over two financial years.

The financial plight was exacerbated with a new sponsor withdrawing only one month after entering into an agreement with Netball Australia in September 2022. The Victorian Government via its tourism agency Visit Victoria quickly stepped into the breach signing a $15m agreement over four and a half years through to 30 June 2027.

The question is whether a public agency can generate value from such an investment, at a time when there is significant cost of living pressures for its constituents. The alternative view would be to question why Victoria taxpayers are subsidizing a national sport.

In the world of professional sport, a $15m sponsorship over four and a half years is not substantial. Nonetheless, the minimum salary of $43,000 for netballers in the elite competition is more that the AFL Women's league at $39,184, although substantially lower than cricket where the female cricketers who play both the 50 over and 20 over formats earn $86,000 annually[180].

The incumbent Victorian Labor Government was first elected November 29, 2014. Once a governing period nears a decade, financial performance becomes very easy to assess by looking at the years prior to being elected and the governing period itself.

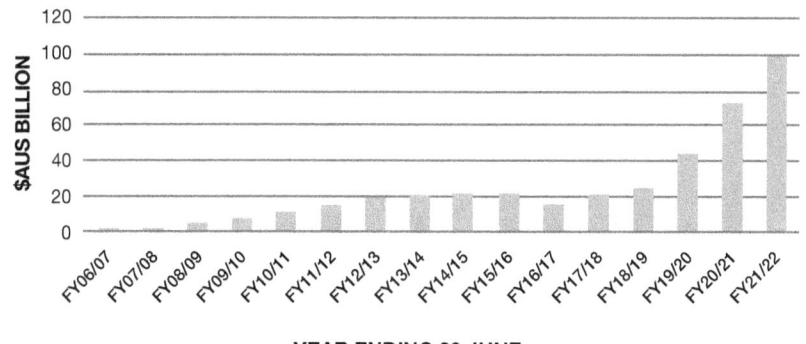

VICTORIAN GOVERNMENT NET DEBT

YEAR ENDING 30 JUNE

Net debt was effectively managed for the first four-year term of the government. Then the first four months of the onset of the global pandemic saw net debt increase by 75 percent. In the following twelve months, the Victorian capital Melbourne would become recognized as the most locked-down city in the world, with the net debt of June 30, 2019, almost tripling by June 30, 2021, and quadrupled by June 30, 2022.

Despite the burgeoning debt, the Victorian Government stepped in to sponsor a national sport and league, presumably in the belief that inbound tourism for select matches of interest would see the investment returned via the tourism dollar. It was a small investment in the overall scheme of things, but made, however, in the context of Victorian households, the second most-populous state, experiencing a drop in their living standards, placing seven out of eight state and territories in disposable household income[181].

GROSS HOUSEHOLD DISPOSABLE INCOME PER CAPITA BY STATE AND TERRITORY

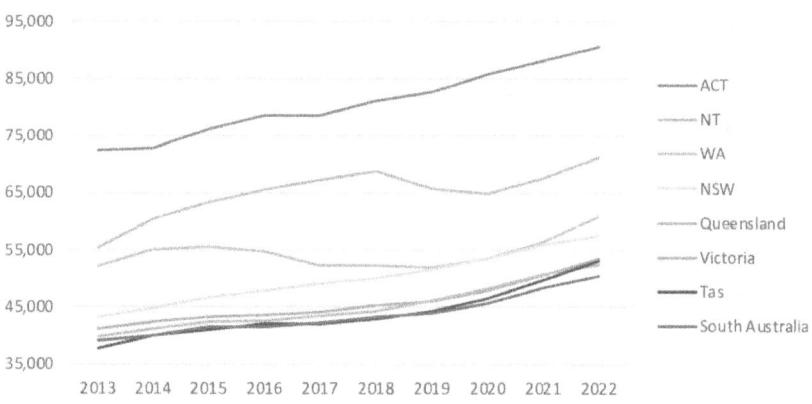

The reasons for the Australian Capital Territory and the Northern Territory dominating so significantly would be another book in itself - suffice to say, government spending once again distorts markets and resource allocation.

Despite having no asset base and the game of netball

facing an existential crisis, the Netball Players Association continued to seek pay increases for elite athletes.

The purpose of reflecting on public net debt in both the United States and Australia, and the financial performance of Netball Australia is to highlight the need to choose your business partners carefully. Governments are no different to any commercial partner. They have requirements in exchange for any monetary support which may or may not be aligned with the best interests of a sporting code. One of those requirements which appears universal is that government support cannot be seen to be material in propping up a commercial operation. Otherwise, voters will quite rightly take elected officials to task on whether the investment is in the public interest.

13. Exiting the pandemic: How different sports fared

IN SETTING THE SCENE FOR this book, the third chapter provided a business performance baseline for major sports by looking at the year 2020, the broader economic climate and the initial onset of the global COVID-19 pandemic. This chapter analyzed the varying sporting league responses to evolving government public health policy settings and the broader pandemic disruption. This included contrasting sporting codes in the US with Australian sports codes. From the NBA moving their post-season into a Florida Disney World bubble, to the NFL implementing safety protocols to get the season underway and then finding ways to complete the season. The NFL season was completed despite ongoing outbreaks impacting individual teams and varying public health measures implemented by individual US states causing the San Francisco 49ers to relocate to Arizona for the final weeks of the 2020 season.

Today, more than a full three calendar years have passed. Data is available to review balance sheets and assess how the referenced sports survived and re-positioned themselves for future success. It goes without saying, in any comparative assessment, that there has been a sliding scale from those who have experienced merely a blip on their way to continued success, down the ladder of success to those that continue to face existential threats today. Let's look at how the NFL, AFL, NRL, Cricket Australia, and Rugby Australia all fared navigating Covid and getting through to the other side of the pandemic.

At one level, there is no such thing as an existential threat in sport. If a professional league runs out of capital, it can still exist as a grass roots volunteer-run sporting code. That outcome, however, is not an aspiration for any league, their players, their fans, nor on their risk registers.

Reflecting on shutdowns enforced by governments across the world, businesses in retail, hospitality, cinema operators, travel, and aviation all lost access to customers with little to no notice; with no assurances for how long lockdowns would last, or when lockdowns would be enacted again. It was incredibly inspiring to see small-business owners pivot to new products and services, or move to open online purchasing, or restaurants moving to solely takeaway menus, all in the hope of keeping the business alive and its people and infrastructure in place for long enough until a return to normality.

Small businesses, who may have been considered lifestyle businesses with no access to capital to batten down the hatches and ride out the storm, were faced with options of either closing down (albeit with some ongoing liabilities in place such as leases) or borrowing against personal assets to extend the business lifespan. If there ever was such a thing as a lifestyle business, this scenario does not feel like a lifestyle one would choose.

National Football League (NFL)

To reflect on where the NFL has been over the past three calendar years, comparing salary caps limits over the past decade provides great insight.

NFL Salary Cap by Year[182]
2024: $255.4m ($30.6m increase)
2023: $224.8m ($16.6m increase)
2022: $208.2m ($25.7m increase)
2021: $182.5m ($15.7m decrease)
2020: $198.2m ($10.0m increase)
2019: $188.2m ($11.0m increase)
2018: $177.2m ($10.2m increase)
2017: $167.0m ($11.73m increase)
2016: $155.27m ($11.99m increase)
2015: $143.28m ($10.28m increase)
2014: $133.0m ($9.4m increase)

The juggernaut that is the NFL experienced only a slight blip on its ongoing growth trajectory. It should not be downplayed that the level of effort that went into assuring the 2021 season proceeded was herculean. Herculean can be achieved with capital. The players and game came together both on a reduced salary cap in the face of the unknown and working through safety protocols that continued to evolve throughout the preseason and the season. In just one year after the blip, the salary-cap jumped back to a level that was consistent with the previous growth trend. It is as if the 2021 adjustment never existed.

Concurrently as the pandemic was beginning to set in, the NFL concluded its new media distribution rights agreement in March 2021 covering the period 2023 through 2033. The collective series of deals worth was worth more than US$100b and provided long-term revenue certainty and ongoing access to working capital. Of course, accompanied by obligatory contract commitments.

The same momentum cannot be said of some of Australia's major sporting codes. Australian Rules and Rugby League have been able to achieve a similar bounce back to the NFL. Cricket Australia and Rugby Union have not.

Australian Football League (AFL)

In the three years since 2016, the AFL was able to double its asset base reaching a high of $238.8m for the 2019 financial year. The last four months of the financial year ending June 30, 2020 coincided with the onset of the pandemic. The AFL experienced a dip in revenue of 15 percent. Corresponding expense reductions meant the asset base dropped just 3.5 percent over this same four-month period. The next financial year the asset base dropped another 12.8 percent before rebounding strongly to recover all losses and regain the historical growth trend demonstrated over the last decade.

Table 13. Australian Football League Financial Position by Financial Year Ending June 30 (AUD '000)

Year	Revenue	Surplus/ (Deficit)	Total Assets	Total Liabilities	Net Assets
2023	1,063,547	126,860	725,002	283,903	441,099
2022	944,370	113,277	754,594	440,355	314,239
2021	738,137	(29,487)	658,707	457,745	200,962
2020	674,816	(8,378)	628,097	397,648	230,449
2019	793,939	27,858	487,487	248,660	238,827
2018	778,596	25,714	536,090	325,121	210,969
2017	752,622	60,344	476,649	291,554	185,095
2016	569,856	(15,455)	203,678	78,927	124,751
2015	558,674	3,648	206,260	66,054	140,206
2014	528,230	13,320	186,191	49,633	136,558
2013	502,699	18,229	174,648	51,410	123,238

It would be fair to say that while the AFL took a little longer than the NFL to regain its growth trajectory, timing was certainly one of the factors for the variance. The AFL season was underway when lockdowns started to commence in Australia during March 2020, whereas the NFL had completed the Super Bowl in February 2020 with the new season not scheduled to commence until September providing some invaluable planning time.

The key piece, however, was the AFL being able to secure a loan of more than half a billion Australian dollars against the asset that is Marvel Stadium. Access to capital was efficient and substantial, and secured because of the AFL's burgeoning asset base. Marvel Stadium was purchased by the AFL in 2016 for $200m and was now worth more than one billion dollars in 2020[183].

National Rugby League (NRL)

The NRL experience was similar to that of the AFL, albeit at half the quantum. The NRL's asset base too had doubled in the three years since 2016 reaching a high of $120.7m in 2019. The last four months of the financial year ending June 30, 2020 coincided with the onset of the pandemic and resulted in the asset base being crippled by 20.5 percent. No real harm was done, however, with losses recovered the next year and another sport back on track in terms of historical growth trajectory.

Table 14. National Rugby League Financial Position by Financial Year Ending June 30 (AUD '000)

Year	Revenue	Surplus/(Deficit)	Total Assets	Total Liabilities	Net Assets
2023	701,145	58,183	345,354	85,291	260,063
2022	593,798	62,903	285,760	83,880	201,880
2021	575,080	43,057	264,524	125,547	138,977
2020	419,673	(24,742)	242,325	146,405	95,920
2019	555,914	28,983	271,833	151,171	120,662
2018	499,940	45,954	246,630	159,248	87,382
2017	377,004	(6,421)	226,786	175,708	51,078
2016	375,709	(8,649)	251,702	194,082	57,620
2015	353,842	(18,655)	194,299	128,030	66,269
2014	350,900	20,200	199,600	114,677	84,923
2013	320,300	45,300	188,074	123,383	64,691

Cricket Australia

Cricket Australia is a different kettle of fish. The asset base had reached a high of AUD$150m back in 2016. This had already been eroded by 35 percent by the end of the 2019 financial year dropping to $97.7m before the onset of COVID-19.

You will recall from the chapter on culture that cricket, being an international game, experiences revenue fluctuations on a four-year cycle based on the timing of the biggest drawcards of England and India visiting Australia. While that premise may be true, it does not account for the 35 percent decline in the asset base before the global pandemic.

The financial year accounting for the first four months of a COVID-19 impacted society, resulted in Cricket Australia's asset base declining another 44 percent down to $54.6m.

This was followed by India visiting Australia for a test series in the financial year of 2021 lifting the asset base by 8.9 percent, and England visiting Australia for a test series in the financial year of 2022. The asset based eroded another 17.9 percent back down to $48.8m.

Exiting the pandemic: How different sports fared

It does not matter which way you cut it; the bottom line is ... the bottom line says ... cricket is a game in significant decline.

The financial year ending June 30, 2023 acquitted the receipts of a three-test match series against South Africa and a two-match test series against the West Indies. The year after, Cricket Australia will be acquitting receipts of a three-test match series against Pakistan and another two test matches against the West Indies.

As covered in the chapter on culture, the ongoing impact on brand of the Sandpapergate scandal, resignation of captain Tim Payne, and the replacement of coach Justin Langer are not as easy to measure as the numbers on a balance sheet. The balance sheet is a lag indicator of a shift in consumer sentiment and business performance.

Table 15. Cricket Australia Financial Position by Financial Year Ending June 30 (AUD '000)

Year	Revenue	Surplus/ (Deficit)	Total Assets	Total Liabilities	Net Assets
2023	426,643	(16,894)	170,339	138,438	31,901
2022	391,004	(10,655)	214,664	165,869	48,795
2021	414,705	4,862	265,201	205,751	59,450
2020	390,098	(43,155)	195,178	140,590	54,588
2019	485,901	9,902	240,785	143,042	97,743
2018	399,265	(10,759)	276,128	188,287	87,841
2017	303,490	(51,295)	317,717	219,117	98,600
2016	339,787	35,727	371,412	221,517	149,895

In 2023, financial head winds for Cricket Australia have only been exacerbated and not just because of inflationary pressures reducing the entertainment and discretionary spend of the consumer base. Cricket's revenue share model appears now to be a race to the bottom. Apparently, no-one ever reviewed the operating model for scalability. It is just not plausible that an asset base could decline by 67.4 percent over six years and lay claim that the sport is in a sound position. Capital is king and the dwindling asset base means Cricket Australia's access to capital is reduced going forward.

Rugby Australia

Rugby Australia's financial position is even more tenuous than Cricket Australia. The financial year for Rugby Australia ends December 31 each year, whereas the other three codes run to June 30 each year. This means that Rugby Australia had ten months to work through from the onset of the pandemic, resulting in revenues dropping from $111.7m in 2019 down to $66.0m in 2020. The bounce back in 2021 was significant, but the net asset base remains in the negative. It is a deep hole, and one that will take many years to work back out from. Or fold to the wolves of private equity knocking on the door accompanied by inevitable changes in how the game is packaged.

Table 16. Rugby Australia Financial Position by Financial Year Ending December 31 (AUD '000)

Year	Revenue	Surplus/ (Deficit)	Total Assets	Total Liabilities	Net Assets
2022	129,249	8,191	69,214	72,902	(3,688)
2021	98,583	(4,503)	58,981	70,861	(11,880)
2020	65,991	(27,111)	56,524	63,893	(7,369)
2019	111,742	(9,485)	59,185	40,856	18,329
2018	119,677	5,204	69,929	43,157	26,772
2017	149,911	17,632	66,660	29,541	37,119

After access to capital, the second key learning from professional sports in responding to the global pandemic is that business trajectories are all about momentum. Once you have it, you need to ride the wave. Once you lose it, getting it back is not a quick fix.

Jim Collins uses the analogy of business pushing a gigantic heavy flywheel. The first rotation is the slowest, and then you keep pushing and future rotations get faster. What businesses do not want to do is the heavy turning for ten rotations, then turn attention to a different flywheel and start with the first hardest rotation again. Success stems from ramping 10 turns of the flywheel up to a billion rotations. Collins argues that the essence of strategy boils down to three questions: where to place a business's big bets, how to protect the flanks, and how to extend the victories. Any strategy that does not account for exploiting the victories is incomplete and inadequate[184].

At an operational level, hall of fame coach Bill Walsh encourages doubling down once momentum has been gained[185]:

> "When things are going best is when you have the opportunity to be the strongest, most demanding, and most effective in your leadership. A strong wind is at your back, but it requires an understanding of the perils produced by victory to prevent that wind from blowing you over."

The NFL, AFL, and NRL have momentum. Cricket Australia and Rugby Australia do not.

14. Conclusion

GIVEN THE SPORTING-WORLD EXPERIENCES, ONE universal business truth remains unchallenged – it is a first principle that capital is king. And this remains true too for all businesses. When things are going well, greater access to capital enables a business to double-down on investments and expand market reach. When things are challenging, greater capital affords better flexibility to address risks.

If you accept that proposition, then there is not really such a thing as a lifestyle business. Investors may use that term because the operating model tabled before them does not afford scaling opportunities. Or the founder demonstrates reticence to adapt the operating model. Or the founder seems to have other outside interests that distracts them from focusing 60–80 hours a week on growing their business. Or the founder seems comfortable with the current returns they are generating from the business even though it is obvious to an external reviewer that a slight change in market conditions will have a material impact.

This is not a debate on issues of wealth creation and issues of equality, where some sports have succeeded in engaging the corporate world, while others have not. It is simply to reinforce the point that capital is king. Within this context, the best time to start building your capital base is today. Not tomorrow. Not reinvesting from strategic reserves in the hope that a new business model emerges in two years' time. Start the accumulation phase today, however that might be achieved.

For large publicly listed companies, timing and maximizing value aside, it is a relatively straight forward exercise to tap the market for capital. For private businesses, it is a little different.

There can be a temptation for private businesses to keep capital as liquid as possible to respond to any unexpected market fluctuations. Ideally, however, a private business will not have large sums of cash sitting idle in a bank account earning minimal interest that disappears after inflation. And while it is possible to tap private investors to come into your business, you really want to be doing this as a way of scaling what is already a successful business model rather than in a market downturn fending off the wolves because the valuation will be substantially lower.

Ultimately, the important consideration is to realize that capital is a tool. It can be parked in higher growth assets such as property that might not be liquid. Nonetheless, it can be borrowed against should an emergency arise. The strategic imperative is to keep growing the capital base. The larger the capital base the bigger investment capability you hold to delight your customers and grow your market share.

I mentioned earlier that the term "investment" really needs to be stricken from the political class's lexicon. There is another word that should be similarly treated – the use of the word "funding". Necessity is the mother of invention, not government funding. You hear all the time business owners lament "if only we had extra funding" we could achieve success. The reality is, if you are dependent on government hand-outs, you do not have a business. You have not found a product/market fit. And rarely will extra "funding" see you through to success. It simply buys time for the business. Thus, the role of government funding needs to be questioned.

That is not to say there is not a role for seed funding, or demonstration projects that incentivize private resources being applied to government priority areas. The point here is that government funding is not free money. You are asking for the ability to amortize that funding amount across the rest of the tax-paying base. This call to arms, that is more funding, has become particularly prevalent in the era of the social enterprise. A founder sees a gap in the market. The gap exists because the customer base either does not desire the service or is unwilling to pay a fee commensurate with the cost of delivering the service, so the fallback is that government should pick up the imbalance.

While most of us would expect government to intervene in instances of market failure and, as a general responsibility, support the most vulnerable citizens, this is not the same as expecting the tax-paying base to fund the lifestyle aspirations of a founder who has been unable to achieve a viable product/market fit. No-one is entitled to have their passion project funded by non-users of the product or service.

The hypothesis for this book has been that all businesses and working professionals can learn something from the business playbooks of major sporting leagues. There is a tendency for non-fans to dismiss pro sports as being over-hyped and over-remunerated, living off the back of media rights and crazed fan bases that pay over-the-odds to attend games, stream games and purchase the merchandise of their favorite sporting teams.

To remove the perception biases of non-sports fans, the analysis has been couched in the business context of sports needing to rapidly respond to evolving government health policy edicts during the onset of COVID-19. Just like all businesses, pro sports too needed to explore different ways to keep the lights on and their fan bases engaged. Then this analysis has the benefit of hindsight by being able to review progress of these pro sports three years after the onset of COVID-19, demonstrating that successful leagues experienced a mere blip on their historical growth trajectories, while others faced and continue to face existential threats.

The main reason professional sports provide such strong analogies to broader business settings is that they are a people-focused operation.

Many of the lessons covered in this book apply across new entrant workers, a team leader, a manager, an executive, the divisional units within the operations, and the wider business as whole. The lens changes but the business context does not.

Talent is the most critical factor of production in businesses, and so too in professional sports. We have covered talent identification and acquisition including the need to take a longer-term view towards talent pool development using the NFL example.

From drafting quarterbacks and war gaming how key drivers of decisions may be weighted, to reviewing the talent pipeline funnel from colleges scouting and acquiring high-school talent, through to the NFL draft, evaluations are made over years to determine the talent desired to ensure teams are best placed to succeed.

Outside of professional sports, bigger businesses and brands are actively supporting university students, and industry events to ensure they monitor and identify talent. It is simply roulette if businesses wait for turnover, and then place an advert on a digital job board expecting that respondents will be sufficient to raise the talent level inside their operations. It is an approach that relies on luck and the cards to fall your way.

Conversely, if all the seats at your table are filled, you cannot let that be a barrier of agility and being able to secure talent that suddenly becomes available. Snooze you lose. Los Angeles Rams head coach Sean McVay didn't when he secured Matthew Stafford as his quarterback from the Detroit Lions, nor did it get in the way of securing wide-receiver Odell Beckham Junior when he became available during the season. History shows the Rams went on to win Super Bowl LIV defeating the Cincinnati Bengals 23–30.

As we covered in chapter four, if the capability of your people is crucial to your future success, your human capital pipeline needs to be a disciplined funnel approach, and your evaluation of talent needs to be a science.

Not all positions contribute equally to a winning formula. The process involves assigning value to roles and responsibilities, evaluating potential, and always developing your talent. Yes, you need to treat all team members fairly, but that does not mean treating everyone the same. All people are different. Strengths and weaknesses are different, experiences and attitudes, values and commitment, and their ability to develop new skills in specific areas. Leaders must constantly be making assessments on value whether that is current market segments, prospective new market segments, potential new territories, regulatory frameworks and market upside in other countries, new infrastructure, retiring old infrastructure, potential new products, retiring older product lines or your human capital.

From organization design to departmental expectations and returns, to individual contributions and potential growth trajectories. Your human capital is the critical factor of production. Businesses should always be looking to lower their overhead and cost of production, and this may mean increased machinery and automation, commoditizing some product lines. It may even mean a reduction in headcount or using offshore manufacturing as part of an evolving operating model. Nonetheless, the business still needs to invest in reinventing itself and remaining relevant and contemporary in the future, and that cannot be achieved without talent; talent who is generally focused on areas higher up the value chain.

These sporting analogies on talent identification, acquisition, and development are not intended to encourage business owners or executives to be hoovering up as much talent as the key to future success. It needs to be a carefully managed process. Why the sporting analogy works so well is because there are limited seats on the bus, and these principles cannot be separated or treated in isolation from roster management.

In the introductory chapter, I referenced the paradox of a sports fan, that being, when a team performs poorly, fans openly criticize specific players, call for such players to be moved on, or call for the sacking of coaches or boards. Professional sports as a business takes fail fast to an entirely different level. While fans may be in agreement of such an approach in supporting their favorite franchise, it would be rarely an approach that they would support or find acceptable in their own workplaces.

Nonetheless, effective roster management is crucial for any business. Using the microeconomics analogy from earlier, there are scarce resources that need to be assigned values, and trade-offs will occur in allocating those scare resources to satisfy business objectives. You base those decisions on the best available yet imperfect information.

In the NFL, the pre-season starts with a 90-man roster progressively reduced throughout the pre-season, first to 85, then to 80, before a final 53-man playing squad is settled on. For those who miss out, there is a small waiver window where they are available to any other franchise. If the opportunity is taken up by another franchise, that would mean the receiving franchise needs to cut another player to free up space for the new signing. After the waiver window closes, each franchise can sign an additional sixteen players to a practice squad. The players who trained with you throughout the offseason may or may not be available when the practice squads are signed. At any point during the season, another franchise can sign a player off your practice squad, again only if a spot on their 53-man player roster is freed up.

The mindset in professional sport is to always be looking to get better. If there is organic turnover in business, it is not a case of looking to replace like for like. It is how to replace like for better, and not settling for going backwards in a position unless it is a strategic decision allowing resources for an upgrade in an area of higher priority. This can mean giving current talent who has not yet reached their ceiling a development opportunity higher up the organization chart.

Conversely, if you are always recruiting higher-level talent, there must also be a science to facilitating exits, otherwise the risk is headcount gets away from you, and you are building inefficiencies into your business model. Worse still, you may by default create two-speed operations internally that will inevitably lead to cultural challenges downstream.

The other lesson professional sports offer is that if you are playing from behind, it is a legitimate strategy to pay overs to entice desired talent to make the transfer to your operations. In salary-cap leagues however, such an approach is not without risk. What is paid to one resource means there is less investment capability for other areas. If you picked the right talent to back, they have the capability of lifting the performance of others in your team. A higher pay cheque does not guarantee this, however, so choose wisely.

Business is more like Major League Baseball where there is no salary cap. Small to medium enterprises are not going to have the opportunity to pay overs in order to attract higher-level talent and make a jump up the league ladder. That is where job design and transferrable skills come into play. If your job design is fluid and a science, rather than having job descriptions remaining static for years, it is possible to recruit from outside your industry by focusing on transferable skills. Finding skilled players at a reduced cost. Much like NFL teams giving Australian punters who are without any gridiron experience an opportunity to learn and develop within their structures. It's not a plug and play solution, but they can become contributors quickly with the right support because of their transferrable skills.

At the opposite end of the spectrum, when do you let mature talent go? Whether salary expectations can no longer be met, or your organization can no longer provide relevant development opportunities? This too is a double-edge sword. Ideally, there would be other team members ready to step up and continue their own career development at a reduced cost without the unit skipping a beat. That said, how many times do you see a franchise let a mature talent walk, only for them to experience years in the doldrums because they have been unable to adequately replace. Momentum is lost, and a prolonged drop in performance ensues.

By now, it should be apparent that the number-one lesson businesses can apply from professional sport is recognizing the value of competition. Even in the NFL, which I would consider the closest metaphor for a free-market economy, recognizes the value of competition. It is a free-market economy by having one representative from each of the 32 franchises on an executive committee, all with the intention of growing the reach and influence of their own franchise's brand while recognizing that strong competition supports that objective rather than hinders it.

The salary cap and draft act as mechanisms for balancing out inequity over time, ensuring robust competition and no one team always dominating. Outside of this, there is little government intervention (a metaphor for the NFL executive committee) and no distortion of the market allowing supply and demand to drive consumer behavior. How to value a position, how to value a player, how to design a trade package, electing to securing a mature playing talent through free agency or a young yet to be proven talent secured through the draft. These are all decisions driven solely by the laws of supply and demand. All teams at different stages of their journey will place different values on different investment decisions.

Professional leagues are only valuable because teams compete, and there is a winner and a loser. There are dynasties from time to time, however, this is rare and extremely difficult to achieve. The same teams do not make the playoffs every year. And the sprinkle of unexpected result adds to the theatre. This keeps fans vested in the fortunes and journeys of their team. There will be ups, and there will be downs. Each require responses from management and the players, and the mood of the fans will swing accordingly.

Competition is one of those words that have been weaponized in today's world. There is not really any difference between a private monopoly or a public monopoly – the absence of competition means there is no yardstick for understanding the degree to which excellence is being achieved or otherwise. Any operating challenges are passed onto customers via increased costs simply because they can.

Conclusion

Nobel Prize winning economist Alvin E. Roth is acclaimed for his research on market design particularly in markets where price and monetary exchange is amoral. For example, organ donation is not an auction marketplace. Roth prosecutes the case that there are three key characteristics most present when markets fail: the absence of market thickness, an inability to avoid congestion, and an inability to make participation safe and simple.

He uses the analogy of a market operating freely being like a wheel that can turn smoothly because it has an axle and well-oiled bearings. Market design is about providing the axle and keeping the bearings well oiled[186].

Sometimes the political imperative uses the public policy lever to create cost recovery markets in areas of public services. The pendulum swings between public agency and then outsourcing to a private company when there is an imperative to lower the cost. It does not matter which way the pendulum has swung, if market thickness remains absent, congestion results. Whether public or private, monopolies are best avoided and do not best serve the intended customer

When you have market thickness, you have competition. Competition to lower operating inefficiencies on one hand while also striving for excellence through innovation and new ways to create value on the other hand.

Thickness of teams, thickness of leagues. The embodiment of the best of the best competing and striving for excellence, knowing that at the end of each season, there can be only one winner.

Life in professional sports is short, and that is across all levels: at the governing body level, at the franchise-as-a-business level, at the team level, and the individual player level. While there must be an eye towards the future, stocks rise or fall in the here and now. Execution is everything.

Success does not happen by chance. Thus, each franchise needs its North-Star metric. Sure, it could be to win the competition in the forthcoming season, however, there needs to be a sense of pragmatism about building towards something.

For the Wests Tigers in the NRL or the Gold Coast Suns in the AFL who have not made the playoffs since 2011, or the New York Jets in the NFL who last appeared in the playoffs in the 2010, some building blocks need to be put in place. Strengthening the roster, qualifying for the playoffs, then consistently positioning the team to compete for a championship.

For sporting franchises, landing on that key metric is critical to aligning energies and feeling confident you are heading in the right direction. Then your philosophy and scheme will dictate how you will get there, those plans and concrete actions reflecting your values and beliefs.

In golf, below the professional level is a handicap system designed to smooth out inequity in competitions. The handicap system ensures each player focuses on their best, and if they play to their best, they will be a chance to win. In the absence of a handicap system, there really is not a competition. If a player has a handicap of 18 and was to play a round sans handicap against another player who has a handicap of 10, the higher handicap player would need to play their best round ever and hope the other player would play somewhere near their worst round to have any chance. The higher handicapper could not start the round with the mindset of beating their previous best round by ten shots. They would need to conjure up a plan and execute it to achieve an incremental improvement, not worried about how the other player was performing, just focusing on what they needed to do to achieve their best.

Everything about professional sports is geared towards

improving the one percenters. The coaching mindset that drives individual and team performance improvement with an expectation that this occurs each and every day. At times it appears like indoctrination.

At the level of the individual, the process is a focus on instilling accountability. The coaching mindset embeds accountability with common catch cries:
- Do your job.
- Control the controllable.
- Separation comes from preparation.
- Champions are made when no-one's looking.
- The road to greatness is always under construction.
- It is the biggest game because it's the next game.
- Every play matters.
- Small steps in the right direction lead to great results.
- Bend don't break mentality.
- Are you stacking days, or are you letting the days stack on you?
- The tough times are really when people separate themselves.
- Consistency is the truest measure of performance.
- Going to be empowered, not entitled.
- Gotta be a champion before you ever gonna win a championship.
- All gas, no brake.
- The best ability is availability.

Unless you are stepping on the gridiron, don't be a gunner. Don't be that person. Be accountable. Always look to add value. In many ways, a playing career is a single-person game. A commitment to realizing your own full potential for the team to achieve its potential.

At the team level, strive for a team-first mentality and

raise the comradery in the locker room. Everyone has a role to play, sacrificing personal interest for what is in the team's best interest. Do your job. What secures the opportunity to perform on the biggest stage is the grind. Team members holding themselves and each other accountable to team standards. A mutuality to trust and team first.

At the front-office level, the process is about crafting a vision of the desired state, and then building the culture to make that happen. Sometimes the talent is developed from within, sometimes the talent acquired externally. Business leaders determine roles and responsibilities and assign value to those responsibilities. Being disciplined and creating a science to talent identification, evaluating potential and acquisition. Finding new pathways to secure talent when the market conditions are prohibitive – what does the job design look like and what are transferable skills that can be sourced from elsewhere? Finding new talent that can enable, irrespective of the season timeline.

At the coaching level, it is about establishing the standard and embedding the standard. Standards cannot be compromised. The standard is the standard. Lifting standards over time. Taking action if the standards cannot be met. You cannot fool the players.

The coaching mindset and becoming elite is a process. There is no finish line. Once you have settled on a roster list, it is all about focusing on realizing the potential of each player on the team and the team as a collective. Every team member needs reps (repetitions), so that situational awareness is optimal, the body and mind operate without fear and execute as planned in response to foreseeable circumstances and minimizing the potential for the players and team to shrink in the big moments. Quality and deliberate practice; iron sharpens iron; culture is built brick by brick.

Across all four categories of individual, team, front office and coaching staff, common characteristics for success are demonstrating being all in, demonstrating grit and having a go irrespective of the circumstances, using a chip on the shoulder to form a steely resolve and winning mindset. Competition is an enabler not a barrier.

Grit is not limited to winning. Grit involves having a crack even when you are outgunned. There is a grind involved to become elite. Firstly, the grind to become proficient, and then the grind to be able to deliver higher performance higher sustained over time. Elite is not just capability and capacity. It must result in achievement.

For businesses, the biggest lessons to take from professional sports is adopting a positive and growth mindset.

In baseball, it is called swinging for the fences.

In cricket parlance, keep your head down and hit sixes.

Endnotes

Chapter 2. Why the NFL is the perfect metaphor for the free-market economy

1. Dusan Randjelovic, "Most profitable sports leagues", Athletic Panda Sports, June 3, 2020, https://apsportseditors.org/others/most-profitable-sports-leagues/
2. Mike Ozanian and Justin Teitelbaum, "The World's 50 Most Valuable Sports Teams 2023", Forbes, September 8, 2023
3. Ryan Gosling, "Who Owns the NFL and Its Brand?" Pro Football Network, 7 February 2023, https://www.profootballnetwork.com/who-owns-the-nfl-and-nfl-brand/

Chapter 3. The unexpected time out: What happens to sport when a once-in-a-lifetime pandemic hits?

4. "Security Sensitive Biological Agents Regulatory Scheme Newsletter – Special Issue March 2020 – Coronavirus disease 2019 (COVID-19)", Australian Government Department of Health, March 4, 2020, https://webarchive.nla.gov.au/awa/20220427082954/https://www1.health.gov.au/internet/main/publishing.nsf/Content/ohp-ssba-news-COVID-19
5. Naaman Zhou, "Anatomy of a coronavirus disaster: how 2,700 people were let off the Ruby Princess cruise ship by mistake", The Guardian, March 24, 2020, https://www.theguardian.com/world/2020/mar/24/anatomy-of-a-coronavirus-disaster-how-2700-people-were-let-off-the-ruby-princess-cruise-ship-by-mistake
6. Prime Minister of Australia, media release: "$130 billion JobKeeper payment to keep Australians in a job", March 30, 2020, https://pmtranscripts.pmc.gov.au/release/transcript-42766
7. "Coronavirus (COVID-19) dashboard", April 12, 2020, Australian Government Department of Health, https://www.health.gov.au/sites/default/files/documents/2020/04/coronavirus-covid-19-at-a-glance-12-april-2020_0.pdf

8 Parliament of Victoria Public Accounts and Estimates Committee, "Inquiry into the Victorian Government's response to the COVID-19 pandemic", February 2021, https://www.parliament.vic.gov.au/file_uploads/PAEC_59-08_Vic_Gov_response_to_COVID-19_pandemic_YKNbjt2Y.pdf
9 Prime Minister of Australia, media release: "New deal secures potential COVID-19 vaccine for every Australian", August 19, 2020, https://pmtranscripts.pmc.gov.au/release/transcript-42985
10 Media release: "AstraZeneca and Oxford University announce landmark agreement for COVID-19 vaccine", AstraZeneca, April 30, 2020, https://www.astrazeneca.com/media-centre/press-releases/2020/astrazeneca-and-oxford-university-announce-landmark-agreement-for-covid-19-vaccine.html
11 "History of Rugby League", NRL Operations, accessed July 13, 2023, https://www.nrl.com/operations/history-of-rugby-league/
12 "The birth of Rugby League in Australia", National Film and Sound Archive of Australia, accessed July 13, 2023, https://www.nfsa.gov.au/collection/curated/birth-rugby-league-australia
13 "Australian National Accounts: National Income, Expenditure and Product, June 2021", Australian Bureau of Statistics, Released September 1, 2021, https://www.abs.gov.au/statistics/economy/national-accounts/australian-national-accounts-national-income-expenditure-and-product/jun-2021
14 Channel Nine, "Operational Initiatives", March 30, 2020, https://cdn-api.markitdigital.com/apiman-gateway/ASX/asx-research/1.0/file/2924-02219812-2A1216711?access_token=83ff-96335c2d45a094df02a206a39ff4
15 "NRL announces new broadcast deal with Nine", Foxtel, NRL.com, May 28, 2020. https://www.nrl.com/news/2020/05/28/nrl-announces-new-broadcast-deal-with-nine-foxtel/
16 Max Mason, "NRL, broadcasters reach new deal", *Australian Financial Review*, May 28, 2020, https://www.afr.com/companies/media-and-marketing/nrl-broadcasters-reach-new-deal-20200528-p54xf0
17 Troy Whittaker, "NSW Premier gives green light for crowds up to 10,000 from July 1", NRL.com, June 14, 2020, https://www.nrl.com/news/2020/06/14/nsw-premier-gives-green-light-for-crowds-up-to-10000-from-july-1/
18 Dan Walsh, "Rep stars cop financial hit to maintain top 30 squads in new pay deal", NRL.com, January 19, 2021, https://www.nrl.com/news/2021/01/19/players-agree-to-6-per-cent-cut-in-new-pay-deal/
19 "The History of Australian Football", AFL, accessed July 13, 2023, https://www.afl.com.au/about-afl/history
20 Damian Barrett, "'Most serious threat in 100 years': AFL postpones

season", AFL, March 22, 2020, https://www.afl.com.au/news/389109/most-serious-threat-in-100-years-afl-postpones-season
21 Victorian COVID-19 data, Coronavirus Victoria, accessed July 7, 2023, https://www.coronavirus.vic.gov.au/victorian-coronavirus-covid-19-data
22 Damian Barrett, "Fixture rewrite: Vic clubs forced north for R6-7, return date unknown", AFL, July 3, 2020, https://www.afl.com.au/news/460394/fixture-rewrite-vic-clubs-forced-north-for-r6-7-return-date-unknown
23 Stephanie Zillman, "Queensland will completely close its border to visitors from Victoria from midday Friday amid state's coronavirus outbreak", ABC News, July 9, 2020, https://www.abc.net.au/news/2020-07-09/coronavirus-queensland-closes-border-to-visitors-from-victoria/12429934
24 Queensland Premier, media release: "Queensland border closed", Queensland Government, August 5, 2020, https://statements.qld.gov.au/statements/90322
25 Damian Barrett, "NAB, ANZ come to the party as AFL secures huge loan", AFL, March 30, 2020, https://www.afl.com.au/news/390294/nab-anz-come-to-the-party-as-afl-secures-huge-loan
26 Jake Niall, "AFL to seek $500m plus loan during unprecedented crisis", The Age, March 24, 2020, https://www.theage.com.au/sport/afl/afl-to-seek-500m-loan-during-unprecedented-crisis-20200324-p54dj7.html
27 Andrew Ramsey, "CA announces staff cutbacks due to coronavirus", Cricket.com.au, April 16, 2020, https://www.cricket.com.au/news/cricket-australia-staff-stood-down-coronavirus-covid19-impact/2020-04-16
28 Press conference: *"An update from CEO Kevin Roberts"*, Cricket Australia, April 21, 2020, https://www.cricketaustralia.com.au/media/announcements/kevin-roberts-cricket-australia-ceo-update-press-conference-april-21-covid19/2020-04-21
29 Dave Middleton, "CA reveals $40m cut to budget, redundancies", Cricket.com.au, June 17, 2020, https://www.cricket.com.au/news/cricket-australia-job-budget-cuts-40-roles-40-million-covid-19-shield-earl-eddings-nick-hockley/2020-06-17
30 Stephanie Chalkley-Rhoden, "Cricket Australia reaches pay deal with players' association after bitter standoff", ABC News, August 3, 2017, https://www.abc.net.au/news/2017-08-03/cricket-australia-reaches-pay-deal-with-players/8765040
31 Dave Middleton, "CA announces full international summer schedule", Cricket.com.au, May 28, 2020, https://www.cricket.com.au/news/cricket-australia-international-schedule-2020-21-india-new-zealand-west-indies-zimbabwe-afghanistan/2020-05-28
32 Match Results, Indian Premier League official website, IPLT20.com,

accessed July 13, 2023, https://www.iplt20.com/matches/results/2020
33 Dave Middleton, "It's on! Dates, venues for India tour confirmed", Cricket.com.au, October 28, 2020, https://www.cricket.com.au/news/australia-india-schedule-tests-odi-t20-international-fixture-dates-venues-tickets-border-gavaskar/2020-10-28
34 "Buildcorp Super W finals postponed, and Pathways programs suspended", Rugby Australia, March 17, 2020, https://australia.rugby/news/2020/03/17/super-w-postponement-covid
35 "Rugby makes significant cuts as COVID-19 impacts hit hard", Rugby Australia, March 31, 2020, https://australia.rugby/news/2020/03/31/covid-19-staffing-decision
36 "Statement regarding Wallabies Captains' letter", Rugby Australia, April 21, 2020, https://australia.rugby/news/2020/04/21/wallabies-captains-letter
37 "Raelene Castle statement", Rugby Australia, April 23, 2020, https://australia.rugby/news/2020/04/23/raelene-castle-statement
38 "Rugby Australia receives World Rugby funding boost", Rugby Australia, May 15, 2020, https://australia.rugby/news/2020/05/15/rugby-australia-receives-world-rugby-funding-boost
39 Beth Newman, "Wallabies' July Test matches postponed", Rugby.com.au, May 15, 2020, https://www.rugby.com.au/news/2020/05/15/july-tests-postponed
40 "Statement on Sunwolves' participation in Vodafone Super Rugby AU", Rugby Australia, June 1, 2020, https://australia.rugby/news/2020/06/01/statement-on-sunwolves-participation-in-vodafone-super-rugby-au
41 "Vodafone Super Rugby AU Season Draw released", Rugby Australia, June 11, 2020, https://australia.rugby/news/2020/06/11/vodafone-super-rugby-au-season-draw-released
42 "RugbyAU and RUPA agree updated interim pay deal", Rugby Australia, July 1, 2020, https://australia.rugby/news/2020/06/30/rugbyau-and-rupa-agree-updated-interim-pay-deal
43 "Rugby Australia welcomes SANZAAR's decision regarding The Rugby Championship", Rugby Australia, September 11, 2020, https://australia.rugby/news/2020/09/11/rugby-au-welcomes-sanzaar-decison
44 "SANZAAR confirm draw for 2020 Rugby Championship", Rugby Australia, September 24, 2020, https://australia.rugby/news/2020/09/23/rugby-championship-draw-announcement
45 "Rugby Australia thanks New Zealand Rugby and New Zealand Government", Rugby Australia, September 15, 2020, https://australia.rugby/news/2020/09/15/ra-new-zealand-thanks
46 "SANZAAR confirm 2020 Tri-Nations Series to kick-off 31 October", Rugby Australia, October 16, 2020, https://australia.rugby/news/2020/10/16/sanzaar-confirm-new-2020-draw
47 "Rugby Australia unveils landmark broadcast deal", Rugby Australia,

November 9, 2020, https://australia.rugby/news/2020/11/08/rugby-australia-unveils-landmark-broadcast-deal

48 "First Travel-related Case of 2019 Novel Coronavirus Detected in United States", Centers for Disease Control and Prevention, January 21, 2020, https://www.cdc.gov/media/releases/2020/p0121-novel-coronavirus-travel-case.html

49 "2019–20 NBA Season Updates, March 13–20 Archive", NBA.com, March 21, 2020, https://www.nba.com/2020-season-update-archive1

50 "NBA Board of Governors approves competitive format to restart 2019-20 season with 22 teams returning to play", NBA.com, June 5, 2020, https://www.nba.com/news/board-of-governors-approves-nba-return-official-release

51 "Cumulative Cases by Days Since 50th Confirmed Case", Johns Hopkins Coronavirus Resource Center, accessed July 11, 2023, https://coronavirus.jhu.edu/data/cumulative-cases

52 "NFL salary cap will increase to $198.2M in 2020", NFL.com, March 15, 2020, https://www.nfl.com/news/nfl-salary-cap-will-increase-to-198-2m-in-2020-0ap3000001106260

53 Thomas Barrabi, "Coronavirus prompts NFL Draft to go 'fully virtual' – NFL coaches, executives will conduct their drafts from home", Fox Business, April 6, 2020, https://www.foxbusiness.com/sports/coronavirus-nfl-draft-virtual-format-2020

54 Kevin Seifert, "NFL tells teams to have facility reopening protocols in place by May 15", ESPN, May 6, 2020, http://www.espn.com/nfl/story/_/id/29144226/nfl-lays-carefully-developed-protocols-reopen-team-facilities

55 "NFLPA advises players not to work out together", ESPN, June 20, 2020, https://www.espn.com/nfl/story/_/id/29339696/nflpa-advises-players-not-work-together-due-coronavirus

56 Nick Shook, "Roger Goodell writes letter to NFL fans as training camps start across US", July 27, 2020, https://www.nfl.com/news/roger-goodell-letter-nfl-fans-training-camps

57 "Introduction to COVID-19 Policies and Procedures", NFL-NFLPA COVID-19 Educational Materials, NFL.com, July 17, 2020, https://www.nfl.com/playerhealthandsafety/health-and-wellness/covid-19/nfl-nflpa-covid-19-educational-materials

58 "Transcript of Briefing by NFL Chief Medical Officer Dr. Allen Sills on COVID-19 Testing", NFL.com, August 13, 2020, https://www.nfl.com/playerhealthandsafety/health-and-wellness/covid-19/transcript-briefing-nfl-chief-medical-officer-dr-allen-sills-covid-19-testing

59 "Media Alert: Update On NFL COVID-19 Testing", BioReference Laboratories, accessed July 13, 2023, https://www.bioreference.com/media-alert-update-on-nfl-covid-19-testing/

60 Ian Rapoport and Tom Pelissero, "Titans fined $350K for COVID-19

violations; Raiders could be next," NFL.com, October 25, 2020, https://www.nfl.com/news/titans-fined-at-least-300k-for-covid-19-violations-raiders-could-be-next

61 "NFL Football Attendance – 2020", ESPN, accessed July 13, 2023, http://www.espn.com/nfl/attendance/_/year/2020

62 "GDP (current US$) – United States, Australia, China, India, Canada, Japan, Germany, United Kingdom, France, Italy, Brazil, Russian Federation, Spain, Indonesia, Mexico, Netherlands, Switzerland, Saudi Arabia, Turkey, Korea, Rep.", World Bank national accounts data and OECD National Accounts data files, World Bank, accessed July 13, 2023, https://data.worldbank.org

63 "GDP (current US$) – United States, Australia, China, India, Canada, Japan, Germany, United Kingdom, France, Italy, Brazil, Russian Federation, Spain, Indonesia, Mexico, Netherlands, Switzerland, Saudi Arabia, Turkey, Korea, Rep.," World Bank national accounts data and OECD National Accounts data files, World Bank, accessed July 13, 2023, https://data.worldbank.org

64 "Labour Force, Australia, June 2020", Australian Bureau of Statistics, accessed July 13, 2023, https://www.abs.gov.au/statistics/labour/employment-and-unemployment/labour-force-australia/jun-2020

65 "Employment and Earnings, Public Sector, Australia, 2019–20 financial year", Australian Bureau of Statistics, November 12, 2020, https://www.abs.gov.au/statistics/labour/employment-and-unemployment/employment-and-earnings-public-sector-australia/2019-20

66 "Counts of Australian Businesses, including Entries and Exits, July 2017 – June 2021", Australian Bureau of Statistics, August 24, 2021, https://www.abs.gov.au/statistics/economy/business-indicators/counts-australian-businesses-including-entries-and-exits/jul2017-jun2021

Chapter 4. Talent identification and acquisition: building a championship winning roster

67 Ben Rolfe, "How does the NFL salary cap work in 2021", Pro Football Network, June 2, 2021, https://www.profootballnetwork.com/how-does-nfl-salary-cap-work-2021/

68 "Kyle Shanahan on Super Bowl Regrets, Trading Up for Lance, Taking the SF Job, and Coaching With His Dad", Flying Coach with Sean McVay and Peter Schrager, The Ringer, July 7, 2021, https://www.theringer.com/2021/7/7/22566190/kyle-shanahan-on-super-bowl-regrets-trading-up-for-lance-taking-the-sf-job-and-coaching-with-his-dad

69 "Kyle Shanahan on Super Bowl Regrets, Trading Up for Lance, Taking the SF Job, and Coaching With His Dad", Flying Coach with Sean McVay and Peter Schrager, The Ringer, July 7, 2021, https://www.theringer.com/2021/7/7/22566190/kyle-shanahan-

on-super-bowl-regrets-trading-up-for-lance-taking-the-sf-job-and-coaching-with-his-dad
70 "Kyle Shanahan on Super Bowl Regrets, Trading Up for Lance, Taking the SF Job, and Coaching With His Dad", Flying Coach with Sean McVay and Peter Schrager, The Ringer, July 7, 2021, (48:57min), https://www.theringer.com/2021/7/7/22566190/kyle-shanahan-on-super-bowl-regrets-trading-up-for-lance-taking-the-sf-job-and-coaching-with-his-dad
71 "Aaron Rodgers Draft Day Slide, 2005 Caught in the Draft", NFL Films, NFL YouTube Channel, accessed July 10, 2023, https://www.youtube.com
72 "Tom Brady College Stats", Sports-Reference.com, accessed July 10, 2023, https://www.sports-reference.com/cfb/players/tom-brady-1.html
73 "The Brady 6: Journey of the Legend No One Wanted", NFL Films, NFL Films YouTube Channel, accessed July 10, 2023, https://www.youtube.com/
74 "Tom Brady", Armchair Expert with Dax Shepard, Episode 243, September 10, 2020, (35:03min), https://armchairexpertpod.com/pods/tom-brady
75 "Full Scorecard of South Africa vs England 5th Test Durban South Afrida 3-14 March 1939", ESPN Cricinfo, accessed July 11, 2023, https://www.espncricinfo.com/series/england-tour-of-south-africa-1938-39-61688/south-africa-vs-england-5th-test-62657/full-scorecard
76 "The Ten Fastest Bowlers In Cricket History", Wisden, December 18, 2020, accessed July 9, 2023, https://wisden.com/stories/the-ten-fastest-bowlers-in-cricket-history
77 "West Indies in Australia 1975/76", Wisden, accessed July 9, 2023, https://wisden.com/comp/3072/west-indies-in-australia-1975-76/results/2
78 "Ashleigh Barty, Player Stats," WTA Tour, accessed July 9, 2023, https://www.wtatennis.com/players/318033/ashleigh-barty#overview
79 Carly Adno, "Ellyse Perry's dual-international career could be over after Matildas squad snub", Fox Sports, April 1, 2014, https://www.foxsports.com.au/football/ellyse-perrys-dualinternation-al-career-could-be-over-after-matildas-squad-snub/news-story/a2c4e0a5f6772404b577fa97db2d4bc
80 "Ellyse Perry profile and biography, stats, records, averages, photos and videos", ESPN Cricinfo, accessed July 11, 2023, https://www.espncricinfo.com/player/ellyse-perry-275487
81 "Bo Jackson Stats", Major League Baseball, MLB.com, accessed July 9, 2023, https://www.mlb.com/player/bo-jackson-116446
82 "Deion Sanders Major League Baseball Stats", ESPN.com, accessed July 9, 2023, https://www.espn.com/mlb/player/stats/_/id/2176/deion-sanders

83 "Bo Jackson NFL Career Stats", NFL.com, accessed July 9, 2023, https://www.nfl.com/players/bo-jackson/stats/career

84 Jim Callis, "2018 Draft bonus pools, pick values – Royals have largest allotment, followed by Tigers, Rays", MLB.com, May 28, 2018, www.mlb.com/news/2018-mlb-draft-bonus-pools-pick-values-c269930084

85 "Ben Graham of the Geelong Cats Career AFL Stats", Footywire.com, accessed July 9, 2023, www.footywire.com/afl/footy/pc-geelong-cats--ben-graham

86 Grant Gordon, "Eagles sign OT Jordan Mailata to four-year, $64m extension", NFL.com, September 11, 2021, https://www.nfl.com/news/eagles-sign-ot-jordan-mailata-to-four-year-64m-extension

Chapter 5. Talent development

87 Good Morning Football, NFL, July 27, 2021, https://twitter.com/gmfb/status/1419673877706428417

88 Press Conference: "Kyle Shanahan Evaluates the Performance of Jimmy Garoppolo and Trey Lance", 49ers.com, August 3, 2021, www.49ers.com/video/kyle-shanahan-evaluates-the-performance-of-jimmy-garoppolo-and-trey-lance

Chapter 6. The secret sauce of success: grit

89 "NFL Films Presents Matthew Stafford Mic'd Up in Game-Winning Heroics vs. Browns (2009)", NFL Films, NFL Films YouTube Channel, accessed July 10, 2023, https://www.youtube.com

90 "Ohio State QB Justin Fields Takes HUGE Hit vs Clemson 2021 College Football", PSC Highlights YouTube Channel, accessed July 10, 2023, https://www.youtube.com

91 "On This Day: Sattler Plays With Broken Jaw", Rabbitohs, April 19, 2018, https://www.rabbitohs.com.au/news/2020/09/19/on-this-day-sattler-plays-with-broken-jaw/

92 "Rabbitohs v Bulldogs Grand Final 2014 Match Centre", NRL, accessed July 10, 2023, https://www.nrl.com/draw/nrl-premiership/2014/grand-final/rabbitohs-v-bulldogs/

93 "Roosters v Storm Grand Final 2018 Match Centre", NRL.com, accessed July 10, 2023, https://www.nrl.com/draw/nrl-premiership/2018/grand-final/roosters-v-storm/

94 "Dee Ford: 'I Haven't Put My Best Ball on Tape Yet'", 49ers Press Conference, 49ers.com, August 6, 2021, https://www.49ers.com/video/dee-ford-i-haven-t-put-my-best-ball-on-tape-yet

95 "Alex Smith feels 'very much lucky to be alive' after suffering broken leg", ESPN YouTube Channel, accessed July 10, 2023, https://www.youtube.com

96 "Kyle Shanahan on Super Bowl Regrets, Trading Up for Lance, Taking the SF Job, and Coaching With His Dad", Flying Coach with Sean McVay

and Peter Schrager, The Ringer, July 7, 2021, https://www.theringer.com/2021/7/7/22566190/kyle-shanahan-on-super-bowl-regrets-trading-up-for-lance-taking-the-sf-job-and-coaching-with-his-dad

97 "Kyle Shanahan on Super Bowl Regrets, Trading Up for Lance, Taking the SF Job, and Coaching With His Dad", Flying Coach with Sean McVay and Peter Schrager, The Ringer, July 7, 2021, https://www.theringer.com/2021/7/7/22566190/kyle-shanahan-on-super-bowl-regrets-trading-up-for-lance-taking-the-sf-job-and-coaching-with-his-dad

98 Abhishek Mukherjee, "John Edrich, 39, and Brian Close, 45, show exemplary courage against frightening West Indies attack", Cricket Country, July 13, 2016, https://www.cricketcountry.com/articles/aging-john-edrich-and-brian-close-show-exemplary-courage-against-frightening-west-indies-attack-28791

99 "Second Tied Test: Bradman Museum", Bradman Museum YouTube Channel, accessed July 10, 2023, https://www.youtube.com

Chapter 7. Roster management: where fluidity and proactivity are business enablers

100 Nick Shook, "Broncos trade star LB Von Miller to Rams for two 2022 NFL Draft picks", NFL.com, November 1, 2021, https://www.nfl.com/news/broncos-trade-star-lb-von-miller-to-rams

101 John Middlekauff, "Three and Out with John Middlekauff podcast", the Volume, March 17, 2020

Chapter 8. Scheme and philosophy (aka your north star)

102 "NFL Mission and Values", NFL, May 30, 2019, accessed July 9, 2023, https://www.nfl.com/news/mission-and-values

103 Judy Battista, "Patriots Adhere to Bottom Line to Stay on Top", The New York Times, August 8, 2004, https://www.nytimes.com/2004/08/08/sports/pro-football-patriots-adhere-to-bottom-line-to-stay-on-top.html

104 Jeffri Chadiha, "How a franchise altering decision by a rookie GM can be traced back to a chance meeting in a college classroom", NFL.com, October 3, 2017, https://www.nfl.com/news/sidelines/stanford-connection

105 JC Tretter, "Setting a New Standard for Guaranteed Contracts", NFL Players Association, April 12, 2022, https://nflpa.com/posts/setting-a-new-standard-for-guaranteed-contracts

106 Grant Gordon, "Jets trade Sam Darnold to Panthers for three Draft Picks", NFL.com, April 5, 2021, https://www.nfl.com/news/jets-trade-sam-darnold-to-panthers-for-three-draft-picks

107 "NFL 2021 Draft Tracker", Spotrac, accessed July 18, 2023, https://www.spotrac.com/nfl/draft/2021/

108 Press Conference: "Head Coach Brandon Staley on Getting Ready for

the Kansas City Chiefs", Chargers.com, October 6, 2021, https://www.chargers.com/video/brandon-staley-press-conference-kansas-city-chiefs-week-3-2021-x5813

109 "Kyle Shanahan on Super Bowl Regrets, Trading Up for Lance, Taking the SF Job, and Coaching With His Dad", Flying Coach with Sean McVay and Peter Schrager, The Ringer, July 7, 2021, https://www.theringer.com/2021/7/7/22566190/kyle-shanahan-on-super-bowl-regrets-trading-up-for-lance-taking-the-sf-job-and-coaching-with-his-dad

110 "Matt LaFleur and Robert Saleh on Reaching the Pinnacle of the Profession and Coaching for and Against Aaron Rodgers", Flying Coach with Sean McVay and Peter Schrager, The Ringer, May 26, 2021

111 "Kyle Shanahan on Super Bowl Regrets, Trading Up for Lance, Taking the SF Job, and Coaching with His Dad", Flying Coach with Sean McVay and Peter Schrager, The Ringer, July 7, 2021, https://www.theringer.com/2021/7/7/22566190/kyle-shanahan-on-super-bowl-regrets-trading-up-for-lance-taking-the-sf-job-and-coaching-with-his-dad

112 Press Conference: "Head Coach Brandon Staley on Getting Ready for the Kansas City Chiefs", Chargers.com, October 6, 2021, https://www.chargers.com/video/brandon-staley-press-conference-kansas-city-chiefs-week-3-2021-x5813

113 Colin Cowherd, The Herd Podcast, Fox Sports Radio, December 17, 2021

114 John Middlekauff, Three and Out podcast, The Volume, November 9, 2021

115 Good Morning Football, NFL.com, March 19, 2021, https://twitter.com/gmfb/status/1372910733932003330?lang=en

Chapter 9. All in: Culture and Legacy

116 First Take, ESPN, January 3, 2022, https://giantswire.usatoday.com/2022/01/04/ryan-clark-takes-aim-joe-judge-calls-new-york-giants-coach-liar/

117 Angela Duckworth, "Grit: The Power of Passion and Perseverance", Random House UK, 2019, p.295.

118 Jim Collins and Bill Lazier, "Beyond Entrepreneurship BE 2.0, Turning Your Business into an enduring Great Company", Random House Business, 2020.

119 "Aaron Rodgers talks Packers, pays tribute to Kenny Mayne on Mayne's final show", SportsCenter, ESPN YouTube channel, May 24, 2021, https://www.youtube.com

120 "Kyle Shanahan on Super Bowl Regrets, Trading Up for Lance, Taking the SF Job, and Coaching With His Dad", Flying Coach with Sean McVay and Peter Schrager, The Ringer, July 7, 2021, https://www.theringer.com/2021/7/7/22566190/kyle-shanahan-on-super-bowl-regrets-trading-up-for-lance-taking-the-sf-job-and-coaching-with-his-dad

121 "Records for Test Matches – Most Matches as Captain", ESPN Cricinfo, accessed July 14, 2023, https://www.espncricinfo.com/records/most-matches-as-captain-283746
122 "Cricket Australia and Australian Cricketers' Association sign new 12-month MOU", Cricket Australia, May 12, 2022, accessed July 9, 2023, https://www.cricketaustralia.com.au/media/announcements/mou-resign/2022-05-12

Chapter 10. Coaching Mindset

123 Angela Duckworth, "Grit: The Power of Passion and Perseverance", Random House UK, 2019, p. 231.
124 "Matt LaFleur and Robert Saleh on Reaching the Pinnacle of the Profession and Coaching for and Against Aaron Rodgers", Flying Coach with Sean McVay and Peter Schrager, The Ringer, May 26, 2021, https://www.theringer.com/2021/5/26/22454288/matt-lafleur-robert-saleh-reaching-the-pinnacle-coaching-for-and-against-aaron-rodgers-and-benihana
125 "Rich Eisen Show", Cumulus Podcast Network, June 21, 2023.
126 Dabo Swinney, "Columbus Valley Area High School Football Awards Luncheon", December 13, 2017, Sportsvisions YouTube Channel, https://www.youtube.com
127 "Kyle Shanahan Reviews The Start of The 49ers Offseason Program", 49ers.com, 49ers Press Conference, May 25, 2022, https://www.49ers.com/video/kyle-shanahan-reviews-the-start-of-the-49ers-offseason-program
128 "Mike McDaniel Talks Game Planning for Packers with Question Marks at Running Back", 49ers.com, 49ers Press Conference, September 23, 2021, https://www.49ers.com/video/mike-mcdaniel-talks-game-planning-for-packers-with-question-marks-at-rb
129 Bill Walsh with Steve Jamison and Craig Walsh, "The Score Takes Care of Itself – My Philosophy of Leadership", The Penguin Group, 2009, p. 142
130 Bill Walsh with Steve Jamison and Craig Walsh, "The Score Takes Care of Itself – My Philosophy of Leadership", The Penguin Group, 2009, p.150
131 "Kyle Shanahan Shares Final Updates Before San Francisco vs Chicago", 49ers news conference, 49ers.com, October 29, 2021, https://www.49ers.com/video/kyle-shanahan-shares-final-updates-before-sfvschi
132 Colin Cowherd, "The Herd Podcast", Fox Sports Radio, September 22, 2021
133 Bill Walsh with Steve Jamison and Craig Walsh, "The Score Takes Care of Itself – My Philosophy of Leadership", The Penguin Group, 2009, p. 161
134 Interview with Earl Woods on ABC television show *"That's*

Endnotes

Incredible" hosted by Pro Football Hall of Fame QB Fran Tarkenton, 1981, accessed July 3, 2022, https://www.youtube.com

135 "Venus Williams", International Olympic Committee, accessed July 9, 2023, https://olympics.com/en/athletes/venus-williams

136 Colin Cowherd, "The Herd Podcast", Fox Sports Radio, April 1, 2022.

137 Richard Williams, "12 and 11-year-old Venus & Serena Williams interview", Trans World Sport, 1992, accessed July 3, 2022, https://www.youtube.com

138 "Best of Charlie Woods at 2021 PNC Championship", PGA Tour YouTube channel, accessed July 9, 2023, https://www.youtube.com

139 "Archie Manning", StatMuse, accessed July 9, 2023, https://www.statmuse.com/nfl/player/archie-manning-12923

140 Angela Duckworth, "Grit: The Power of Passion and Perseverance", Random House UK, 2019, p. 51

141 Bill Walsh with Steve Jamison and Craig Walsh, "The Score Takes Care of Itself – My Philosophy of Leadership", The Penguin Group, 2009, pp. 143–144

142 Simon Sinek, "Performance v Trust", Simon Sinek Facebook page, accessed July 9, 2023, https://www.facebook.com

143 "The Morning After Matthew Won Super Bowl LVI", "The Morning After with Kelly Stafford", Action Park Media, February 15, 2022, https://www.podcastrepublic.net/podcast/1585848116

144 "Coaching Character Initiative", Student Government Association, University of Alabama, April 12. 2012, (54:50min), accessed July 5, 2022, www.youtube.com

145 "Deebo Samuel", Spotrac, accessed July 9, 2023, https://www.spotrac.com/nfl/san-francisco-49ers/deebo-samuel-29071/

146 "Deebo Samuel: 'I Just Love the Game'", 49ers news conference, 49ers.com, August 2, 2022, https://www.49ers.com/video/deebo-samuel-i-just-love-the-game

147 "NFL's biggest contracts for 2018", NFL.com, accessed July 9, 2023, https://www.nfl.com/photos/nfl-s-biggest-contracts-for-2018-0ap3000000915508

148 "NFL's biggest contracts for 2019", NFL.com, accessed July 9, 2023, https://www.nfl.com/photos/nfl-s-biggest-contracts-for-2019-0ap3000001022730

149 "Ranking the NFL's biggest contracts for 2020", NFL.com, accessed July 9, 2023, https://www.nfl.com/photos/nfl-s-biggest-contracts-for-2020

150 "Ranking the NFL's biggest contracts for 2021", NFL.com, accessed July 9, 2023, https://www.nfl.com/photos/ranking-the-nfl-s-biggest-contracts-for-2021

151 "John Lynch, Class of 2021", Pro Football Hall of Fame, accessed July 9, 2023, https://www.profootballhof.com/players/john-lynch/

Chapter 11. Customer experience, go-to-market and your distribution platform

152 Tom Goodwin, "The Battle Is For the Customer Interface", Tech Crunch, March 4, 2015, https://techcrunch.com/2015/03/03/in-the-age-of-disintermediation-the-battle-is-all-for-the-customer-interface/
153 "The Story of Netflix", Netflix.com, accessed July 4, 2023, https://about.netflix.com/en
154 "Disney's Bob Iger: How acquisitions become an ecosystem", Masters of Scale Podcast with Reid Hoffman, March 2, 2021, https://mastersofscale.com/bob-iger-part-1/
155 Brooks Barnes and John Koblin, "Disney's Big Bet on Streaming Relies on Little-Known Tech Company", New York Times, 8 October 2017, https://www.nytimes.com/2017/10/08/business/media/bamtech-disney-streaming.html
156 "The Walt Disney Company Reports Third Quarter and Nine Months Earnings for Fiscal 2022", The Walt Disney Company, August 10, 2022, https://thewaltdisneycompany.com/the-walt-disney-company-reports-third-quarter-and-nine-months-earnings-for-fiscal-2022/
157 "2023 Quarterly Earnings – First Quarter Earnings", Netflix.com, April 18, 2023, https://ir.netflix.net/financials/quarterly-earnings/default.aspx
158 "NFL completes long-term media distribution agreements through 2033 season", NFL.com, March 18, 2021, https://www.nfl.com/news/nfl-announces-new-broadcast-deals-running-through-2033-season
159 Brian Steinberg, "NBC's 'Sunday Night Football' Kicks Off Season With Logo Change", Variety, September 7, 2017, https://variety.com/2022/tv/news/nbc-sunday-night-football-logo-design-change-1235362390/
160 Jonathan Shieber, "Fox gets deeper into streaming with $440 million acquisition of Tubi", Tech Crunch, March 18, 2020, https://techcrunch.com/2020/03/17/fox-gets-deeper-into-streaming-with-440-million-acquisition-of-tubi/
161 Media Release: "NFL Network to Launch November 4; NFL Total Access to Serve as Centerpiece", NFL.com, July 10, 2003, https://www.nfl.info/nflmedia/NFL%20Network/NetworkLaunchDate.htm
162 "NFL and Sky Sports unveil 'Sky Sports NFL' as part of five-year partnership", Sky Sports NFL, August 14, 2020, https://www.skysports.com/nfl/news/12118/12047354/nfl-and-sky-sports-unveil-sky-sports-nfl-as-part-of-five-year-partnership
163 Andrew Cohen, "NFL Game Pass Expands to Australia, Brazil, India, Japan and Mexico", Sports Business Journal, October 7, 2019, https://www.sportsbusinessjournal.com/Daily/Issues/2019/10/07/Technology/nfl-game-pass-181-countries-territories-football-overtier-streaming.aspx
164 "NFL launches exclusive streaming subscription service NFL+",

NFL.com, July 25, 2022, https://www.nfl.com/news/nfl-launches-exclusive-streaming-subscription-service-nfl
165 "NFL completes long-term media distribution agreements through 2033 season", NFL.com, March 18, 2021, https://www.nfl.com/news/nfl-completes-long-term-media-distribution-agreements-through-2033-season
166 Michael Schneider, Monica Marie Zorrilla, "Top 100 Telecasts of 2021: 'NCIS', 'Yellowstone', NFL Dominate, as Oscars Fail to Make the Cut", Variety, December 29, 2021, https://variety.com/2021/tv/news/top-rated-shows-2021-ncis-yellowstone-squid-game-1235143671/
167 "NFL Rule Book", NFL, Section 1, Article 3, accessed July 4, 2023, p. 12. https://operations.nfl.com/the-rules/2022-nfl-rulebook/
168 Kevin Ota, "ESPN Fantasy Football: 11 Million Players Sets New All-Time Record", ESPN.com, September 14, 2022, https://espnpressroom.com/us/press-releases/2022/09/espn-fantasy-football-11-million-players-sets-new-all-time-record
169 "UNDISPUTED and THE HERD Score Most-Watched Shows Ever on FS1", Fox Sports Press Pass, January 19, 2022, https://www.foxsports.com/presspass/blog/2022/01/19/undisputed-herd-score-watched-shows-ever-fs1/
170 Rachel Nelson, "The Herd With Colin Cowherd Surpasses 70 Million Podcast Listens in 2019", FOX Sports Radio, January 13, 2020, https://foxsportsradio.iheart.com/content/2020-01-12-the-herd-with-colin-cowherd-surpasses-70-million-podcast-listens-in-2019/
171 By Variety, "YouTube officially shuts down original content group", NBC News, January 19, 2022, https://www.nbcnews.com/pop-culture/pop-culture-news/youtube-officially-shuts-original-content-group-rcna12643
172 ESPN News Services, "Pat McAfee Show coming to ESPN in multiyear deal", ESPN, May 17, 2023, https://www.espn.com.au/espn/story/_/id/37664316/pat-mcafee-show-coming-espn-multiyear-deal
173 Brian Eckhouse and Dev Merrill, "Closed Movie Theaters Leave Void From Small Towns to Big Cities", Bloomberg, December 10, 2021, https://www.bloomberg.com/news/articles/2021-12-10/closed-movie-theaters-leave-void-from-small-towns-to-big-cities

Chapter 12. Politics and sport: there is no escaping the macroeconomic environment

174 "Government expenditure, percent of GDP", International Monetary Fund, accessed July 6, 2023, https://www.imf.org/external/datamapper/exp@FPP/AUS/USA
175 Daniel Conifer, "At least $38b in JobKeeper went to companies where turnover did not fall below thresholds, data finds", ABC News, November 2, 2021, https://www.abc.net.au/news/

2021-11-02/38b-in-jobkeeper-went-to-companies-where-turnover-did-not-fall-/100586310
176 Sarah Martin, Nick Evershed, Josh Nicholas, "Budget 2022: analysis reveals Morrison government funneling billions into must-win marginal seats", The Guardian, March 29, 2022, https://www.theguardian.com/australia-news/2022/mar/29/analysis-reveals-morrison-government-funnelling-billions-into-must-win-marginal-seats
177 "What is the national debt", Fiscal Data, The US Department of Treasury, accessed July 9, 2023, https://fiscaldata.treasury.gov/americas-finance-guide/national-debt/
178 "Community participation in Commonwealth Games Sports", AusPlay July 2022, Australian Sports Commission, https://www.clearinghouseforsport.gov.au/research/ausplay/results/previous-data-releases/historical-publications
179 Annual Reports, Netball Australia, accessed July 6, 2023, https://netball.com.au/annual-reports
180 Jackson Graham, "'No more money': Netball pay dispute fuels fears of talent drain", Sydney Morning Herald, February 27, 2023, https://www.smh.com.au/sport/netball/no-more-money-netball-pay-dispute-fuels-fears-of-talent-drain-20230226-p5cnqa.html
181 John Kehoe, "Victorians get poorer under Labor's Andrews as state debt balloons", Australian Financial Review, November 22, 2022, https://www.afr.com/policy/economy/victorian-incomes-lag-under-labor-s-andrews-as-state-debt-balloons-20221121-p5bzzl

Chapter 13. Exiting the pandemic: How different sports fared

182 Dallas Robinson, "NFL Salary Cap History Throughout the Years", Pro Football Network, March 13, 2023, https://www.profootballnetwork.com/nfl-salary-cap-history/
183 Joel Smith, "A look at AFL Stadium Deals and Revenue", Austadiums, August 1, 2021, https://www.austadiums.com/news/1034/a-look-at-afl-stadium-deals-and-revenue
184 Jim Collins and Bill Lazier, "Beyond Entrepreneurship 2.0 – Turning Your Business into an Enduring Great Company", Penguin Random House, United Kingdom, 2020, pps183–189
185 Bill Walsh with Steve Jamison and Craig Walsh, "The Score Takes Care of Itself – My Philosophy of Leadership", The Penguin Group, 2009, p. 146

Chapter 14. Conclusion

186 Alvin E Roth, "Who Gets What and Why", First Mariner Books, 2016, United State of America, p. 13

www.ingramcontent.com/pod-product-compliance
Lightning Source LLC
Chambersburg PA
CBHW071853290426
44110CB00013B/1131